VISIONS *of* AUSTRALIA

VISIONS
of
AUSTRALIA

Impressions of the Landscape

1642–1910

ERIC ROLLS

Lothian
BOOKS

Thomas C. Lothian Pty Ltd
132-136 Albert Road, South Melbourne, 3205
www.lothian.com.au

National Library of Australia
Cataloguing-in-Publication data:

Rolls, Eric C. (Eric Charles), 1923- .
    Visions of Australia: impressions of the landscape 1642-1910.

    ISBN 0 7344 0445 X.

    1. Australia - History. 2. Australia - Description and
    travel. 3. Australia - Social life and customs. I. Title.

    994

Cover and text design by Black Widow Graphic Design
Cover image: *Gigantic Lily*; inset image: *Curryong*; watercolours by
    Dorothy E. Paty, 1805–1836, in *Wild flowers around Newcastle N.S.W.*.
    By permission of the National Library of Australia.
Typeset by Cannon Typesetting in 12/14pt Baskerville
Printed in Australia by Griffin Press

Contents

Preface

This book remakes the perception of Australia. Henry Lawson, Adam Lindsay Gordon and others wrote well enough to daub a permanent drab coat over its loveliness. They saw it through the eyes of settlers trying to build farms with insufficient land, insufficient money and insufficient knowledge. The casual first European observers of country and city found them beautiful. The land was mostly open. Trees grew singly or in clumps and belts of varying size, grasses grew in well-spaced tussocks. In places, especially in Tasmania, there were magnificent tangles of forest. And everywhere, from the cold wet valleys of Tasmania through the hot sandy plains of the Red Centre to the tropical north, shrubs and flowers bloomed for most of the year.

Visions of Australia records the opinions of one hundred of those who saw the land one to three hundred years ago and the cities as they developed. They transform the modern notions of a harsh landscape into a garden of wildflowers; they transform the early wood and canvas huts fronting streets of mud and dust into buildings of extraordinary elegance; they transform the European people from drunken and licentious convicts and opportunists into members of a society intelligent, vigorous, adaptable and proud; they transform Aboriginal Australians into highly intelligent people with great artistic ability.

We found manuscripts in every state in Australia and in England. One hundred did not exhaust the total; it merely fitted the required length of the book. It would have been easy to find two hundred or more.

Some writings were simply sterile business and uncommitted, few were hostile. Admittedly, the early Dutch explorers found 'little of good' on the west coast, but that part of Australia does not present its best to those arriving by sea.

Australia seldom flaunts itself; it reveals its wonders quietly. Very strangely, a few early comers were so unobservant that they found our flora and fauna lacking. Louisa Anne Meredith countered that idea directly: 'The notion that our flowers have no scent is as ridiculous as the idea that our birds have no song'. The Pied Butcherbird has the finest voice of all birds. Mary Bundock and her fellow passengers on *Harry Turner* in 1833 'smelt a new scent in the air' while they were still at sea. Wattle was in bloom and an offshore wind carried the scent to them. Exploring the early artists was a particular joy. So many exceeded our expectations, so many, like the writers, found wonder in their new country.

The extracts have been ordered chronologically and, for ease of reference, have been divided into time periods roughly equating with major shifts in Australian history. The comprehensive index and bibliography will help guide readers to specific entries.

Research was made joy by the enthusiastic help we received from libraries. It was wonderful to email requirements to a library a few days before we went, and on arrival find trolleys loaded with books and manuscripts waiting for us. I use the plural because, as always, Elaine van Kempen did a lot of the work with me.

I especially thank Jennifer Broomhead, Wendy Holz, Kathy Spinks and Linda West of the Mitchell Library; Susan Killoran of Harris Manchester College, Oxford; Sally Blake of the State Library of Victoria; Prue McDonald and Carmel McInerny of the State Library of South Australia; Tony Marshall of the State Library of Tasmania; Elizabeth Hibbard of the John Oxley Library; Gwen Griffin of the Port Macquarie Historical Society; Edwin Wilson of the Royal Botanic Gardens Sydney; Andrew Lyne of the Australian National Herbarium and Kylie Rees of the Royal Australian Historical Society. Suzanne Ridley and Ophelia Cowell made a lot of early discoveries for this book. Two books were essential to our selection of pictures: Joan Kerr's *The Dictionary of Australian Artists* and Bernard Smith's *European Vision and the South Pacific*.

I thank the Literature Board of the Australia Council for grants that allowed me to fit this book in as an extra to other work.

Eric Rolls
June 2002

PRE-1788

ABEL JANSZOON TASMAN, TASMANIA, 1642

Abel Janszoon Tasman, for whom Tasmania is named, made two journeys to Australia. In 1642 Anthony van Diemen, Governor-General of Holland, sent him to find a quicker route south of Australia to Chile and Peru, who had both proclaimed their independence from Spain. The Dutch knew of Australia from three previous expeditions, one resulting in the appalling aftermath of the wreck of Batavia *on Houtman Abrolhos.*

Tasman set out from Batavia (now Jakarta in Java) in his yacht *Haemskirk* accompanied by the flyboat (fast boat) *Zeehain*. Although both were remarkably high in bow and stern to weather high seas, the Roaring Forties gave them such rough passage Tasman headed northeast out of the constant wind and, about four o'clock in the afternoon of 24 November, he saw land 'bearing E. by N., distant from us by conjecture ten miles [German miles, approximately 40 English miles or 64 kilometres]'.

Tasman, an experienced and expert cartographer, surveyed and mapped the island from where he sighted it round the east coast to either North Bay or Marion Bay south of Maria Island, which he named for Governor van Diemen's wife. Parties went ashore in search of fresh water but then the seas got up again. Tasman himself did not go ashore to plant a claimant flag. His carpenter was a strong swimmer, so a boat rowed him as close to the surf as was safe, and he swam ashore and planted the Dutch flag near four prominent trees. The Dutch Government ignored the acquisition.

High winds drove Tasman off the island. He sailed southeast, sighted the south island of New Zealand, and then travelled back to Java via Fiji.

He described it as a 'happy voyage'. But the proposed sea lane seemed too long and too difficult, so van Diemen sent Tasman out again in 1644 to find a route to the north of Australia. This time he had three ships. Once again high winds and wild seas turned him back when he was nearing Torres Strait. He took refuge in the Gulf of Carpentaria, mapped its southern and western boundary, and then charted hundreds of kilometres of coastline from Melville Island down to present Roebourne in Western Australia. The secretive Dutch Government suppressed his journals and maps. It was not until 1744 that his map of *Hollandia Nova* was published. Matthew Flinders praised its accuracy. Of Tasman's work in the Gulf he wrote:

No particulars were known of the discovery of the south and western parts, — not even the name of the author, though opinion ascribed it with reason to Tasman, — so the chart was considered as little better than a representation of fairy-land, and did not obtain the credit which it was now proved to have merited. Henceforward, the Gulph of Carpentaria will take its station among the conspicuous parts of the Globe in a decided character.

Tasman admired Australia for its position. As an adjunct to his map he wrote:[*]

It is impossible to conceive a country that promises fairer from its situation than this TERRA AUSTRALIS; no longer incognita, as this map demonstrates, but the Southern Continent Discovered. It lies precisely in the richest climates of the World. If the islands of SUMATRA, JAVA and BORNEO abound in precious stones and other valuable commodities; and the MOLUCCAS in spices; NEW GUINEA and the Regions behind it must by a parity of reason be as plentifully endowed by Nature. If the Island of MADAGASCAR is so noble and plentiful a country as all authors speak it, and Gold, Ivory, and other commodities are common in the southern part of Africa from MELINDA down to the CAPE OF GOOD HOPE, and so up again to C.GONSALEZ, here are $\frac{e}{y}$ same latitudes in CARPENTARIA, NEW HOLLAND and NEW ZEALAND. If PERU overflows with silver, if all the mountains of CHILI are filled with Gold, and this precious metal and stones, much more precious, are $\frac{e}{y}$ product of BRAZIL, this continent enjoys the benefit of the same position, and therefore whoever perfectly discovers it and settles it will become infallibly possessed of territories as rich, as fruitful, and as capable of improvement as any that have been hitherto found out, either in the EAST INDIES or the West.

[*] The translator used the space saving inversion of 'ye', $\frac{e}{y}$, the old-fashioned version of 'the'.

WILLEM DE VLAMINGH, ROTTNEST ISLAND, OFF THE WESTERN AUSTRALIAN COAST, 1696-97

Willem de Vlamingh was born in 1640 in Oost-Vlieland, a town in an island off the coast of Holland (now the Netherlands). He learnt seacraft while whaling and catching walruses off the east coast of Greenland and islands north of Russia in the Arctic Ocean. Already the animals in close water had been overharvested. He made repeated voyages into these dangerous and difficult waters, sometimes stopping to chart unknown coasts. Willempie Cornelis, whom he married in 1668, saw him sometimes.

Because of his exceptional experience, the United East India Company offered de Vlamingh permanent employment. He joined the company in November 1688 and made two successful trading trips round the Cape to Batavia. Since he had then proved himself in all waters, the Company offered him command of three vessels to search for the remains of one of their ships so long overdue they knew it had come to grief. The Company also wanted him to make a final exploration of the South Land to see if it held any prospects for settlement. They thought it not improbable that the wreck of the ship would be found on the coast of Western Australia; perhaps the crew may have got ashore and survived.

De Vlamingh set out from the Texel roads on 3 May 1696, at first in company with 130 whalers bound for Greenland and three other cargo ships bound for the West Indies and Ceylon.

The Company and de Vlamingh recognised the importance of fresh vegetables in avoiding scurvy. Captains regularly lost 60 per cent of their crew on long voyages. Despite his care, de Vlamingh arrived at the Cape of Good Hope, a regular victualling and refitting port for all ships, with one out of seven of his crew affected. Since part of his specific instructions were, 'Having come to the Cape mentioned shall allow the ship's crews to restore and rest themselves properly and to give them fresh food, to eat as much as will be possible', he spent seven weeks there rebuilding crew and ships.

De Vlamingh found no trace of the missing ship. He landed on Rottnest Island and surveyed the coast from Swan River to Dirk Hartog Island. That coast presents an unattractive face to those who do not know it. De Vlamingh was instructed to send an armed party of 80 men 80 miles (130 kilometres) inland. Lack of fresh water negated that adventure. A party rowed 10 or 12 kilometres up the Swan River and brought back Black Swans dead and

Swartte Swaane drift op het Eyland Rottenest.

VIEW OF THE SWAN RIVER
Engraving in F. Valentin, *Oud- en Nieuw Oosst-Indiën*, 1724– 26 (University Library, Amersterdam),
by courtesy Royal Australian Historical Society

alive. Parties went ashore in other places to the north in unsuccessful attempts to contact the inhabitants known to be watching them. One trip was cut short because several men incautiously ate seeds of cycads that the native people had been roasting before they were disturbed, and 'after an interval of about three hours I and five more of the others who had also eaten of the said fruit began to vomit so violently that there was hardly any distinction between death and us'. The roasting of this excellent carbohydrate has to be followed by much washing to dispel a poison that can be deadly.

On Dirk Hartog Island a party sent ashore made the wonderful discovery of a pewter plate attached to a post by Dirk Hartog in 1616. It bore this inscription:

Willem de Vlamingh, 1696–97

1616

DEN 25 OCTOBER IS

HIER AENGECOMEN HET SCHIP

DEENDRACHT VAN AMSTEADAM

DE OPPERKOPMAN GILLIS MIBAIS

VAN LVICK SCHIPPER DIRCK HATICHS

VAN AMSTERDAM DE 27 DITO

TE SEIL GEGHM NA BANTVM

DE ONDERCOOPMAN JAN STINS

DE OPPER STVIERMAN PIETER DOEKES

VAN BIL ANNO 1616

De Vlamingh took the plate and replaced it with an inscribed hammered pewter plate of his own showing the date, the names of his ships and the most important members of his crew. (Hartog's plate is now in the Netherlands History section of the Rijksmuseum, de Vlamingh's in the Fremantle Museum.)

Rottnest Island (originally Rottenest) was named for the many Quokkas which de Vlamingh thought were rats 'nearly as big as cats, which had a pouch below their throats in to which one could put one's hand'. Despite much study of these little wallabies, the purpose of the throat pouch is still unknown.

De Vlamingh was enthusiastic about the sandalwood on Rottnest, so were the Chinese when first sent samples. Roots, trunks and branches of *Santalum spicatum* are still valuable exports from Western Australia.

[December] the 31st [1696] Monday in the morning the wind from WSW to S, stiff topsail breeze. After breakfast I went ashore with our bookkeeper and sent our longboat ashore with a party of hands to cut firewood which was to be had there in abundance and very fine of fragrance just like rosewood, of which I have had some in our own boat full taken on board, and let our bookkeeper examine the island further. On coming back reported to have found nothing more than related above. Back on board towards the evening the steersmen who had been on board reported that he and all the crew had seen much smoke rise up on the mainland coast: by evening the wind as before until the morning.

7

1697

January the 1st Tuesday in the morning the wind and weather as before, sent our longboat again to fetch firewood. Have seen smoke rising in several places along the mainland coast. By the evening the wind and weather as before until the evening.

[January] the 2nd Wednesday in the morning the wind as above. After breakfast sent our longboat ashore to cut firewood. In the forenoon went ashore with our bookkeeper and found there the finest wood in the world, from which the whole land was filled with a fine pleasant smell. Have searched through everything and taken a sample on board because it is unknown to us. Careened our ship to cleanse her. As before, saw smoke rise in several places on the mainland coast and have made our sailing order to put to sea at the first opportunity; wind and weather as before until the morning.

JAMES COOK, BUSTARD BAY, OFF THE QUEENSLAND COAST, 1770

Some teachers still tell their pupils that Captain Cook discovered Australia. It was probably discovered 600,000 years before him by an adventurous party of Homo erectus *drifting and paddling down from the Indonesian island of Flores. Natives of Papua New Guinea had been trading down the coast of Queensland as far as Rockhampton for hundreds, probably thousands, of years. But they kept no written records.*

Cook was a literate master mariner and a superb cartographer. He was born in Yorkshire in 1728 and, as a boy, worked as a farm labourer. His schooling was brief. At the age of 17 he was apprenticed to a shopkeeper who offered no future to an adventurer, so he got out of that agreement. He then signed indentures with a local coal-shipper who first gave him a thorough grounding in coastal navigation then took him trading with Sweden, Germany, Poland and Finland in the Baltic Sea. He learnt so quickly that after eight years he was offered command of one of the vessels.

Cook transferred to the Royal Navy when the Seven Years' War broke out in 1755, although he had to begin as an able seaman. In two years he was master of a vessel. He took part in British attacks on French positions in the St Lawrence River and in the capture of Quebec. During that two-year campaign, he assisted expert surveyors and draftsmen in drawing up a large-scale chart of the St Lawrence River.

After another successful campaign and more surveying, Cook returned to Portsmouth in 1762 with a commendation to the Admiralty that he was a man of 'genius and capacity'. At the request of the governor of Newfoundland, he then made extensive surveys of the coast of Newfoundland complete with sailing directions into the harbours. This work added to his reputation.

Moreover, his observation of the 1766 eclipse of the sun earned him the notice of the Royal Society, which was planning observations of the transit of Venus, expected to take place on 3 June 1769. This fitted in with the desire of the Admiralty to know what was in the South Pacific. Cook was chosen for both jobs.

On 26 May 1768, as Lieutenant James Cook, he sailed for Tahiti in HM Bark *Endeavour*. The *Endeavour* was somewhat overcrowded with scientists including Joseph Banks, Daniel Solander, who had studied botany in

Sweden under the famous Carolus Linnaeus, and an astronomer Charles Green, to observe the transit of Venus across the sun in Tahiti. The main aim of the voyage, however, was to find out what land was in the South Pacific.

Cook spent six months charting the coastline of New Zealand, then sailed for New Holland, laying claim to it as New Wales by raising a flag on Possession Island off the tip of Cape York.

Cook's wife, née Elizabeth Batty, saw little of him – about three years altogether. They married at the end of 1762 before he left for the surveys in Newfoundland.

A year after his return from his first voyage, he was sent on a second three-year voyage to crisscross the southern Pacific in search of a major landmass south of New Holland. Although a third voyage to find a northern route from the Pacific to the Atlantic resulted in the discovery and mapping of islands unknown to Europeans, it was a disaster for Cook. He was killed during an altercation with the previously friendly inhabitants of Hawaii.

Contemporaries described Cook as a tall man. Height is relative. His parents were certainly not tall by today's standards. The outlandish removal of a house that his parents lived in to the Fitzroy Gardens, Melbourne, allows one to see the double bed that they slept in. It is 125 centimetres long.

This passage from Cook's journal describes Bustard Bay between Bundaberg and Rockhampton. On most modern maps the northern head is identified as Bustard Head, but the bay is not named. The longitude quoted by Cook for its position is hundreds of kilometres out. His chronometers were faulty, as Kenneth Slessor told in 'Five Visions of Captain Cook':

> Two chronometers the captain had,
> One by Arnold that ran like mad,
> One by Kendal in a walnut case,
> Poor devoted creature with a hangdog face...
>
> All through the night-time clock talked to clock,
> In the captain's cabin, tock-tock-tock,
> One ticked fast and one ticked slow,
> And time went over them a hundred years ago.

[Cook's journal] **Wednesday 23rd May** [1770]. Early the next morning I went ashore with a party of men, in order to examine the country, accompanied by Mr. Banks, Dr. Solander, the other gentlemen, and Tupia... We landed a little within the south point

of the bay, where we found a channel leading into a large lagoon...
In this place there is room for a few ships to lie in great security,
and a small stream of fresh water; I would have rowed into the
lagoon, but was prevented by shallows. We found several bogs and
swamps of salt water, upon which and by the sides of the lagoon,
grows the true mangrove, such as is found in the West Indies and the
first of the kind that we had met with. In the branches of these
mangroves, there were many nests of a remarkable kind of ant, that
was as green as grass: when the branches were disturbed they came
out in great numbers, and punished the offender by a much sharper
bite than ever we had felt from the same kind of animal before.
Upon these mangroves also we saw small green caterpillars in great
numbers. Their bodies were thick set with hairs, and they were
ranged upon the leaves side by side like a file of soldiers, to the
number of twenty or thirty together. When we touched them we
found that the hair on their bodies had the quality of a nettle, and
gave us a more much acute though less durable pain... Upon the
shore we saw a species of the bustard, one of which we shot, it was
as large as a turkey, and weighed seventeen pounds and a half. We all
agreed that this was the best bird we had eaten since we left England,
and in honour of it we called this inlet Bustard Bay. It lies in
latitude 24 deg. 4 min., longitude 208 deg. 18 min. The sea seems to
abound with fish, but unhappily we tore our seine to pieces at the
first haul. Upon the mud-banks, under the mangroves, we found
innumerable oysters of various kinds; among others the hammer
oyster, and a large proportion of small pearl oysters; if in deeper
water there is equal plenty of such oysters at their full growth,
a pearl fishery might certainly be established here to very great
advantage.

SIR GEORGE YOUNG, ENGLAND, 1785

Sir George Young never saw Australia, but for years he tried to persuade the British Government to send him out to settle New South Wales. Like Tasman he saw the advantages of its position.

Young was an experienced seafarer. Born in Dorset in 1732, he joined the Royal Navy as a thirteen-year-old. One of the few to survive the sinking of his ship in a cyclone, he then joined the East India Company's marine. For seven years he sailed the Indian Ocean and the China Sea in trading ships, for the last three years as midshipman.

When the complicated Seven Years' War broke out, Young rejoined the Royal Navy which directed its hostility at French possessions. He made a name for himself in several successful ventures including the capture of the great French fortress on Cape Breton Island off Nova Scotia.

He returned to England when the war ended and married Elizabeth Bradshaw. They had four children in the next four years, and then Young was given command of *Cormorant* carrying 14 guns. In further trouble with the French, in 1778 he took part in the Siege of Pondicherry, then a French possession in southeast India. After almost three years away he returned home to find his wife had died. Later the same year he married Anne Battie, daughter of a wealthy doctor. He used the timber of two old ships as framing for a big house on the Thames in Berkshire.

In 1781, the Admiralty gave Young command of the Royal Yacht, *William and Mary*. His friendship with the Prince of Wales aided that appointment. Despite frequent applications, he never again saw active service. The King knighted him for his work in the East and he was promoted to Admiral by seniority.

Young first proposed a settlement on Madagascar. The trading monopoly of the East India Company precluded that. His application for a venture to New South Wales was made in conjunction with James Maria Matra, a minor diplomat who had been a midshipman on Cook's *Endeavour*. Although the government adopted many of Young's ideas, he played no part in the settlement. In May 1788, he and his partners put in a final bid, this time for a grant of Norfolk Island 'to them and their heirs for ever'. He wanted to grow New Zealand flax and cultivate pine for masts. That application also failed.

Young's proposals for New South Wales exist in five forms, all presented in a book of beautiful format by Alan Frost, *Dreams of a Pacific Empire*, published by Resolution Press, Sydney, in 1980.

The following quote is from the final corrected printed version of 21 April 1785, which avoids the difficulty of the old-fashioned 'f' with a half bar for the letter 's'.

Its great extent, and relative situation, with respect to the eastern and southern parts of the Globe, are material for consideration:

Botany Bay, or its vicinity, the part that is proposed to be first settled, is about two thousand leagues from Lima and Baldavia, with a fair, open navigation; and there is no doubt but that a lucrative trade would soon be opened with the Creole Spaniards, for English manufactures: or suppose we were again involved in a war with Spain, HERE are ports of shelter and refreshment for our ships, should it be necessary to send any to the South Sea.

From the coast of China, it lies about fifteen hundred leagues, and nearly the same distance from the East Indies; from the Spice Islands, about seven hundred leagues, and about six weeks run from the Cape of Good Hope.

The variety of climates included between the forty-fourth, and tenth degrees of latitude, give us an opportunity of uniting, in one territory, almost all the productions of the known world: to explain this more fully, I will point out some of the countries which are situated within the same extent of latitude, on either side of the Equator; they are China, Japan, Siam, Italy, Persia, Arabia Felix, Egypt, Greece, all Turkey, the Mediterranean Sea, India, Spain, South of France and Portugal, with Mexico, Lima, Baldavia, and the greatest part of the Pacific Ocean; to which may be added the Cape of Good Hope, &c. &c.

From this review, it will, I think, be acknowledged, that a territory so happily situated, must be superior to all others, for establishing a very extensive commerce; nor is it mere presumption to say, the country is every way capable of producing all kinds of spice; likewise the fine oriental cotton, indigo, coffee, tobacco, with every species of the sugar-cane; also tea, silk and madder.--- That very remarkable plant, known by the name of New Zealand Flax Plant, may be cultivated in every part, and in any quantity our demands may require; its uses are more extensive than any vegetable hitherto known; for, in its gross state, it far exceeds any thing of the kind for cordage and canvas, not subject to dry-rot, and may be obtained at a much cheaper rate than those materials, which at present we get from Russia... not to mention the great probability for finding, in such an immense country, metals of every kind. At a time when men are alarmed at every idea of emigration, I wish not to add to their fears by any attempt to depopulate the parent state; the settlers of New South Wales are principally to be collected from the Friendly Islands, and China; all the people required from England, are only a few that are possessed of the useful arts, and those comprised among the crews of the ships sent out on that service; and the natives, no doubt, may in time, be brought to unite in this society ... The heavy expence government is annually put to, for transporting, and otherwise punishing the felons, together with the facility of their return, are evils long and much lamented; THERE is an asylum open that will considerably reduce the first, and wholly prevent the latter.

Had I the Command of this Expedition, I should require a Ship of War, say the Old Rainbow, now at Woolwich, formerly a Ship of 40 Guns, as the best constructed for that Purpose of any in the Navy, with only half her lower Deck Guns, and 250 Men; 100 of which should be Mariners; a Store Ship likewise, of about 600 Tons Burthen, with 40 Seamen and 10 Marines; and a small Vessel of about 100 Tons, of the Brig or Schooner kind, with 20 Men, both fitted as Ships of War, and Commanded by PROPER OFFICERS.

1788−1809

ARTHUR BOWES SMYTH. LORD HOWE ISLAND. 1788

As ship's surgeon, Arthur Bowes Smyth attended 109 convict women and eight children aboard Lady Penrhyn of the First Fleet. He did not stay in Sydney, making a round trip to take on tea in China and then home, to die six months later at the age of 40.

Born in 1750, Arthur was the seventh of 10 children of Thomas Smyth, Overseer of the Poor in Essex. There is no record of his studying medicine, but for years he practised successfully as surgeon and midwife in Tolleshunt D'Arcy, Essex. He attracted high fees. An IOU in the office of the Agent-General for New South Wales in London shows a charge of £6-15-0 for treating a broken 'legg'. That is equivalent to $6000 today. For midwifery duties, he arranged with the parish for a fee of one shilling and sixpence above what they usually paid for the delivery of women in their care.

Originally appointed as doctor to the crew, Bowes Smyth's experience made him an excellent choice to replace the doctor appointed to the convict women when that doctor suddenly became too ill to travel.

Bowes Smyth was proud of his work. He recorded in his journal of 17 April 1787:

GRASS TREES

From *The Journal of Arthur Bowes Smyth*, 1788, 'I have etch'd the likeness...& is no very bad resemblance of it', Mitchell Library, State Library of New South Wales

This day I attended (at the request of Mr Balmain) on the woman wt. the fractured leg [she was Balmain's patient on *Alexander* – they had not yet left port], & removed the Bandage and dressed it up again; before the Bandage was removed the woman was in the most excruciating pain, but very soon after removing it she became perfectly easy and continued so.

He was needed as an obstetrician. On 15 November 1787 he noted: 'This day, Ann Morton one of the women on board our ship, delivered of a Boy'. On 1 December 1787, 12 days out of the Cape of Good Hope, he wrote with deep satisfaction:

In the *Lady Penrhyn* only 2 Women have died since leaving England; one 82 Yrs. of Age of a Dropsy wh. had long rain'd upon her & the other of a Consumption, sent on board the *Lady Penrhyn* in the last stage thereof, from the *Friendship* whilst we were at the Cape of Good Hope.

Bowes Smyth did not like the convict women despite his attentive care,

... since every day furnishes proofs of their being more harden'd in their Wickedness — nor do I conceive it possible in their present situation to adopt any plan to induce them to behave like rational or even human Beings — perpetually thieving the Cloaths from each other, nay almost from their backs may be rank'd amongst the least of their crimes (tho' it is the Crime for which most of them are in their present disgraceful situation).

Nor did he have any sympathy for an energetic lover when they were anchored in Port Jackson.

March 25th [1788] This Eveng. abt 7 o'Clock died John Fisher, Seaman on board our Ship of a Dysentery — several of the men on board had the same disorder & recover'd, & I attributed the death of this young man (abt. 20 years old) in a great measure to his own imprudence, in swimming on Shore naked in the middle of the night to one of the Convict women wt. whom he had formed a Connection & who had a child by him while on board — he wd. lye abt. wt. her in the woods all night in the Dews, & return on board again a little before day light, whereby he caught a most violent cold & made his disorder infinitely more putrid than it wd. otherwise have been, (if he did not wholey occasion it by such improper conduct).

The bird life on Lord Howe Island, innocently unaware that human beings are predators, astounded Bowes Smyth. The killing was not wanton. All were valuable food; all were eaten.

This forenoon [16 May 1788] I went shore wt. Captain Sever & Mr. Watts in the Pinnace; we went thro' an openg. in the reef over which the Sea broke wt. a tremendous noise & swell. We landed in Hunter's Bay & saw great numbers of Boobies, Pidgeons, & many other birds. The Capt. & Mrs. Watts return'd to dinner but as Mr. Anstis was coming on shore after dinner I continued there hunting Birds &ca. in the woods — Mr. Anstis & the Steward wt. several of the Ships Company came in the Afternoon & stay'd on Shore all night. The sport we had in knockg. down Birds &ca. was great indeed tho' at the Expence of tearing most of the Cloaths off our backs. We made a fire under the trees & supp'd upon part of our Game broil'd — wh. was very sweet & good, the Pidgeons were the largest I ever saw. We afterwards slept in thick great coats carried on shore for that purpose, cover'd over wt. the leaves of the Cabbage tree, which are here innumerable & many of them so small & tender that you may cut them down with a pocket knife. — When I was in the Woods amongst the Birds I cd. not help picturing to myself the Golden Age as described by Ovid to see the Fowls or Coots some White, some blue and white, others all blue wt. large red bills & a patch of red on the top of their heads, & the Boobies in thousands, together wt. a curious brown bird abt. the size of the Landrail in England walking totally fearless & unconcern'd in all part around us, so that we had nothing more to do than to stand still a minute or two & knock down as many as we pleas'd wt. a short stick...

The Pidgeons also were as tame as those already described & wd. sit upon the branches of the trees till you might go & take them off with your hand or if the branch was so high on wh. they sat, they wd. at all times sit till you might knock them down with a short stick — many hundreds of all the sorts mention'd above, together wt. many Parotts & Parroquetts, Magpies & other Birds were caught & carried on board our Ship & the Charlotte...

After discribing the number & tameness of the feather'd inhabitants of this Island, I must take notice that our Surprise was no less in the morng. upon going into the pinnace to fish with hooks & lines in the Bay within side the reef. The water in many parts not more than 4 or 5 ft. deep wt. a fine white sandy bottom wt. Coral, Brain stones & many other Marine plants growing at the bottom, wt. the Sun shining bright upon them, & the inumerable quantities & varieties of fish swimg. amongst this Coral Grove (if I may be allow'd the Expression) exhibited such a novel & beautiful a scene as but few places in the World I believe will afford. The fish bit so very fast that in abt. 2 or 3 hours we had caught some hundred weight -- & the Pinnace was half Loaded — the Bait made use of was a piece of flesh of the Boobies of wh. we had some hundreds also (alive & dead) in the pinnace — I must not omit to mention that this Island produces, Broad Beans (exactly in pod, size & taste the same as the Windsor Bean) Scurvy Grass, Samphire, Endive & Spinnage. The fish we caught in the space of 3 hours served the whole ships Company 3 days.

Burenda Boundary.

WATKIN TENCH, SYDNEY, 1791

Watkin Tench was born at Chester in the western country of Cheshire some time between May 1758 and May 1759. His father, Fisher Tench, was a dancing master. With his wife Margaret, or Margarita, they ran 'an academy of dancing and a most respectable boarding school'. They certainly gave their son Watkin a good education. His books show a wide knowledge of Latin and English classics and he read modern French literature.

When the American War of Independence seemed certain to break out, Tench joined the Marine Corps with the rank of second lieutenant. His two-year service in North America ended when a French squadron drove his ship ashore at Delaware Bay. He spent three months as a prisoner of war.

Back in England when the war ended, he was put on half pay. When the call came for volunteers for a corps of marines to sail with the First Fleet 'for the protection of the settlement intended to be made there, as well as for preserving good order and regularity among the convicts', he offered his services and was accepted.

Tench spent four years at Port Jackson with the rank of captain-lieutenant. While there he wrote *A Narrative of the Expedition to Botany Bay; with an Account of New South Wales, its Productions, Inhabitants, &c., to which is subjoined A List of the Civil and Military Establishments at Port Jackson*. It was published in London in 1789 and ran into three editions. Translations were published in France, Sweden, Holland and Germany.

Tench liked the look of the place:

> The general face of the country is certainly pleasing, being
> diversified with gentle ascents, and little winding vallies, covered
> for the most part with large spreading trees, which afford a
> succession of leaves in all seasons. In those places where trees are
> scarce, a variety of flowering shrubs abound, most of them entirely
> new to an European, and surpassing in beauty, fragrance, and number,
> all I ever saw in an uncultivated state: among these, a tall shrub,
> bearing an elegant white flower, which smells like English May, is
> particularly delightful [probably a *Leptospermum* or a *Melaleuca*].

But he was cautious about its prospects.

[An] adventurer, if of a persevering character and competent knowledge, might in the course of ten years bring matters into such a train as to render himself comfortable and independent, I think highly probable.

However, he thought the land was too distant and export too difficult for any fortunes to be made. Ruthless go-getters soon proved that estimate wrong.

In June 1789, Tench led a party 'through a country untrodden before by an European foot' and found the Nepean River. He left for England in December 1791, where he wrote *A Complete Account of the Settlement at Port Jackson*, published in 1793. He states:

... no climate, hitherto known, is more generally salubrious ... to this cause I ascribe the great number of births which happened, considering the age and other circumstances of many of the mothers. Women, who certainly would never have bred in any other climate, here produced as fine children as ever were born.

Still cautious in his appraisal, he correctly nominated whaling as offering the best immediate business. Until the 1820s when wool replaced it, whale oil was the principal export of the Colony.

Tench remained in service. He married Anna Maria Sargent after his return from Australia. During the war with France on 6 November 1794, his ship HMS *Alexander* of 74 guns became separated from the rest of the Channel Fleet. Three French seventy-fours attacked. In a desperate engagement she beat off two of them killing 450 French sailors, but by then she was a near wreck with 40 of her own men dead, so she struck her colours (surrendered) to the third. Tench spent six months in Brittany as a prisoner of war, mostly on parole. That gave him material for another good book published in 1796, *Letters Written from France to a Friend in London*. Having no children of their own, when his wife's sister and her husband died a couple of years apart, he and Anna adopted their four children in 1821. He retired in 1827 with the rank of lieutenant colonel and died in 1833.

From *A Complete Account of the Settlement…* I quote his finely detailed and sympathetic description of Aboriginal men and women fishing.

Summoned by the calls of hunger, and the returning light, he starts from his beloved indolence, and snatching up the remaining brand of his fire, hastens with his wife to the strand, to commence their daily task. In general the canoe is assigned to her, into which she puts the fire, and pushes off into deep water, to fish with hook and line, this being the province of the women. If she have a child at the breast, she takes it with her. And thus in her skiff, a piece of bark tied at both ends with vines, and the edge of it but just above the surface of the water, she pushes out regardless of the elements, if they be but commonly agitated. While she paddles to the fishing-bank, and while employed there, the child is placed on her shoulders, entwining its little hands around her neck, and closely grasping her hair with its hands. To its first cries she remains insensible, as she believes them to arise only from the inconveniency of a situation, to which she knows it must be inured. But if its plaints continue, and she supposes it to be in want of food, she ceases her fishing, and clasps it to her breast. An European spectator is struck with horror and astonishment, at their perilous situation: but accidents seldom happen. The management of the canoe alone appears a work of unsurmountable difficulty, its breadth is so inadequate to its length. The Indians, aware of its ticklish formation, practise from infancy to move in it without risk. Use only could reconcile them to the painful position in which they sit in it: they drop in the middle of the canoe upon their knees, and resting the buttocks on the heels, extend the knees to the sides, against which they press strongly, so as to form a poize, sufficient to retain the body in its situation, and relieve the weight which would otherwise fall wholly upon the toes. Either in this position, or cautiously moving in the centre of the vessel, the mother tends her child; paddles her boat; broils fish; and provides in part the subsistence of the day. — Their favourite bait for fish is a cockle.

The husband in the mean time warily moves to some rock, over which he can peep into unruffled water, to look for fish. For this purposes he always chuses a weather shore; and the various windings of the numerous creeks and indents always afford one. Silent and watchful he chews a cockle, and spits it into the water. Allured by the bait, the fish appear from beneath the rock. He prepares his fish-gig, and pointing it downward, moves it gently towards the object, always trying to approach it as near as possible to the fish, before the stroke be given. At last he deems himself sufficiently advanced, and plunges it at his prey. If he has hit his mark, he continues his efforts and endeavours to transpierce it, or so to entangle the barbs in the flesh, as to prevent its escape. When he finds it secure he drops the instrument, and the fish, fastened on the prongs, rises to the surface, floated by the buoyancy of the staff. Nothing now remains to be done, but to haul it to him, with either a long stick, or another fish-gig (for an Indian, if he can help it, never goes into the water on these occasions) to disengage it, and to look out for fresh sport.

But sometimes the fish have either deserted the rocks for deeper water, or are too shy to suffer approach. He then launches his canoe, and leaving the shore behind, watches the rise of prey out of the water, and darts his gig at them to the distance of many yards. Large fish he seldom procures by this method; but among shoals of mullets, which are either pursued by enemies, or leap at objects on the surface, he is often successful. Baneelon [probably much closer to the sound of his name than Bennelong as it is usually written] has been seen to kill more than twenty fish by this method, in an afternoon.

RICHARD ATKINS, SYDNEY, 1792

Richard Atkins was born in 1745, the fifth son of Sir William Bowyer.
By an extraordinary provision in a will, Richard had to change his name to Atkins.
He entered the army, but all that is known of his career there is that he was
Adjutant of the Isle of Man militia in 1783.

He must have had legal training since he was appointed magistrate shortly after his arrival in Sydney in February 1791. By 1802, he was judge advocate.

His legal opinions were respected at first, but he was an alcoholic. A judge who delivered sentences of death while drunk earned opprobrium. When Macquarie took over as Governor on 1 January 1810, he replaced Atkins and sent him to England to appear in court as one of Governor Bligh's witnesses. Atkins lived obscurely after the court martial that cleared Bligh. He died in 1820.

The *mss Journal of a Voyage to Botany Bay* that Atkins kept from 1791 to 1810 is strange reading. It shows a learned man given to long philosophical arguments with himself. He wrote pages on light, considering it scientifically and artistically. He wrote more pages on sight as the main sense, even more on the advantages of society and a consideration of man as head of the animals:

> ... the natural superiority of man over the other animals is a
> necessary result of the great number of instincts with which
> his mind is endowed.

Atkins includes many poems, some long. On 12 April 1793 after the entry, 'Wind West. Ther. 78', he wrote out the whole of 'Elegy Written in a Country Churchyard' without attribution. The first line is cross-referenced in Italian to Dante and the second last line to Petrarch.

Some poems were apparently written by him, such as the declamatory 'Ode to Fancy by an untaught Muse'.

> O thou keen power! whose radiant eye
> Can thousand shadowy forms descry
> That cheat corporeal sight...

Atkins had frequent violent pains in the stomach and several times recorded being 'taken excessive ill, so much so that my life was in the most iminent danger'. On 7 June 1795 he asks, 'For what do I get by drinking? I lose the friendship of my best friends, I lose my health, I lose my reputation, I lose my happiness altogether'.

He wrote pages on religion and a long discussion in English and French, 'On the Shortness of Life'. When he wonders, 'What hearts are inaccessible to love? What situations in life can put us under the restriction of a passion so involuntary?' he wonders in French.

One woman left him because of his drinking, but his three illegitimate children by other women lived with him.

There is one unexpected entry in the journal that sensitises the philosophy:

> A gentleman was asked by a Lady to make a rhyme for Ring.
> Your husband gave to you a Ring
> Sett round with diamonds fair,
> You gave to him a better thing
> A Ring sett round with hair.

Despite his sitting in judgment when drunk, Atkins had a genuine compassion for those he sentenced. On 26 June 1792 when the Colony was desperately short of food, he wrote, 'I am obliged to punish those whose hunger drove to steal a few cobs of corn or a turnip. I most sincerely pray to God that this may soon end'.

In this quote from his journal, it is startling to find Sydney known as 'the camp'.

> [April 1792] Mild and regular weather, the sea breeze sets in generally about 11 o'clock. This Evening I walked by myself to the Brick fields, about a mile from the Camp, for so Sydney is call'd, from its having been the Spot they pitch'd their tents on their first landing; A very good road is made the whole way to it through the wood, where trees of immense size border it on both sides, their lofty and wide spreading Branches look beautiful. The timber is of no value but for burning, almost every tree is rotten at the heart, very hard and heavy and coarse grained, emitting great quantities of Gum like Dragons Blood, but without its properties, and is totally useless. The underwood is mostly flowering shrubs, some of whom are now in blossom of the most vivid and beautiful Colours imaginable and many of them most delicately formed. An arm of the sea appears thro' the wood and beyond it another wood rising

gradually to a moderate height which terminates the prospect...

24 [April 1792] Continuance of fine weather. The quantities of fish in the harbour is amazing, mostly Mullet, I should imagine the fishery under proper regulations might be of great advantage, indeed if any thing has happened to the Atlantic, (the Ship sent to Bengal for provisions,) or should they neglect to send us a Store Ship from England, something must be thought of for the support of the Colony which is at present in a very tickilish situation...

6 [June 1792 – he was then living in Parramatta] The continuance of fine pleasant weather at a time of year (the beginning of Winter) shews the excellence of the climate, indeed every thing is in a continual state of vegetation, The Woods are in constant foliage for tho' they shed their leaves, yet they are only shoved off by the succeeding Leaves.

BY WATER TO PARRAMATTA WITH A DISTANT VIEW OF THE WESTERN MOUNTAINS
Taken from the Windmill Hill at Sydney, James Heath 1757–1834, Rex Nan Kivell Collection
NK3374/8, National Library of Australia

On 14 November, he set out from Parramatta with a friend and four armed men to walk to the Nepean River. On the first night, they had a thoroughly Australian picnic.

> ... at last at a distance we perceived a large pond, which we immediately made for and on its bank we sett the Kettle boiling and made some excellent Soup of 1 Duck 1 Pidgeon 1 Crow and 3 Magpies and some salt pork.

LUIS NÉE, BOTANY BAY, 1793

Antonio Joseph Cavanilles published Anales de Historia Natural, No.3 *in March 1800 in Spain. In it he included '"Observations on the soil, natives and plains of Port Jackson and Botany Bay;" being mainly a quotation from the general description of the colony made by Luis Née, botanist on the Malaspina Expedition, Mar.–Apr. 1793.'*

Captain Alexandro Malaspina had a more cultured upbringing than either Young or Cook. He was born on 5 November 1754 to an aristocratic and distinguished Italian family in northern Tuscany. He studied at the Clementine College in Rome and learnt navigation as a Knight of the Order of Malta. He joined the Spanish Navy and soon rose to the rank of Captain.

Aware that Spain was rapidly losing the world to British and French adventurers, Malaspina presented a plan on 10 September 1788 of a major exploratory expedition to Antonio Valdés, Spanish Minister of Marine. Apart from scientific studies, he suggested an examination of the British settlement in New Holland and the Liu Qiu or Ryukyu Islands, a chain of islands including Okinawa in the far south of Japan where Britain had no intention of establishing a colony. The islands were rich in agriculture and manufacturing; they attracted artists and artisans of high order and they were a major trading centre between China, Korea and Japan. Malaspina had misinterpreted something he read.

With two ships in his charge, Malaspina sailed for the Pacific in 1789. After examining ports in South America and the west coast of North America, he turned southwest to the Philippines, southeast to New Zealand, then northwest to Port Jackson, ostensibly for a rest and a refit, in reality to spy. He arrived on 12 March 1793 and unloaded an Andalusian cow, presumably because it no longer produced milk. Malaspina did not think much of the British settlement. On his return, he too was sent on an unsuccessful search for a northwest passage. He eventually lost government favour. Believing that Spain would be better off if she established trading posts on the Pacific Rim rather than trying to dominate distant lands, he worked politically to persuade the King. The furious King threw him into prison, where he languished for seven years.

Luis Née, his botanist, was French, born in 1734. He was working in the Jardin de la Prioria de la Real Bótica when asked to join the southern expedition. He collected in Uruguay, Argentina, Chile, Peru, Ecuador, the

Philippines and Mexico, where he travelled into the interior. After his Australian collecting he disembarked at Talcahuano in Chile, crossed the Andes, travelled through Argentina collecting all the way and picked up the expedition waiting for him in Buenos Aires. In Australia he collected several specimens of more than a thousand species.

The population of Jackson occupies the worst part of the colony and its surroundings are hardly suitable for cultivation, being rocky, sandy and very arid land. The very pleasant colonists have done their best to utilize the land around their dwellings by force of persistent and heavy work. Half a league from the town on both sides of the river the soil is very different, presenting on all parts a virgin and fertile land. The port is secure and sheltered, the disembarkation excellent, wood is abundant, the water delicious, although distant from the port; and the police admirable in spite of men being attached to it who were the scourge of their homeland. Two miles from the port may be seen the ranch which the Governor ordered built, located on a fertile plot, with a stake fence, and within the enclosure a good house and abundant water. The land between the ranch and the tile works is not inferior in quality and it is certain that all of it will be cultivated when the resources of the colony are greater...

I went out to study plants every day when the rains did not prevent it. I always started my excursions at nine o'clock in the morning because until then a copious dew, which was the equivalent of a good rain, persisted. Thus I covered several times and in various directions the hills immediately around Jackson, always collecting valuable plants. I set aside one day to go to Botany Bay and I left the town at four in the morning, accompanied by two armed soldiers to defend me against any attacks that the natives of the country might attempt. I found the narrow tracks overgrown with dense scrub so heavy with dew that in very little time I was wet to the skin; and the land arid, with no other moisture than the light rains retained in two or three marshes. Some short stretches had trees, others were covered with beautiful shrubs and plants and the rest almost without vegetation...

I was getting close now to the coast and half a league before arriving at the Bay, I found a valley and an arroyo of fresh water in such quantity that it would be sufficient to make the soil fruitful. In great part it is marshy and could be used for rice cultivation, and when the stored waters are released and the land dried, converted into gardens of corn, maize etc. I also found a large river which the natives visit in their canoes in order to fish when they cannot do so in the ocean and I crossed it on a tree trunk which serves as a bridge there during low tide. My walk was slow and roundabout, as it always should be with a botanist... I arrived at last on the beach where I examined for more than a league towards the east. Close to the sea all the land is made up of loose sand, and between the sea and the surrounding hills are rivulets and marshes of brackish water which can be drunk. On the beach I found three species of orachs, one of which was in fruit; three convolvulus, one very like soldanela, two ranunculas; and among many other plants three geraniums, one similar to the columbine and another to the grossularioides of Linneaus; in the marshes some rushes and three new droseras; a little further away from the sea the casuarina, the mangrove, common also in the Philippines and various species of banksia with very curious cryptograms. The multitude of plants that grow there is so great that to collect and know them even slightly, it would be necessary to live many years in the vicinity of the Bay.

THOMAS FYSHE PALMER, PORT JACKSON, 1795

Thomas Fyshe Palmer arrived at Port Jackson on 25 October 1794 as one of the five celebrated Scottish Martyrs. Born in Bedfordshire, England, to wealthy parents of high standing, he had an impressive career at Queen's College, Cambridge, eventually adding Bachelor of Divinity to Master of Arts. Once ordained, he became Church of England curate at Leatherhead in Surrey. While there, he dined with the formidable Samuel Johnson in London. According to Boswell, one of their discussions concerned the inadequate pay of county clergy. A Unitarian society had just been established in London and their ideas attracted Palmer. He was beginning to question the doctrines of the Church of England.

The Unitarians were first acknowledged as a religious body in Transylvania in 1600. Its members met controversy in several countries. They insisted on intellectual freedom and on critical methods of studying the Bible, and they refused to accept that doctrinaire agreement (the specific interpretations of the Bible by a religion) is necessary to salvation.

Although he had a brilliant future with the established Church of England, Palmer offered his services as a Unitarian preacher. From his base in Dundee, he frequently preached in Scottish towns and cities and formed Unitarian societies wherever he went. Pamphlets began to circulate refuting his doctrines.

Palmer then became involved with the Friends of Liberty, which had its headquarters in Dundee. This body advocated necessary political reform: the removal of the very high war tax which people were finding increasingly difficult to pay, general suffrage and a shorter term for elected parliaments. Palmer did no more than correct the grammar of a handbill addressed to the public and water down the more offensive statements. However, he did send it to a printer with an order for 1000 copies. For that he was arrested on a charge of sedition, found guilty of treason by a compliant jury at the circuit court, Perth, and sentenced to seven years' transportation.

Palmer spent some months in irons in the hulks working with convicted felons. With two of the Martyrs tried on equally flimsy grounds, he was then put aboard *Surprise* with a gang of convicts bound for Port Jackson. So bad was his treatment on board that Palmer thought the captain had been told to make sure he did not reach Port Jackson. James Ellis, a good friend who was travelling as a free settler, alleviated his condition as much as possible.

Palmer arrived with such good recommendations to Lieutenant-Governor Grose that he was treated as a special prisoner, unable to return home until his term was spent, but to live as a free man provided he did not engage in politics.

Although his health was affected by dysentery contracted in the hulks, Palmer became a successful farmer and, in partnership with James Ellis, built a boat to trade with Norfolk Island. When his sentence was due to expire, he combined with several others to build *El Plumier*, intending to trade extensively on their way home. The trip was a disaster. They could buy no goods in New Zealand, although they waited weeks. A native war prevented their landing at Tongatapu, but they were welcomed at the nearby island of Fiji. Island to island trading halted when they struck a reef. After getting the vessel repaired they sailed for Macao, one of the few Chinese ports then open. Violent storms drove them about the Pacific until they ran out of supplies, so they risked putting into the Spanish port of Guguan, one of the Northern Mariana Islands, even though Britain and Spain were at war. The Governor seized the crew as prisoners of war. Palmer had no medicine to counteract his returning dysentery and he died on the island in June 1802.

Palmer wrote two letters from Australia to Reverend H. Williamson, Unitarian minister in Dundee, saying in one, 'I have no scruple in saying it is the finest country I ever saw'.

The following quote is from a portion of a letter in the archives of Harris Manchester College, Oxford. It was written to an unknown recipient on 16 September 1795 and signed 'Your affectionate humble servt. Thos. Fyshe Palmer'.

The climate is delicious the air so salubrious that there is no occasion for short allowance to whet the appetite. You are hungry soon after dinner. Some impute this to a defect in the nutriment the beast receives. This must be a mistake. No cattle are more fat. The kine (what there are of them) have the coats of race horses, glossy as sattin & not a rib to be seen. There is a very good proportion of most excellent ground. Some of it producing with most wretched farming 40 Bushels of wheat per acre & from 50 to 80 of Indian Corn. If 2 or 3 thousand head of cattle were imported & the military monopoly put an end to. I am persuaded that this settlement like Norfolk Island might immediately support itself. But unless an alteration soon takes place the officers will make princely fortunes & the place be ruined.

This place would afford infinite entertainment. It is certainly a new world, a new creation. Every plant, every shell tree fish & animal, bird, insect different from the old. I believe it to be rich in minerals, especially iron, the ore of which is in immence quantities on the surface of the ground. Cook found the compass affected as he sailed along the coast which he attributed to the iron. The grape vine thrives with the utmost luxuriance, & wine tolerably good is already produced. This will be the staple article of commerce. Possibly copper & coal & fine wood might be carried to advantage to India. A ship is now loading with the latter. We are beginning today to distill the essential oil of peppermint from the leaves of a peppermint tree to send thither.

MATTHEW EVERINGHAM, BLUE MOUNTAINS, NEW SOUTH WALES, OCTOBER 1795

In 1985, Valerie Ross published The Everingham Letterbook, Letters of a First Fleet Convict. *She had earlier published three volumes about Matthew Everingham and his wife Elizabeth. The third volume,* Cornstalks — A Genealogy, *is an indexed list of their 8000 descendants of which Valerie Ross is one. A few months after the third volume was published, Valerie Ross was told of a small, dilapidated brown leather notebook with three letters by Everingham and three newspaper cuttings in the Archives of the University of Melbourne.*

It had come in 1964 with a mass of documents from a Western District grazing property owned by the Ritchie family. During the 1840s and 1850s, one of their forebears was a ship's surgeon with a special interest in penal settlements. Somehow he came by the book and it lay unnoticed among station records for more than 100 years. It also lay unnoticed in the library archives until May 1981, when it was brought out for inclusion in a display of 'Images of Yesterday'. A friend of an Everingham descendant recognised it.

Very little is known of Everingham before his arrival in Australia as a convict in the First Fleet, with a little more than two years remaining to serve. When he was 15 years old, he stole two law books from Samuel Shepherd, a 24-year-old barrister, and sold them. Shepherd prosecuted him and he received a seven-year sentence. Shepherd was later raised to the Privy Council, knighted and made Lord Chief Baron of the Court of Exchequer in Scotland.

Shepherd seems to have thought that the lad, Everingham, had learnt his lesson and took a continued interest in his welfare in Australia, even sending him a 'very liberal donation (in this part of the world a Nabob's fortune)'. Everingham wrote all three newsy letters to Shepherd in gratitude for 'the many incontestable proofs I have received of your friendship'.

The year 1791 was particularly eventful for him: on 13 March he married Elizabeth Rimes who had been transported on *Neptune* in the Second Fleet, his time expired on 7 July and a few weeks later he settled on a farm at The Ponds, northeast of Parramatta, now the suburb of Rydalmere. In 1792, he held the deed to 20 acres and he was prospering.

I have now settled 15 months and my little Farm thank God seems
to promise pretty well My wife has got pretty well and really a
good one she is. I have 5 acres of India Corn one of English wheat
about half an Acre of Barley Pumkins Melons callavans [callavance,
pulses]. &c in abundance, all seem to thrive well. I have two Sows
big with Piggs some poultry and a hive of this Country's bees
[*Trigona carbonaria*] they are exceedingly small In three months
I am to maintain myself & family Independent of the public store,
and do the best I can for myself. Next year I hope I shall be able
to maintain two men off the store. I have now one...

The chief story in the letters is of an attempted crossing of the Blue
Mountains in December 1795. There is no other record of this expedition
and it was very nearly successful. Two neighbouring farmers accompanied
Everingham: John Ramsay, formerly a sailor transported for robbery, and
William Reid, who had come as a sailor on the First Fleet and obtained his
discharge from the navy in Australia. Reid later commanded various ships;
he discovered Lake Macquarie and possibly sailed through Bass Strait
before Bass and Flinders.

The Blue Mountains venture probably ended at Mount Irvine eight
kilometres west of present Bilpin, or possibly at Mount Tomah to the south-
west. From either site, it was not too hard going to accomplish a crossing.
They turned back because they were out of food and because Everingham's
shoes had fallen to pieces – he was barefoot.

... by 10 o'Clock we found ourselves right on the Mountains
and were now convinced that we had been fortunate enough to
hitt on the right road, about 12 o'Clock We were on the Top of
the Mountain [Mount Bowen, southwest of Kurrajong] and could
look down on all $\frac{e}{y}$ Country round with a heartfelt pleasure the
prospect was really delightfull for many miles we could behold all
the Country round except to the Northwd where lay more
mountains for Us to encounter. The day was very clear and at an
amazing distance we could observe the sea rolling against the Shore
The Hawksbury river and all its different windings thro' the
low Country. The different Settlements we could discover by
their various smoak asscending. as far as ever our eyes could discern
(to the Southwd a fine level Champagne Country where the Cows
Strayed) some thousands of natives little fires...

It was Dinner time and when We had sufficiently feasted our Eyes, We had our little repast on the Top of this mountain.

We had taken a bladder of brandy with us to take a little now and then to Cheer our spirits

On the Top of the mountain I had the honour to drink yours and Mrs Shepherd's good health in a hearty glass of it The Mountain in honour to the Judge Advocate of this Country was named by Us Mount Collins

On the very top of it there is a bare spot with a bush bearing a flouer the Colour and Smell Much resembling Lavender [a Mint Bush, either *Prostanthera violacea* or *P. caerulea*]. We sat under it to eat our dinner and it was named by my desire Shepherd's Bush.

We descended this mountain and crossed a very deep Cut of water & Slept at the foot of the Mountain opposite that night.

We started at day light but it was near half after Eleven before we reached the Top of this Mountain, being higher than the former Mountain, our view was not near so good, the ground being covered with brush Stinging Nettles And briers which obstructed our walking greatly the Timber heavy and lofty quite of different Species to what we had ever seen in the Country before — We climbed up a very lofty Tree to find the best road to the next Mountain

We descended this Mountain that night and Slept at the foot of it; In the morning we begun to cross the valley before us in order to asscend the other mountain; by three in the afternoon we had reached the Top, from which we had a view that made us amends for our disappointment at $\frac{e}{y}$ last [probably Mount Tootie north of present Bilpin].

We now found the mountains were Intersected in two places by two terrible chasms, the Hawksbury river takes it direction out of the Mountains goes thro one and another river named Macarthur [probably Bowen's Creek] runs thro' the other, suppose to empty itself in Port Stephens We now found, we had got quite to the outside of this Chain of Mountains, and further to the Nthwd about 30 miles apparently was another chain more lofty and dreadful than those we were on,

Determined to descend and Steer directly over for them, we found after about 3 hours search a place to descend with safety We went for the night into a Clift of a rock where there was a Cavity like an Oven Capable of holding 200 men

In the night there was some little Rain with a deal of Thunder and lightning. Never in my live was my soul Struck with such awful admiration, the echoing of the Thunder about those terrible Rocks and mountains was sublimely grand, how insignificant the report of a broad side of great Guns appeared to this. It was to the hearer as if the very rocks and mountains were rending from their bottoms, each flash of forked livid fire seem'd regularly to keep time with each dreadful report; when first the flash appeared I could see all the Country before Me, then in a second or two, would come rumbling along the Thunder dreadful to hear. In three or four reports I had entirely lost my hearing and was in a manner petrified It at last ceased, & became quite Calm, the rest of the night tho' we were very tired was not spent in sleep but in discanting accord g to our little ability on the awfulness and majesty of $\frac{e}{y}$ Supreme being and our own littleness and insignifficancy while we stood trembling under a rock at the very terror of his sounds

MATTHEW FLINDERS, BARRIER REEF, 1802

Matthew Flinders had a short life — he died when he was 40 years old — but his work for Australia was profound. We owe him the name of the country. After the publication of A Voyage to Terra Australis *in 1814, in which he suggested 'Australia' was a better name, it gradually came into universal use. Islands, ranges, bays, a genus of trees and a river are named for him.*

Born in 1774 in Lincolnshire, Flinders entered the Royal Navy at the age of 15 and soon became a midshipman. He served under Captain William Bligh on a two-year expedition to the South Seas in search of breadfruit. He saw action in a naval engagement, then in 1795 sailed for Sydney aboard HMS *Reliance* under Captain Hunter. George Bass was the ship's surgeon.

Discovery in any sort of vessel was Flinders's passion. He told friends in England that if the plans for a voyage were read over his grave, he would leap out to join it.

Soon after his arrival in Sydney, George Bass joined him in an extraordinary survey of the coast to Botany Bay and into Georges River. Their vessel was *Tom Thumb*, 2.5 metres long. Several months later, Flinders surveyed more of the south coast in a bigger *Tom Thumb*. Over the next few years he took part in more discoveries, including the encircling of Van Diemen's Land to prove it was an island.

Flinders returned to England in 1800 and published the results of his explorations dedicated to Sir Joseph Banks.

Banks was influential in Flinders's promotion to commander and his appointment in January 1801 as captain of HMS *Investigator*, a more fitting name to carry his plans than *Xenophon*, the vessel's previous name. He married Ann Tyler in April that year and sailed for Sydney in July, leaving his bride at home. His instructions were to survey the coast of Australia. The French Government issued him a passport stating that, although England and France were at war, Flinders was on a voyage of discovery and he was not to be interfered with.

In June 1803, Flinders arrived back in Port Jackson with his job complete. He had circumnavigated Australia. *Investigator* was a near wreck and fit for no more exploring. There was no other ship available to him so Governor Philip Gidley King suggested he travel as a passenger to England to present his work to the Admiralty and to request another vessel. He boarded *Porpoise*, which was wrecked about 1200 kilometres north of Sydney. Ninety-four survivors were cast on a sand cay. Flinders navigated the ship's cutter back to Sydney for help.

To get his charts and papers to London, he took command of *Cumberland*, a small schooner. On the way to the Cape of Good Hope he wrote a letter dated 24 September 1803 to Governor King thanking him for his help but explaining that the trip was difficult:

> I am now sitting on the bed locker, with my knees up to my chin for a table to write on, and in momentary expectation of the sea coming down the companion and sky light... writing here is like writing on horseback on a rainy day.

He was troubled with 'bugs, lice, fleas, weavels, mosquitos, cockroaches, large and small, and mice... I shall set my old friend Trim [his famous cat] to work upon the mice'. Finally, the old vessel began to leak so badly, Flinders turned north to Île de France (Mauritius). And there, despite his passport, the malicious French governor imprisoned him for almost seven years.

Flinders arrived in London in 1810 to overdue honours, but his health was broken. His wife, who had waited nine years for him, knew him for less than another four. However, he completed writing *A Voyage to Terra Australis*.

In this extract from his work, Flinders is on the Barrier Reef near the Northumberland Islands southeast of Mackay. He is trying to find a shipping lane through the maze of reefs.

> In the afternoon I went upon the reef with a party of the gentlemen, and the water being very clear round the edges, a new creation, as it was to us, but imitative of the old, was there presented to our view. We had wheat sheaves, mushrooms, stag's horns, cabbage leaves, and a variety of other forms, glowing under water with vivid tints of every shade betwixt green, purple, brown, and white, equalling in beauty and excelling in grandeur the most favourite parterre of the curious florist. These were different species of coral or fungus, growing, as it were, out of the solid rock, and each had its peculiar form and shade of colouring: but whilst contemplating the richness of the scene, we could not long forget with what destruction it was pregnant.
>
> Different shells in a dead state, concreted into a solid mass of a dull white colour, composed the stone of the reef. The negro heads were lumps which stood higher than the rest; and being generally

dry, were blackened by the weather; but even in these, the forms of the different corals, and some shells were distinguishable. The edges of the reef, but particularly on the outside where the sea broke, were the highest parts; within there were pools and holes containing live corals, sponges and sea eggs, and cucumbers [trepang]; and many enormous cockles (*chama gigas*) [Giant Clams, now *Tridacna gigas*] were scattered upon different parts of the reef. At low water, this cockle seems most commonly to be half open, but frequently closes with much noise; and the water within the shells then spouts up in a stream, three or four feet high: it was from this noise and the spouting of the water that we discovered them, for in other respects they were scarcely to be distinguished from the coral rock. A number of these cockles were taken on board the ship, and stewed in the coppers; but they were too rank to be agreeable food, and were eaten by a few. One of them weighed 47½ lbs. [21.6 kilograms] when taken up, and contained about 3 lbs. 2 oz. of meat; but the size is much inferior to what was found by Captain Cook and Bligh, upon the reefs of the coast further northward, or to several in the British Museum; and I have since seen single shells more than four times the weight of the above shells and fish taken together.

HENRY WATERHOUSE, PORT JACKSON, 1802

Henry Waterhouse was an officer on HMS Sirius of the First Fleet. He returned home with the ship, and then came back in 1795 as second captain of HMS Reliance. Matthew Flinders was midshipman, George Bass surgeon.

In 1796, Governor John Hunter sent Waterhouse as captain of HMS *Reliance* and William Kent, Hunter's nephew, as captain of HMS *Supply* with commissary John Palmer to buy livestock at the Cape, particularly cattle and Afrikaner fat-tail sheep, a good mutton breed. When the main purchases had been made, Palmer was offered a small flock of merinos by Mrs Gordon, widow of a colonel recently killed in action. The sheep had been bred from a gift from the King of Spain to the Dutch Government at the Cape. Colonel Gordon seems to have taken over the sheep because no one else was interested in them. Palmer was not interested either. He wanted meat, not wool. Kent and Waterhouse bought the sheep privately, 13 each. They knew nothing about wool and bought them perhaps as a speculation, perhaps out of curiosity to see how they fared in the Colony.

They did not fare well on the voyage home. Captain Waterhouse wrote:

> The passage to Port Jackson is generally made in 35 to 40 days, this one 78... we met with one gale of wind the most terrible I ever saw or heard of, expecting to go to the bottom every moment.

The animals ran out of food, 'they lived on air most of the time'. The cattle and fat-tail sheep stood it well enough. Kent lost all his merinos except one ram. Waterhouse lost four, five or six of his – he did not remember exactly. There were three merino rams and five or six ewes left alive. Waterhouse isolated the ewes and mated them only to the merino rams; the rams were also available for mating with the Cape fat-tails and other little hairy ewes from Bengal. Australia's wool industry had begun, though few then realised it. The merinos were at first delicate and there was insufficient meat on them. However, when Waterhouse left the Colony, he had 99 merinos to sell at a good price. William Cox bought them.

Supply arrived back as 'a complete mass of rotten timber', and unfit for further use. *Reliance* needed a great deal of repair. The available timbers greatly impressed Waterhouse.

In speaking of the Timber of New South Wales, and of its utility
for naval purposes, I confine myself to what experience I had of it
in His Majesty's ship *Reliance*, whilst under my Command.

In 1797 on a Passage from the Cape of Good Hope to New
South Wales, in a Calm, three heavy Seas broke on board the Ship,
smashed the Jolly Boat (over the Stern) to pieces, stove the Cabin
dead light in, &c., &c., which, together with Gales of Wind
afterwards, shook the Ship so much, and put her in so leaky a state
that it was necessary to give her a very considerable repair, to do
which the Carpenter thought it necessary to put Eight Riders in of
a side, from the Gunwale down to the Kelson, each in one piece,
which was done, together with relaying the Decks, repairing the
Topsides, and new Waterways, from the Wood of the Country, and
from Trees fallen near where the Ship lay. I afterwards made several
voyages to and from Norfolk Island, and made a Winter's Passage
round Cape Horn to Saint Helena, and from thence to England,
during which time, though the ship encountered many heavy Gales,
and laboured much, not one of the Riders either shrunk, rent, or
when I left the Ship in 1801, were in the least decayed...

I must here remark, that we had not any paint in the Ship, or any
thing that would tend to preserve the Wood in a warm, and
afterwards in a very cold Climate. It is therefore in the same state
as when cut down in the Woods and was not seasoned as Ship
Timber in general is...

It will be necessary to observe, that there is so much resinous
gum in the Wood, that it appears to be impervious to Water — for
many Logs, on the first forming the Settlement in 1788, were cut
down, and rolled into the Water (Salt) to clear the Land — which
Logs when taken up again in 1798, were as sound as when cut down
— not the smallest appearance of decay. The stumps of which Trees
were blown with gunpowder, bored with Holes, and filled with mud
and Water, and of course constantly exposed to the weather — after
remaining in this state more than eleven years, no appearance of
decay shewed itself. I am therefore induced to think the Wood of
New South Wales more durable than Oak or the Teak. Masts have
been made of it, and very fully approved of by the Commanders of
different Vessels in which they were put. In His Majesty's Ship

Buffalo, which returned from New South Wales, there is a Mizen Mast and Bowsprit made of the Wood of New South Wales. The Commander of her so much approved of the Bowsprit, that he solicited the Officers of the Yard not to replace it, and has sailed again for New South Wales with it in. On being got out for the purpose of being examined it *floated.* The Mizen Mast was kept by the Officers of Portsmouth Yard, and is now there for inspection.

Where this Wood has been used for planking a Ship, it has been found of so hard a nature, that a Scraper would hardly touch it — and a Nail drove in, the Carpenter of the *Reliance* said they could not get it out again. The Bolts now in the Riders of the *Reliance* will most probably confirm the assertion.

The Carpenters when getting the timber for the repairs of the *Reliance,* stated, that the Timber necessary was in great abundance, but they were sometimes obliged to go for the crooked Timbers that exactly suited their purpose, some distance, but the Ship was then lying alongside the Rocks in the Town of Sydney. Any quantity of strait or crooked Timber was to be got close to the Water's edge (I mean fit for naval purposes) through the whole Harbour of Port Jackson, which is nearly seventeen miles in length, with almost numberless coves on each side, the parts cleared for cultivation being in general some distance in Land. Rough timber may be fashioned where the Tree is fallen, and in the heaviest Gale of Wind a small Boat can go to any part of the Harbour, it being in general considerably less than a quarter of a mile wide, consequently Water Carriage is always certain.

1810—1821

DAVID DICKINSON MANN, NEW SOUTH WALES, 1810

On 10 January 1798, D.D. Mann was brought before the Old Bailey and charged with fraud. He had held responsible positions in the household of the Duke of Northumberland and of Lord Somerset. He was 22 years old. In July 1799, he arrived in Sydney as a convict aboard Hillsborough *and entered government service, perhaps as a schoolmaster, perhaps as a clerk in the Governor's office. Governor Hunter was so impressed with his conduct that he recommended Mann for an absolute pardon, which he obtained in January 1802. It is certain that he later served in Governor King's office but on Christmas Eve 1805, he was suddenly dismissed. No records tell why.*

Mann was so successful on rented farms that in 1804 he built a stable, carriage-house and a 'commodious' dwelling costing more than £400 on a block of land at the rear of Government House to which Governor King had given him a 14-year lease. He lived there with his wife Elizabeth whom he had married in 1801.

Despite his success, Mann decided to return to England. When he advertised the house for sale, he learnt to his consternation that Governor Bligh refused to honour the lease and intended to pull the house down.

His wife took work in the retail trade and Mann became Collector of Quit-rents. In March 1809, they both left the Colony aboard *Admiral Gambier* in company with Colonel George Johnston, who had asked him to appear as a witness in his impending court martial over the arrest of Governor Bligh.

In London, Mann wrote *The Present Picture of New South Wales; illustrated with Four Large Coloured Views from Drawings taken on the Spot, of Sydney, the seat of Government: with a plan of the Colony, taken from actual survey by public authority... dedicated, with permission to Admiral John Hunter, late his Majesty's Captain-General and Governor in Chief of New South Wales and its Dependencies* which was published in the same year. For some time in London, he used the office address of his brother James, who was an attorney in Edgeware Road. The end of his life is as obscure as the beginning: nothing is known.

It is likely that Hunter was involved in the writing. The end of the book, 'Hints for the Improvement of the Colony', is Hunter's justification for his service (he was out of favour with the authorities), although Mann used it as though they were his own ideas. I quote Mann's observations on 'Climate' and the Colony's children from the book.

Although the climate is variable, yet it is very healthy, and uncommonly fine for vegetation... Frost is known but little; at least, ice is very seldom seen; and, I believe, snow has never yet appeared since the establishment of the colony: Yet on the highest ridges of the remoter mountains, to which I have had occasion to allude as never yet having been passed, snow is to be seen for a long time together; and this circumstance is a proof of their elevation. The usual weather in New South Wales is uncommonly bright and clear, and the common weather there, in spring and autumn, is equal to the finest summer day in England. This purity and warmth of atmosphere, it may be naturally inferred, must be particularly favourable to the growth of shrubs and plants, which flourish exceedingly, and attain to a degree of perfection and beauty which is unknown to the inhabitants of this country. The woods and fields present a boundless variety of the choicest productions of nature, which gratify the senses with their fragrance and magnificence; while the branches of the trees display a brilliant assemblage of the feathered race, whose plumage, "glittering in the sun," dazzles the eye of the beholder with its unmatched loveliness and lustre, and presenting, on the whole, a scene too rich for the pencil to pourtray — too glowing and animated for the feeble pen of mortal to describe with half the energy and beauty which belong to it, and without which description is unfaithful...

The children born in this colony from European parents, are very robust, comely, and well made; nor do I recollect a solitary instance of one being naturally deformed. They are remarkably quick of apprehension; learn any thing with uncommon rapidity; and greatly improve in good manners, promising to become a fine race of people.

JANE MARIA COX. SYDNEY. c.1814

Born Jane Maria Brooks near London in 1806, she came to New South Wales about 1813 with her parents. Her father was a resourceful early settler. He brought his family out in their own ship, which he sold to buy five stores, a country house, a big block of land at the corner of Pitt and Hunter Streets and a stone cottage with a garden.

Jane married Edward Cox, the most successful of the Cox brothers, since a friend of his father left him a substantial property just as he was making his way. He had a good farm at Mulgoa (now a Sydney suburb) south of John Jamison's Regentville. He squatted on the Daby plain, near present Rylstone on the Cudgegong River southeast of Mudgee, and built it into a famous merino stud; he squatted on two big runs east of Coonabarabran on the Castlereagh River and, in 1835, established Namoi Hut where Cox's Creek joins the Namoi River after its course through the Liverpool Plains.

As a child, Jane Cox enjoyed walking about Sydney. She compiled a journal some time in the late 1870s.

After getting settled in our Cottage and getting a Pew in St. Phillip's, my Father and Mother thought after our studies were over, we should walk; round Benalong's Point, (named after a native Chief,) was our favourite. It was by the water side, a raised terrace walk under the Government Domain Wall, a seat at the end, then a steep flight of steps to go up to the higher ground. I remember the natives used to sleep there in little Gunyahs made of Bushes, but our Governess did not like to go too near them as she thought the fish they were eating for supper did not smell well. In our early morning walk we could see very tiny Canoes with a Gin fishing in them quite alone, sometimes a streak of smoke from it, and we supposed she was cooking. Another walk we took across the "Racecourse", which is now Hyde Park. It was exactly the same dimensions but no road through the centre; It had been cleared from large wood as there were still a few stumps of the trees left, but they were soon cut up and cleared away. The only house we visited at out of town was Woolloomooloo House; it was situated a pleasant distance from a white sandy beach quite white and sparkling. We used to see shoals of Blue-backed Crabs running on it. The native shrubs grew down to the water's edge. The natives used to make their fires on the hill side at night, but never came by the front of the house; this House and pretty grounds was built and laid out by Assistant Commissary General Palmer, a gentleman of great taste and a kind heart. There were iron gates supported by stone walls and a stone Palisading up to the House, within which grew Norfolk Island pines and the large blossomed Currajong.

JAMES PORTER, SYDNEY AND PARRAMATTA, 1815

Captain James Porter brought the Hebe into Sydney Harbour on 10 August 1815.
She carried convicts and free men. As soon as he received his instructions from
the Naval Officer, or Captain of the Port, Porter went ashore to wait on
Governor Macquarie.

Porter found

> ... his Excellency attend'd by all the principal officers of the Colony
> both Civil and Military all anxious to hear the unexpected account
> of the War with France and of Napoleon having regain'd the Throne.

Then Porter went back to his ship, brought her up to the moorings, giving 13 guns in salute as he passed the Battery, and came ashore again 'to perform the usual Acts requir'd in the Port regulations'. One of them was decidedly strange:

> To employ the Town Crier to caution the Inhabitants, Publicans
> in particular, not to give credit to any one belonging to the Ship as
> comformable to the Regulations I should not be answerable for the
> payment of their Debts — this is term'd crying down the Credit of
> the Crew & ultimately prov'd highly necessary.

The crew had plenty of time to run up debts. After the slow voyage, the *Hebe* stayed in port for nearly three months. Captain Porter travelled to Liverpool, Parramatta and to the fine properties of John Oxley and the Macarthurs at Camden. He wrote his impressions in his logbook and dated them 5 November, the day he sailed for home.

One of Porter's sons, also called James, settled in New South Wales in 1853. He had eight children. One of his descendants, G.M. Porter, donated Captain Porter's logbooks to the Mitchell Library.

> Sydney Cove is situat'd about 7 or 8 miles from the entrance of
> the Port and forms one of the most compleat little Harbours in
> the World — being well shelter'd from all winds, with good depth
> of water and excellent holding Ground — there is a most capital
> Wharf on the west side of the Cove where ships of 350 Tons

burthen can haul along side and discharge their Cargo, which the Crighton did at the time we were in the Port, all the Colonial Vessels discharge at the Wharf saving a considerable expence of time, labour & Boat hire. Our goods such as belong'd to the ship where land'd with our own boats at Mr Campbells Stores which are very Convenient and large enough to Contain several thousand Tons of Goods...

Building begins to be in a state of much improvement, Brick and Stone Houses are taking place of the Houses built of wood and weather Boards — the Roofs of which are cover'd with Shingles of board cut to the size of Tiles us'd in England and placed in a similar manner — this kind of roof is still prevalent — the Houses in general are not large tho there a few nearly finished of 3 storys high compleatly fitt'd up with every Comfort and convenience after the fashion of Europe...

The vicinity of Parramatta notwithstanding the Ground has been constantly workd since the first settling of the Colony, is the Best Cultivat'd and is more productive than any we saw in our Journey — and such is the natural richness of the Soil that two or three crops are annually taken — tho the seasons for these last 3 years have been so unprecipitous to Cultivation — there are few Aboriginal Fruits here, but the Quantities of Peaches that this country produces is such they could not be consum'd... they feed the Hogs with them, and this is the case all over the Colony, Oranges, Lemons, Grapes, Mulberry thrive here and are annually produced in abundance, the European Fruit Trees do not thrive so well, but there are some which with care it is hoped will be brought to maturity.

Timber fit for all purposes is to be got here in abundance, Ship and House timber, handsome timber for furniture &c — in fact nature seems to have been lavish of everything necessary to promote the Comfort of Man — The lands here when the Seasons are only Moderate produce such abundance of Grain, that they have plenty for home Consumption & admitts of large Exportations to Rio Janiero and other places.

WILLIAM COX, FISH AND CAMPBELL RIVERS, NEW SOUTH WALES, 1815

Among many achievements, William Cox built the first road over the Blue Mountains. He was a man of prodigious energy who was involved in the earliest squatting in northern New South Wales. There have been Coxes on the land and usually in parliament ever since the road was built.

Born in Dorsetshire in 1764, William Cox joined the militia when war broke out with France in 1793. In 1797, he enrolled in the New South Wales Corps as a lieutenant and made a brief visit to Australia, and then returned in 1800 with his wife and four small sons as the newly appointed paymaster of the Corps. Cox came out in charge of a shipload of Irish rebels whom he treated very well. The food was better than on most convict ships and, whenever the weather gave opportunity, he exercised them on deck.

One of the perks of the paymaster's position was the use of the funds in his charge. It acted like an overdraft on which no interest was paid. But any call on the money had to be met immediately. Cox bought Brush Farm (near the modern suburbs of Dundas Valley and Eastwood) from John Macarthur and, under the management of Joseph Holt, built it into a fine farm. Holt was allowed his freedom if he kept out of Ireland. Cox bought more farms in the Nepean-Parramatta area all with government money. Then he was suddenly caught £8000 short.

He assigned his estates to trustees, and farms and stock were put up for auction, the first big auction in the Colony. Two days of sale yielded the funds to repay the Government.

Cox was sent to London to face trial for malversation (improper behaviour in office) – not too serious a charge, but he seems to have escaped any sort of trial. He returned to Sydney in 1810 to become magistrate of the Hawkesbury. He made an excellent magistrate. He did not like the general restriction on movement thought necessary to keep convicts in their allotted places. He issued his own travelling passes. 'Captain Cox's Liberties' they were called. The people loved him.

When he was asked to build the western road, Cox first thought of himself. He demanded a good grant of land. Then he considered his men. He needed about 30 fit convicts and their reward was to be freedom when the road was made. It was completed in six months, an extraordinary achievement: 170 kilometres of good clear track and a dozen or more wooden bridges.

Cox took contracts for public works, gaols, schools, anything the Government needed building in Windsor. Even if he had no training for a job, some of the buildings are still standing to prove his competence. The courthouse at Windsor, begun in 1820, is the best known. It is still in use and such a lovely solid building that one wishes its purpose were more genial than the maintenance of law.

Cox's sons explored for grazing land while he built his *Clarendon* estate at Windsor into a wonderfully productive, self-contained community of about 60 people. He could boast:

> We manufacture cloth for Trowsers and frocks from our coarse wool, also Coarse Blankets, boots and shoes from hides tanned upon the estate, we make our own hemp, we keep a Taylor to make up the Cloathing a smith for a Blacksmiths forge a carpenter also a Wheelwright when we can get one.

Butter and cheese were made in the dairy. He grew grain: maize, wheat, barley and oats. He ran cattle, pigs, sheep and poultry.

This quote is from the journal Cox kept during the building of the road. He is travelling in a western line about 15 kilometres north of Oberon.

> January 1, [1810] — On Thursday, at noon, crossed the river [Fish River] and after proceeding up the hill bent our course west as near as the land would allow. At half-past I made Emu Valley. We here started six kangaroos, killed two, and stopped an hour. At three and a-half got to very fine grazing ground. In 20 minutes after crossed Sidmouth Valley, a most beautiful one; then over the hills, west, until 5, when we came to a dry creek. This ground about three miles over is very fine. Steered north-north-west, and in three-quarters of an hour made a ford on the river, about seven miles due west from our crossing-place, where we remained for the night. Started a kangaroo half-a-mile before we got in, which we killed. At half-past 4, Friday morning, started steering due west. At 6 crossed O'Connell Plains, and at 7 stopped on a point of the river to breakfast. Saw six or eight wild turkeys, and as many kangaroos; one of the latter we killed. At 9 set off again west-north-west, about three miles; then north-north-west, soon after which, seeing

Macquarie Plains, we went down to it on our right, and followed
the course of the river about three miles until we came to the point
where Macquarie and Campbell's rivers unite, at 11.30, where we sat
down for the day. In the afternoon of yesterday crossed Campbell's
River, about three miles. Found it very good pasture for sheep and
cattle. On Saturday morning, at 4.30, started again, and went about
two miles up Campbell's River; then steered due east, until 11
o'clock, without halting. Here meeting with water in a creek, we
stopped to refresh, and remained until 1, when my compass being out
of order we made our way by hills and sun, and arrived at our old
encampment at 6.30, having been the whole length from Macquarie
River up to where we are building a bridge in the day. The day was
cold, with wind from east. No foot men could have performed it in
a day. Fine, dry, healthy hills, gravelly soil, and good grass, and so
thinly timbered, that it resembled parks in England rather than a
forest. There are few gullies and no swamps, but the hills passed
gradually into fine valleys, some of which have fine grass in them.
At Sidmouth Valley I never saw finer grass, or more on the same
quantity of land in a meadow in England than there was here, and
just in a fit state for mowing. The whole of the line, about 20 miles
due west, would make most excellent grazing farms, with the river
in front and the back on east and west line. This is the south side of
the Fish River I am describing. On the north side I have not yet
been, but I see there are some good farms to be had there. Ordered a
bullock to be killed for the use of the people, which I had issued to
them in lieu of giving them a ration of salt pork. It ran to about 12
lbs. a man. Some fish have also been caught this week, and when the
men were mustered this morning they were extremely clean, and
looked cheerful and hearty.

SIR JOHN JAMISON. WARRAGAMBA RIVER.
NEW SOUTH WALES. 1818

Jamison's father, Thomas, came to Australia with the First Fleet as surgeon's mate aboard HMS Sirius. He took up Regentville, a superb farm near where the Western Highway now bridges the Nepean River. It was watered by two creeks as well as the river.

John Jamison was born in 1776 and trained as a surgeon, but he became better known as a naval physician. In 1808 at the request of Charles XIII of Sweden, he cured an outbreak of scurvy in the Swedish Navy. The King acknowledged his brilliant work with the high Order of Gustavus Vasa. On his return to England, the Prince Regent knighted him.

When his father died in 1814, Sir John migrated to Australia and took over the farm where he ran good Devon cattle and some of the first Herefords to come to Australia.

Jamison helped found the Bank of New South Wales. He founded the Agricultural Society and, as president, instigated a valuable experimental garden at Parramatta. He was founder and president of the Sydney Turf Club with his own racecourse at Regentville, and also founded the Australian Racing and Jockey Club.

A good friend of the explorer Thomas Mitchell, Sir John sent cattle to the rich land of the Namoi River as soon as Mitchell returned with news of his discoveries in 1832. Jamison had already extended his cattle breeding to two big farms on the Hunter. The five stockmen he sent with the Namoi cattle offended the Kamilaroi Aborigines who retaliated by killing them all. Jamison sent up more men to muster the cattle and take charge of the station known as Baan Baa, surely an unnerving experience.

When the Bank of Australia failed in 1843 in a general economic calamity, Jamison lost heavily. Perhaps it shortened his life, for he died the next year. In June 1844, a few months before he died, Jamison married Mary Griffiths, the daughter of his dairyman, who had been his housekeeper. During the years of spectacular entertaining at Regentville she would have been the servant in the background. When the indignity of a lowly marriage no longer mattered, he married her as a financial arrangement. He had had seven children by her as well as a few by other women.

So Baan Baa passed to Lady Jamison. T.D. Mutch was a New South Wales politician in the 1920s who, in his later life, compiled a huge and

WA-RA-TA [WARATAH]
John Hunter, 1800 or before, Rex Nan Kivell Collection,
National Library of Australia T12180

PRINCIPAL SETTLEMENT ON NORFOLK ISLAND
George Raper, 1790, National Library of Australia R247; the flag indicates safe landing

VIEW OF PORT BOWEN (now Port Clinton north of Yepoon on Queensland's mid coast)
William Westall, 1802, Mitchell Library, State Library of New South Wales

VIEW OF SIR EDWARD PELLEW GROUP, Gulf of Carpentaria
William Westall, 1802, Mitchell Library, State Library of New South Wales

VIEW OF SYDNEY FROM THE WEST SIDE OF THE COVE
D.D. Mann, 1810, from *The Present Picture of New South Wales…*, Mitchell Library, State Library of New South Wales

FISHING BY TORCHLIGHT, OTHER ABORIGINES BESIDE CAMP FIRES COOKING FISH
Joseph Lycett, c.1817, National Library of Australia R5677

VIEW OF PORT MACQUARIE AT THE ENTRANCE OF THE RIVER HASTINGS, New South Wales
Joseph Lycett, c.1820, National Library of Australia R8737

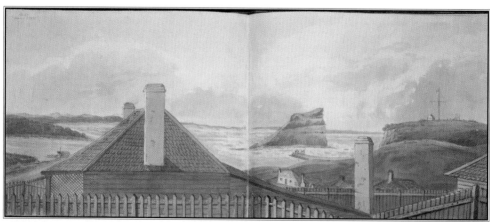

NEWCASTLE, NEW SOUTH WALES, showing Nobby Head
Sophia Campbell, ?1820, National Library of Australia R7271

valuable card index of births, marriages and deaths. He was unkind enough
to refer to the widow as 'Lady' Jamison. She had well earned the honour,
just as Jamison had earned his knighthood.

Jamison frequently entertained visitors at riverside picnics to demonstrate the beauty of Australia, but he never saw his distant stations. Yet he
was venturesome in exploration as well as in business, as this extract from
'Journal of the First Excursion up the Warragamba' discloses. Strangely, the
document was little known until Ralph Mansfield published it more than
15 years later in his *The New South Wales Magazine* of January 1834. John
Wentworth was the brother of William Charles; Robert Johnston of Annan-
dale was one of the sons of George Johnston.

The beautiful Warragamba is now controlled by dams. Much of the river
that Jamison called the Warragamba is now the Cox.

November 15th 1818. — At 5 o'clock this morning, I proceeded
from Regent-Ville, seated on the right bank of the Nepean, and
within a mile of Emu-Ford, on a long-intended attempt to trace as
far as possible the course of the river Warragamba, and, if
practicable, to ascertain its source. In this undertaking, Lieutenant
Robert Johnstone and Mr. John Wentworth, both of the Royal
Navy, obligingly accompanied me. I also took Thomas Jones, my
collector of natural history productions. The boat we embarked in
was twelve feet keel by five feet beam; the crew consisting of
William Morrison, and Gilderoy, *alias* Bob, a black native. We were
victualled for a fortnight, and well equipped for shooting and
fishing sports.

We rowed in a S.S. West direction, up the magnificent course of
the Nepean, which varies from sixty to two hundred yards in width,
and, until near the junction of the Warragamba, a computed distance
of twelve miles, so deep that it appears almost streamless. --- At the
end of two miles, we passed a rill of constantly running water,
forcing its course, from a W.N.West direction, through a deep and
highly romantic chasm of the mountain. Concluding that the stream
must have its rise in the Regent's Glen, I named it "Glenbrook". At
the junction of this brook with the Nepean, I have caught black
mountain perch of a quite peculiar character. --- On proceeding a
little further, we observed a surprising phenomenon in the course of
the river. Instead of *skirting* the mountains, as heretofore, it now

flowed through their very heart, the mountains having been cleft from their summits to afford it a channel, and presenting in the perspective the shape of a wedge. In the bed of this wonderful excavation through solid rock, which, rising on either side from three hundred to a thousand feet in height, assumes a thousand fantastic and sublime shapes, clothed with trees and flowering shrubs from its summit to its base, the river flows for full ten miles. --- At eight o'clock, we passed a considerable stream of water coming from the westward, supposed to be the junction of Cox's River. The great mass of the mountain is here formed of an ochreous yellow sand rock, lying uniformly in horizontal strata of from five to ten feet and upwards. The gloom of this tranquil hollow is materially relieved by the fine forest trees which the fertility of the climate has caused to grow on the rugged banks and up the precipitous face of the mountains, without soil, and supported only by their roots clinging round or fastening into the fissures of the rocks. In this retired spot we saw abundance of wild ducks and a variety of birds, all well known. The river is plentifully supplied with very superior perch, mullet, herrings, gudgeon, and eels...

[Here they are nearing the headwaters of the present Cox River] the Blue Mountain fell back in a circular curve, so as to form what I at first considered to be Pitt's Amphitheatre; but, on proving our course and distance, with several other correcting facts, I found we were then considerably to the southward of it. I therefore named this truly beautiful and picturesque spot, "Macquarie's Amphitheatre", in compliment to his Excellency the Governor. Here trees that are the growth of rich soil only, mostly of the eucalyptus species, and known in the colony by the names of flooded and blue gums, stringy-bark, and apple-trees, formed the open forests, and, together with the richest bladed and native grasses I have seen, vouched for the luxuriance of the soil. The Macquarie Amphitheatre is about six miles in circumference, with a fine river passing down its centre, on the banks of which we collected some rare fossils, and saw some very good coal and excellent limestone, lying in such bulk and quantities as to justify the conclusion that considerable beds exist near the amphitheatre.

[A very wet night on the way home caused him to rejoice in the climate] ... the rain, increasing to a "pour", not only forced its way to us *over* the rocks, but also oozed out of under-fissures, so that we awoke in the middle of the night lying in a not very agreeable shower-bath. Our bedding consisted of a boat-cloak or rug to each, which were as completely soaked as if just drawn out of the river. Comfortless, however, as was our lodging, the rain outside continued so heavily that we were compelled to remain where we were; and so fatigued were we with the labours of the day, that, in despite of hard, wet, uneven rocks, and incessant droppings from above, we soon relapsed into profound sleep.--- But such is the salubrity of this climate, that with all the wettings, hardships, and fatigues to which we were constantly exposed throughout our expedition, we did not experience the slightest indisposition; and we considered the air to be as rarified on the engulphed banks of the Warragamba as at Sydney.

PHILLIP PARKER KING, SOUTH GOULBURN ISLAND, NORTHERN TERRITORY, 1818

Phillip P. King was a very early colonial. He was born on Norfolk Island on 13 December 1791, the son of Philip Gidley King, Lieutenant Governor of the island, and his wife Anna who was eight months pregnant when she arrived after a long, slow journey by sailing ship. Philip Gidley King became the third Governor of New South Wales.

When Phillip Parker King was 11 years old, he was sent to the Portsmouth Naval Academy. From there, he entered the navy and showed bravery in engagements in 1808 and 1809. By 1814, he was a lieutenant in command of his own ship. He had gained such a reputation as a marine surveyor that in February 1817 Earl Bathurst, Secretary of State for the Colonies, sent him in command of an expedition to complete the exploration of the Australian coast. Matthew Flinders's excellent maps ended at Cape Wessel on the northern tip of Wessel Island off the northeast corner of Arnhem Land.

Governor Macquarie bought the 84-ton cutter *Mermaid* for the work. King took a crew of 19, two assistant surveyors, Allan Cunningham as botanist and Bungaree, an Aboriginal Australian who had sailed with Flinders. It was rare for any exploring party, either by land or by sea, to move without Aboriginal guidance.

King spent three years making three circles of the Australian coast and one trip to Macquarie Harbour in southwest Tasmania. When he returned to Sydney in December 1820 *Mermaid* needed a complete refit.

The next year King made another voyage in the brig *Bathurst*, a bigger vessel. On the way north he made a running survey of the western side of the Great Barrier Reef and advised that the inner route was safer and faster than the outer route through the Coral Sea.

King completed a survey of the Western Australian coast, then returned to Sydney to learn that he had been recalled to England. While there he wrote *Narrative of a Survey of the Intertropical and Western Coasts of Australia*, published in two volumes in 1827. Before it was published, he was sent in command of a vessel to survey the southern coasts of South America. Four years work there produced another book.

After his fine work was paid off handsomely, King returned to New South Wales and settled on his farm near St Marys, outside Sydney. He was appointed to the Legislative Council and spent 10 years as Resident Commissioner of the troubled Australian Agricultural Company. In 1855, he became the first Australian to be promoted to rear admiral but he died the following year.

In this quote, King is on South Goulburn Island, off Arnhem Land.

[27 March 1818] As the shores of the bay, in which we had anchored, appeared likely to afford both wood and water, of which articles we were much in want, I was induced to take advantage of the opportunity, and immediately made preparation to commence these occupations. In the evening a pit was dug for water, which oozed so fast into it, that we did not anticipate any difficulty on that head, and the wood was both plentiful and convenient to the beach.

It was now about the termination of the rainy season, and every thing bore the most luxuriant appearance; the grass, which covered the face of the island, was more than six feet high, and completely concealed us from each other as we walked to the summit of the hill, the sides of which were very thickly wooded. Upon the edge

VIEW OF SOUTH WEST BAY GOULBURN ISLAND ('watering party attacked by natives')
P.P. King, 1818, from *Narrative of a Survey...*, Mitchell Library, State Library of New South Wales

of the beach, the *pandanus*, the *hibiscus*, and a variety of other tropical trees and shrubs were growing, and the sand was variegated with the long-stemmed *convolvolus* in full flower.

The trees upon the hills were principally a small sized *eucalyptus*, which we cut for firewood, but the stem was found to be unsound, and totally useless for any purpose excepting for fuel. Among the flowers that were strewed about the island, was a superb shrubby *grevillea*, with scarlet flowers. The *casuarina* grew also near the sandy beach, but it seemed to prefer the exposed parts near the extremities of the sandy projections of the land where no other tree would grow. The wood of this tree appeared to be of a closer grain, and of a darker colour than the species that is usually found upon the north coast.

The only edible fruit that we found was a small black grape: it bore a very inferior resemblance to the common sweet-water grape, but the leaf and habit are altogether different.

The centre of the bay is formed by a sandy beach; it is terminated by cliffs of about forty feet in height, the upper stratum of which appeared to be an indurated clay of a very red colour, occasioned by the ferruginous nature of the rocks and soil; the lower part is a stratum of the whitest pipe-clay, the upper limit of which, from the surface having been washed clean by the late rains, was so defined, and produced so striking a contrast in point of colour, as to give the whole a most remarkable appearance.

WILLIAM KINGDOM JUN., BATHURST PLAINS, NEW SOUTH WALES AND VAN DIEMEN'S LAND, c.1818

In the early 19th century, emigration guides were popular with British publishers and popular with the many emigrants. In 1820, William Kingdom Jun. published the second edition of America and the British Colonies An Abstract of all the most useful information relative to The United States of America and the British Colonies of Canada, the Cape of Good Hope, New South Wales and Van Diemen's Island exhibiting at one view the comparative advantages and disadvantages Each Country offers for Emigration collected from the most valuable and recent publications to which are added A Few Notes and Observations.

Here are Kingdom's prophetic estimates of the capabilities of the Bathurst country:

> To the westward of these mountains the country abounds with the richest herbage, and is upon the whole tolerably well supplied with running water. In the immediate vicinity of them there is a profusion of rivulets.
>
> This large and fertile tract of country is in general perfectly free from underwood, and in many places is without any timber at all. Bathurst Plains, for instance, where there is a commandant, a military depôt, and some few settlers established, have been found, by actual admeasurement, to contain upwards of 60,000 acres, upon which there is scarcely a tree. The great distance of this tract of country, as well as the difficulty of communicating with the capital, will prevent it from assuming an agricultural character: by way, however, of set-off against the manifest superiority which the districts to the eastward of the mountains possess, in this respect, over the country to the westward of them, this latter is much better adapted for all the purposes of grazing and rearing cattle; the herbage is sweeter, and more nutritive, and there is an unlimited range for stock, without any fear of trespassing. There is, besides, for the first 200 miles, a constant succession of hill and dale, admirably suited for the pasture of sheep, the wool of which will without doubt eventually become the principal export of this

colony, and may be conveyed across these mountains at an
inconsiderable expense. A river of some magnitude has lately been
discovered in this western territory by Mr. Oxley, the surveyor-
general of the colony. A deficiency of means prevented this
gentleman from following up his discovery to any distance; but
when he quitted the river its course was northerly, and in latitude
32°48' south, and 148°58' east longitude, running through a beautiful
country; its breadth about 250 yards, and of sufficient depth to float
a line of battle ship. Should this river empty itself on the western
coast of New Holland, as imagined, a distance of at least 2000 miles,
some idea may be formed of its probable magnitude.

Of Van Diemen's Land, under the heading SOIL, &c. he wrote:

In this island, as in New Holland, there is every diversity of soil;
but certainly, in proportion to the surface of the two countries, this
contains comparatively much less of an indifferent quality. Large
tracts of land perfectly free from timber or underwood, and covered
with the most luxuriant herbage, are to be found in all directions,
but more particularly in the environs of Port Dalrymple. This sort
of land is *invariably* of the *very best description, and millions* of
acres still remain *unappropriated, which are capable of being
instantly converted to all the purposes of husbandry. There, the
colonist has no expense to incur in clearing his farm: he is not
compelled to a great preliminary outlay of capital before he can
expect a considerable return: he has only to set fire to the grass,
to prepare his land for the immediate reception of the plough-
share...*

To this very great superiority which this settlement may claim
over the parent colony may be super-added two other items of
distinction, which are perhaps of equal magnitude and importance.
First, the rivers here have sufficient fall in them to prevent any
excessive accumulation of water from violent or continued rains;
and are consequently free from those awful inundations to which all
its rivers are perpetually subject. Here, therefore, the industrious
colonist may settle on the banks of a navigable river, and enjoy all
the advantages of sending his produce to market by water, without
running the constant hazard of having the fruit of his labour, the

golden promise of the year, swept away in an hour by a capricious and domineering element. Secondly, the seasons are more regular and defined, and those great droughts, which have been so frequent at Port Jackson, are here altogether unknown.

JOHN HOWE, HUNTER RIVER, 1819

At the time of Howe's exploration, there was a penal settlement at Newcastle that could be serviced only by boat. The isolation was deliberate. Only secondaries, re-sentenced convicts, were sent there. But John Oxley had returned from a long journey with stories of a big river flowing into a fine bay at Port Macquarie. If good land could be found on the Hunter River, and if an overland route were found to it, the convicts could be transferred to Port Macquarie and the Hunter lands opened to settlers. Governor Macquarie sent John Howe to investigate. He had two free men with him, three convicts and an Aboriginal guide.

This extraordinary man was Chief Constable of Windsor. Howe came to Sydney in 1802, a free immigrant, with a wife and two small daughters. He farmed a grant of 40 hectares at Ebenezer, bought a store at Windsor, then in 1810 set up in business as an auctioneer. He became a builder by chance. Tenders were called for a bridge over South Creek. None were received, so Howe decided to build the bridge himself. It was about 70 metres long, the largest bridge then built in the Colony, and he finished it in seven months. The rows of 15 metre piles were driven three metres into the bed of the creek.

Thereafter Howe, like William Cox, took all the building contracts he could get: streets and roads, wharves at Windsor, and a toll punt across the Hawkesbury with orders from the Governor that no other punt was to ply within three kilometres.

Howe reached the Hunter at a point above present Jerry's Plains. He did not know that it was the Hunter, and there was no chance to explore much of the river. Howe was sick, and the party short of food. He saw enough to declare: 'It is the finest sheep land I have seen since I left England'.

The next year Howe went back with a big party. This time they were certain that the river was the Hunter. They came across convict cedar-getters and followed the river down to the penal settlement. There was no question of the extent of good land. 'In our way down the river', Howe reported, 'we came thro as fine a country as imagination can form and on both sides of the river from upwards of 40 miles (I may say) will at least average two miles wide of fine land fit for cultivation and equally so for grazing'.

This extract is taken from Howe's first trip.

Friday, November 5. [1819] Breakfasted and got ready for
travelling. North to N.N.E. ³/₄ mile. N.E. ⅛ mile to pass a gully.
North ¼ mile. N.W. ½ mile. Went down a gully to make the creek
which we left yesterday afternoon, and with much difficulty
obtained it. N.N.W. ½ mile. Cross the creek, where we found a fine
valley and thinly timbered about ¼ mile over it, but widening as we
get down. W.N.W. 1½ mile. N.W. ½ mile, cross the creek. North 1½
mile. Valley nearly a mile over and fine ground. I think it equal to
Richmond, but not one half the timber. N.N.W. ³/₄ mile. North 1½
mile. The valley not so wide as before, the mountains coming closer
in one place. N.E. ³/₄ mile. North 2¼ miles to a fine fresh water
river [the Hunter]. The last two hours through a fine country
thinly timbered, and the last hour many acres without a tree on it.
One spot, I think, exceeds 50 acres with not 20 trees on it, and very
fine ground. It is evidently flooded, it having left the rubbish where
the bushes were about breast high, but there is sufficient high land
for stock and buildings. It is the finest sheep land I have seen since I
left England. The tide makes in the river, though it does not appear
to flow so high as when we made it. Resolved to follow it down till
to-morrow night, if not longer. Stop to dinner. Caught a few perch.
A great number in the river. The land on both sides very fine, and a
great part of it may be cultivated without felling a tree. Even the
high land is well clothed with grass and lightly timbered, though
mostly thicker than the low ground. The grass on the low ground
equals a meadow in England, and will throw as good a swath, and is
like that native grass which is found where old stockyards have
been. In the afternoon, though much fatigued, we took our course
down the river. E.S.E. ½ mile. N.N.E. ½ mile. At the bottom of the
reach a large bank or beach of gravel, pebbles and sand. The river
widens to near the width of the Hawkesbury at Windsor, and is very
deep. North 1 mile. A rock on the east side of the river and high
land, nearly a mile, gradually sloping to the river. Back ground very
fine and little timber, only a few trees to an acre, and some patches
without. Opposite side of the river, land more level and what timber
is on is of no object. It may be said to be clear. The high land
appears to be about ³/₄ of a mile back, and that very little timber on
it, and the grass very green.

JACQUES ARAGO, SYDNEY AND CAMDEN, 1819

Jacques Etienne Victor Arago, brother of the astronomer Royal of France, arrived in Sydney on 18 November 1819 as draughtsman aboard L'Uranie *captained by Louis de Freycinet. Freycinet had already been in Sydney in 1802 as ensign on Nicolas Baudin's* Le Géographe. *He was one of the few officers to survive scurvy on that terrible voyage.*

Rose, his wife, unexpectedly accompanied him on the three-year scientific expedition. She went aboard dressed as a boy and stowed away. On their return she wrote a book about her adventures.

L'Uranie came into Sydney for a refit that took five weeks, giving Arago plenty of time to explore the town. He spent several days with John Oxley on his Camden grant, Kirkham. Three other members of the crew travelled out to Bathurst.

Arago published *Promenade autour du Monde* in France in 1822. A translation was published in England in 1823. He sketched and painted romantic views of Australia, but his enthusiastic descriptions are not exaggerated and they acknowledge the work of Governor and Mrs Macquarie.

The town of Sydney-Cove, the capital of the county of Cumberland, is situated partly in a plain and partly on a little hill overlooking the south side of the river, so that it resembles an amphitheatre and makes a charming picture. The principal buildings contrast strangely with the old wooden houses that are gradually disappearing, their place being taken by houses of beautiful cut stone decorated with pleasing sculptures, and embellished with balconies in a really fine style. One would imagine that our best architects had deserted Europe and come to New Holland to reproduce their most elegant mansions.

First, on your left is the Governor's spacious residence, surrounded by a magnificent English garden. Its rooms are remarkable for their distribution, their luxury, and pictures of fights between the savages of New Holland. The Governor, who spends part of the year at his Parramatta residence, has not had the poor taste to crowd this fine dwelling with too many sculptures or other ornaments, which almost always offend the eye and spoil the effect.

To the right of Government House, but farther off, is the
regular facade of the splendid barracks in brick and stone; beyond
are the fine outlines of a military hospital ornamented with a
beautiful colonnade, where all day long the patients may breathe the
pure wholesome air. Nearer you distinguish a spacious building,
which is the house of prayer and nearer still on the very harbour
front you see great bond stores. Opposite this store, and on the
other side of the cove, is an unfinished quay where ships may be
careened easily, without incurring the slightest risk. A great number
of other public buildings and private houses help to enhance this
really magnificent landscape; and there is nothing to proclaim that
this town, already so beautiful, is the work of but a few years...

The country I visited was even richer than that visited by the
three travellers who went to Bathurst. I cannot compare its majesty
with anything I have met before. The vast forests in Brazil or the
Moluccas cannot compare with these in New Holland. Having no
spiny grasses, lianas and briars, the Australian woods almost
everywhere exhibit immense plains with smiling verdure, where
flowers grow lavishly intermingled, rich in countless hues and
spreading a delightful perfume...

The only point of resemblance that appears to me to exist
between this country and the one I visited in South America is that
tremendous number of beautiful birds that people the forest. In this
respect Brazil is superior to New Holland. But, although destitute
of that numberous and lively family of humming-birds, and those
amazing varieties of large butterflies, marvellous alike for their
adornment and the variety of their rapid evolutions, the country I
am visiting now can nevertheless count wealth enough to content it.

Among the handsome denizens of its countryside, the white
cockatoo takes pride of place; then come tit-mice, different kinds of
finches, and that prodigious company of little parakeets, green only
or green with red feathers, whose shrill cries at all hours of the day
or night disturb the traveller's meditations...

The day after our arrival we saw a little party of eight aborigines
come down into his property [Kirkham], one of whom had been
chief of a numerous tribe. He was armed with a tomahawk; and so
that I might enjoy an extraordinary sight, Mr. Oxley told him to

climb a very straight tree, over three feet in diameter, promising
him a reward if he climbed to the top of the stout branches in less
than five minutes. The aborigine at once takes the tomahawk from
his belt; he quickly chops the trunk with it, making two notches
two feet apart, and climbs up. Standing in the upper notch, he
throws his tool man's height, it buries itself in the very smooth
stem; he gives a great spring, grips the handle, raises himself, holds
on with the folds of his hard skin and the rough soles of his feet,
and repeats the performance. Never in my life should I have credited
such skill and dexterity. The tree was climbed in six minutes, and
the aborigine did not take but one to climb down. The other poor
wretches about us begged also the favour of climbing trees bigger
still, and Mr. Oxley rewarded their zeal with an ample provision of
food with which he filled their kangaroo skins.

CHARLES JEFFREYS. HOBART TO PORT DALRYMPLE. TASMANIA. c.1819

Jeffreys was born on the Isle of Wight in 1782. He joined the navy when he was 11 years old and was commissioned lieutenant in 1805. He arrived in Port Jackson in the brig **Kangaroo** *in January 1814 accompanied by his wife, Jane.*

Jeffreys was given the job of transporting convicts and free passengers to the Derwent, but turned back on the first trip in May because of heavy weather. Governor Macquarie regarded him as a timid seaman. However Jeffreys delivered his passengers in October. His instructions were to collect a cargo of wheat at Port Dalrymple on the way back. Jeffreys did not travel with his ship to Port Dalrymple; he travelled overland by coach to have a look at the country.

The *Kangaroo* did not get back to Port Jackson until February. Although Macquarie did not believe his explanation for the delay – presumably he had done some private trading – he sent Jeffreys to Ceylon with the remainder of the 73rd Regiment. That was the most successful and most honest trip of his devious career. He named Molle Island (now South Molle) in the Whitsunday group after Colonel George Molle, Lieutenant Governor of New South Wales, and its highest peak, Mount Jeffreys, in honour of himself. Farther north, he named Princess Charlotte Bay after the exceptional daughter of King George IV.

Back in Australia in 1816, Jeffreys made two successful trips to the Derwent with convicts and stores; but Macquarie was still unhappy with him and ordered him to England with the *Kangaroo* with instructions not to call at any port in either of the colonies. Jeffreys pulled into the Derwent with stories of a lost boat and some damage to *Kangaroo* to cover a cargo of spirits he had for sale.

It was discovered at the Derwent that two escaped convicts had been taken aboard in Port Jackson plus others from Hobart. Also aboard was Garnham Blaxcell, a Sydney merchant escaping a big debt to the government. When William Sorell, Lieutenant-Governor, sent a couple of boats to patrol the river, Jeffreys and his crew boarded one of them, attacked the captain and took him and his crew prisoner aboard *Kangaroo*. The next day Jeffreys released them, then sailed for England a few days later. Macquarie expected him to face trial there but Jeffreys escaped prosecution. He wrote a book, *Van Diemen's Land. Geographical and Descriptive Delineations of the Island of Van Diemen's Land,* which was published in 1820.

Jeffreys returned to Hobart with his wife, who had accompanied him to England, and took up a grant of land at Pittwater, northeast of Hobart. He did not prosper as a farmer and died aged 43 years in 1826. Jane remained in the colony and took up an additional grant.

Van Diemen's Land is a strange work. Much of the information was taken directly from the work of surveyor George Evans. Jeffreys made his overland trip in 1814 so, in the passage that I quote here, he is not making an actual trip but leading the reader through Evans's assessments. His description of the great extent of open country in the east and centre led too many settlers to believe that the whole of Tasmania held similar country.

A few miles farther we reach NEW NORFOLK situated at the falls, and on the right bank of the Derwent, it is a fine tract of level country, occupied by a considerable number of settlers from Norfolk Island, who came here at the time that settlement was evacuated [early 1814]. They have formed several valuable farms, on a rich soil, with a great extent of pasturage.

Adjoining these farms, situated on Herdsman's Cove, are the fertile plains of BAGDAD, a small portion only of which is yet granted to individuals. On the south it is well watered by the stream above alluded to, and in the centre by a rivulet, or rather a large chain of ponds, these plains occupy an extent of country of twelve miles in length, and near three in breadth, and are surrounded by moderately high hills. They are but thinly covered with timber, so that in some places, for upwards of half a mile square, there are scarcely a hundred trees standing; while the grass is in general about three feet long.

Bagdad is joined on the west, by a range of country of considerable extent, called the TEA TREE BRUSH. Here is, for about six miles, a beautiful, rich, and even luxuriant pasturage, reaching to a narrow pass between two hills, called THE OVENS, from a number of caves in the side of one of the hills. [He is leading the reader east to the Pittwater district (present Sorell) then turning north.]

Beyond this pass, lies the delightful COAL RIVER DISTRICT, running north and south. This most pleasing and valuable tract of country may be seen, through nearly its whole extent, by ascending the Ovens' Hills...

The author traversed almost its whole extent, from Hobart Town to Launceston and Port Dalrymple on the Tamar, a distance of one-hundred and twenty-five miles in a barouche, with three and sometimes four horses in hand, and yet has not had more than twenty miles of what could, possibly be called a road; the whole being a beautiful level pasture, with but few trees to obstruct the view or the passage.

Having passed the range of hills eastward of the Ovens, in which is found abundance of fine coal, we cross the Coal River, and enter upon a considerable extent of rich pasture land, lying between what are called the Bengal Hills, at its extremity we enter the PITT WATER DISTRICT. To the right of the road are the SWEET WATER HILLS, and the author's estate. On the left is a delightful spot, called Orielton Park, the estate of Edward Lord, Esquire, the principal merchant in the island, who formerly held a commission in His Majesty's service, and, as before stated, administered the government after the death of Governor Collins; this gentleman is without exception the largest land and stock-holder in the island, and to him the colony is indebted for the great improvements effected in the breed of cattle, sheep and horses. His house is situated on one side of an oblong piece of ground, containing about one thousand acres, (part of his park) and is so thinly wooded as to appear somewhat naked; a portion of this is Orielton Race Course, comprising an area of a mile and a half without tree or shrub, but full of fine short bite grass, and a peculiar sort of herbage, very much resembling the sage leaf, but narrower, on which sheep and pigs thrive uncommonly.

CAPTAIN FADDEI FADDEEVICH BELLINGSHAUSEN, AT SEA WEST OF TASMANIA, 1820

Baron Bellingshausen was born in Russia in 1779, a fortunate time for a boy to grow up with a passion for the sea, since Russia had only just gained control of the mouths of its three big rivers emptying into the Black Sea: the Dneiper and the Dneister directly and the Don River into its bay-like Sea of Azov. Turkey had monopolised all trade in that great, busy, difficult Black Sea. It is almost landlocked. The narrow Karadeniz Boğazi (Bosforus) strait, leads through a complication of seas, and another strait, Çanakkale Boğazi (the Dardanelles of the Gallipoli misfortune), leads into the Mediterranean. Winter tempests disturb the Black Sea: a semicircle of high land in the east swirls the winds cyclonically. It was a good place to learn seacraft.

Russia had dreams of building a navy, or at least a fleet of merchant ships. It was common practice for young Russian nobles to take service with the British Navy. They idolised Cook after his magnificent voyages and hankered to take part in a Russian expedition. In 1803, Alexander I sent A.J. van Kruzenstern with two ships to find a good route to the distant Kamchatka Peninsula, a Russian holding that was difficult to service by land. Van Kruzenstern had years of experience with the British Navy and on British merchantmen. He sailed by way of Cape Horn and the Marquesas and Sandwich Islands to Kamchatka, then home via the Cape of Good Hope. The voyage took three years. It was a great feat to encircle the world without a single loss of life. Kruzenstern knew how to treat his men.

Baron Bellingshausen was his fifth officer. That experience, and later command of his own ships, fitted Bellingshausen to lead an expedition to survey the Antarctic. He was out from 1819 to 1821; he travelled farther south than anyone before him. They discovered Peter I Island and Alexander I Land; they explored and mapped Macquarie Island. So accurate were their charts of the Antarctic that the British Admiralty used them until 1931. The voyage rivalled Cook's.

When Bellingshausen made the following entry in his journal, he was not in Australia; he was halfway between the Cape of Good Hope and Tasmania but considerably south of the straight line between those points. He was only 800 kilometres north of the Antarctic Circle. He continued to Tasmania and up to Port Jackson to refit and to establish an observatory on North Head for his astronomer to make a study of the earth's magnetism. He then sailed for the Sandwich Islands, making more discoveries, and returned to Port Jackson to take in stores for the Antarctic work.

More than a century later, my family marvelled at displays of Aurora Australis from our farms at Boggabri and Baradine, but we never saw a display such as Bellingshausen describes. Perhaps he saw the brightest yet known.

[2 March 1820] The mercury in the thermometer stood at night at 27° F. The officers of the watch had only just changed, when we observed a flashing light which appeared from time to time, the cause of which we did not know. Finally, at the close of the second hour after midnight when the clouds became less dense, we beheld one of the most beautiful and impressive phenomena of nature. To the south there appeared two columns of a whitish-blue colour similar to phosphorescent fire, flashing from clouds along the horizon with the rapidity of rockets. Each column was as broad as three diameters of the sun. Then this amazing spectacle spread along the horizon over about 120° and passed the zenith. Finally, towards the end of the phenomenon, the whole sky was filled with similar pillars. We enjoyed and admired this extraordinary sight. The light was so strong and penetrating that opaque objects threw shadows exactly as in daylight when the sun is covered with clouds, and it was possible to read even the smallest print without difficulty.

The phenomenon faded gradually, but lighting the whole horizon throughout the whole night, it was most helpful to us, because though for the past few days it had become quite light from time to time even on the cloudiest nights, the cause of which we had not understood, this light allowed us to proceed much more boldly. The last phase of this display appeared at first as a small bluish-white ball, from which instantly bands of the same colour spread over the vault of the heavens, some extending to the opposite horizon, others reaching the zenith and passing beyond it. Sometimes across the whole of the sky there were feathers of light and sometimes the whole of the sky and even the horizon to the north were covered with light. With the dawn the magnificent sight gradually faded away...

[4 March] During the night the wind continued to blow in sharp gusts with an extremely heavy snowfall, but as soon as the snow ceased to fall, the southern aurora showed in all its magnificence and brightness, quite different from that which we had seen the previous night. The whole vault of the heavens except 12° or 15° from the horizon was covered with bands of rainbow colour which, with the rapidity of lightning, traversed the sky in sinuous lines from south to north, shading off from colour to colour. This spectacle, surpassing all description, aroused in us the greatest wonder and saved us, it may be, from misfortune. When the snow clouds had cleared and the sea was lit up by the aurora, we observed that we were passing close to a huge iceberg to leeward: we considered ourselves fortunate not to have run into it.

GEORGE COX, FROM BATHURST, NEW SOUTH WALES, TO THE TALBRAGAR RIVER NEAR CRABOON, 1821.

George Cox was one of the four sons who came with William Cox and his wife to Sydney in 1800. With two of his brothers and two sons of William Lawson, he took part in the first squatting north of Bathurst, eventually moving to the Liverpool Plains. They kept in advance of settlement and in advance of the law. It was a profitable arrangement. There was society behind as a buffer and free land in front.

After crossing the Blue Mountains, William Lawson did not give up exploring. He made four trips to the north in need of grass for his increasing flocks. In November 1821, he returned to Bathurst to tell the Cox brothers of wonderful country. George went up to see for himself. He took up the country for the Lawsons in partnership with himself and his brother Henry. Their first venture struck trouble.

On 7 February 1822, William Cox wrote from his busy farm, *Clarendon*, near Windsor, to Governor Sir Thomas Brisbane:

> My son Mr Henry Cox is this instant returned from Bathurst
> (and so ill from the heat that he cannot proceed further) with
> information that the Natives have driven away the persons who was
> in charge of the Stock at the River Cudgegong with the exception
> of one man who it is supposed is killed it also appears that the
> natives let the Horn Cattle out of the yards and got possession of
> the sheep that my sons kept there for Rations which they were
> killing when the men came away...

Henry Cox had reason to be exhausted. Life did not move as leisurely in those days as is now supposed. George Cox first saw the country at Munna, north of Mudgee, on 3 December 1821. William Cox's letter was written 66 days later. In that time, George had inspected the country from Munna to the Talbragar and ridden back to Bathurst, a distance of 220 kilometres; Henry and he had established two cattle runs about 130 kilometres north of Bathurst (that involved, not only the mustering and droving of the cattle and the ration sheep and the building of huts and yards, but the organising of provisions for several months for the several men who were left there); and Henry had ridden about 300 kilometres to *Clarendon*, to tell his father of the attack while George sought help at Bathurst.

George Cox described the land he passed through as he followed Lawson's blazed line down the Macquarie River, across the Cudgegong to the Talbragar, in *A Journal kept by Mr George Cox in his late Tour to the Northward and Westward of 'Bathurst' accompanied by Richard Lewis and William Lee, Settlers and having altogether seven persons (including one Native man) and five horses.*

Sunday 1 Dec. 1821 [on the Macquarie River half way between Bathurst and present Dubbo, New South Wales] **Had a fair night and started at ½ past 5 A.M. followed down the river but did not keep its course exactly as we took every advantage of cutting off the bends in it, the Country the first six miles was beautifully grassed and not very high hills, some pretty flatts on the river containing from fifty to two hundred and fifty acres, but not many of them the Apple Tree** [*Angophora floribunda*, indicators of good country] **here begins to make its appearance among the other Timber, but the hills on both sides of the River much steeper and appear rather rocky. We travelled down the South side, the opposite one, appearing to be very rocky and mountainous, caught a very large Kangaroo this morning for Breakfast left this spot at 11, and followed the river the same way as in the morning, the land the first 20½ miles much the same as before, but gradually opened wider on the side we travelled, at the end of this distance we commenced on a very rich flatt of land Gum and Apple Tree growing thereon very large with abundance of grass and herbage of excellent quality, after travelling about a mile on this flatt we came to a very handsome dry and sound plain, containing about one thousand acres, where the Herbs grow equal in richness and abundance to the finest parts of Bathurst, the flatt land from the River back at this plain appear to be about 1½ mile, it may be about ¾ of a mile across; and about one mile on from the plains is the richest and finest feeding that can be conceived...**

Thursday [6 December 1821, Talbragar River Flats near present Craboon]

Left our sleeping station 20 minutes past 5 A.M. and travelled a N.W. course until we again made the river, when we halted on a most beautiful plain Covered with good Sheep herbage, about 3 miles in length and one deep, there appears to be on both sides of

the river a succession of Plains for about 20 miles from 2 to 6 miles in length and one to two in Depth, with a small neck of Timber, dividing them from each other, the grass on the clear lands is short and very rich, but by far the greatest proportion of the Food is herbs of the greatest variety and richness the wild Tares are very luxuriant, as are indeed every other part of the food, the land on these plains is dry, healthy and extremely rich, the Flatts that have Timber at the back of these Plains have an immense quantity of grass, but not the variety of Herbs, although excellent feeding land and the Timber not thick, on the most fertile parts are Apple Tree, the more inferior Box, and the hills Pine Iron Bark and Box with occasionally a little stunted Oak, Stringy Bark and Gum, our dogs and Pack horses as well as some of the men wanting rest we remained here from breakfast time.

G.T.W.B. BOYES, NEPEAN RIVER,
NEW SOUTH WALES 1821, HOBART 1831

George Thomas William Blamey Boyes was born in Hampshire in 1786, the son of a
gentleman and a by-no-means wealthy property owner. His mother died a month after
he was born and he had a disturbed childhood, moving from relative to relative and
school to school. However, some of his schooling introduced him to drawing and
painting with watercolours under the instruction of thoroughly competent artists. He
even took advice, perhaps also instruction, from J.M.W. Turner. He did not become a
great artist, but he did much beautiful work in Australia both with pen and brush.
When the aging John Glover came to live in Tasmania in 1831, Boyes spent 'a very
pleasant evening' with him. 'At about eight Glover pulled out two sketchbooks and,
putting both his hands upon them on the table, said: "Now Sir, your Portfolio – and
we will exchange for the evening".'

It was fortunate for Boyes that he was given the opportunity to work in
Australia. In 1809, he joined the Commissariat of the British Army as a
Treasury Clerk and spent seven years in Spain and Portugal during the
Peninsular Wars. The mountains excited him and he did much sketching
and painting but, promoted deputy assistant commissary-general, he also
got a thorough grounding in requisitioning and managing supplies.

Back in London, retired on half pay and with £100 left in his father's
will, Boyes married Mary Ediss in 1818. By 1822, he was finding it impossible to support a wife, two sons and trips to London to further his painting,
so he went to Coutances in Normandy where living was much cheaper,
expecting his family to join him. Heavily pregnant, Mary refused to go.

Boyes spent several lonely months painting in Normandy, but produced
Coutances, one of his best paintings. Then his finances were rescued by an
upheaval in the commissariat of New South Wales. The head had debunked
with the cash.

Having made his name as a meticulous accountant, Boyes was sent to
help put things right. He arrived in Sydney on 17 April 1824. While waiting
for the arrival of the man who was to head the commissariat, William
Lithgow, Boyes spent several weeks on a farm on the banks of the Nepean
owned by a man he had served with in the Peninsular.

Boyes was posted to Van Diemen's Land as colonial auditor in October
1826. There he wrote many letters to his wife, maintained the diary that he

began in France and painted. He hoped that his wife and family would join him. They did not; but he supported them. In 1832, he got leave of absence and met his dear Mary and children after an absence of 9 years and 17 days.

Boyes returned to take up his position in 1834, this time bringing Mary and their four sons with him. He was appointed legislative councillor in 1840 and colonial secretary in 1842. He died in 1853.

Both his letters and his diaries contain shrewd, acerbic comments. In early letters from Sydney, Boyes wrote, 'There will be everything in this country in time except plenty of water and honest men'.

John Blaxland's daughters were 'the commonest of the common. They are togs for shew – but though they are at every party, the mother can't get them married – the misfortune is that they are shown about till everybody is weary of them'. But four of the six daughters married men of rank.

Although he loved the Nepean, Boyes liked Van Diemen's Land better, calling it 'land of the Mountain and the Flood'. After a visit there on his way to Sydney, he told Mary: 'You have never seen anything half so fine as the Derwent. The river is the most beautiful thing of its kind I have ever met with'.

The following quotes tell of the Nepean, Mount Wellington and of the generation of colonials growing up in Van Diemen's Land.

16th. [March 1824] After raining very heavily for some hours it held up about three o'clock — and I availed myself of the chance to visit once again my favourite river and its rocky banks. The foliage was all loaded with the moisture and the mosses upon the stones looked richer than ever while thousands of rain drops trickled from the trees.

I am off for Sydney the day after tomorrow and considering how many hours I have past here in rambling about the Nepean I cannot think of my departure with indifference. I have bid adieu to the rocks, the woods, the river. If they had been endowed with consciousness and knew how much I loved them, they could not have shed more tears at losing a friend; the lichens, the mosses, Myrtles and Mimosa melted into balmy drops as I passed them, each shrub shook fragrance on my head and perfumed the path. T'was a grey sober twilight sort of evening and but for the tinkling of the little bell bird as I climbed the rugged path that led up the precipitous bank, the silence had been complete. In these wild sequestered scenes there is nothing to remind you of England.

Of animals you meet with the Wallabee — the Kangaroo rat — the native dog, the Opossum and the native cat, all differing in many essentials from those of our own country. The woods swarm with birds, whose notes are entirely new to the European ear — and they are as various as they are discordant. Sometimes when I have been bathing in the Nepean — these feathered savages have set up such a yelling, screaming, shouting, laughing, that fifty natives /from whom they acquired their notes/ could not have exceeded — and it is at first difficult to believe that such sounds do not proceed from human throats celebrating their savage orgies...

February 13th. [1831]

At home all morning. In the afternoon rode Bryant's horse beyond Roseway across the stream and into the woods on the other side. Magnificent scenery — Mount Wellington rearing his giant head above the tall trees at every turn — and the deep purple shadows of the Ravines formed fine contrasts with the bright parts rich with streams of yellow light from the declining sun...

[Hobart Town, 23 October 1831]

They are such beauties, you cannot imagine such a beautiful race as the rising generation in this Colony. As they grow up they think nothing of England and can't bear the idea of going there. It is extraordinary the passionate love they have for the country of their birth, but I believe it is remarked that the natives of a Mountain Land feel stronger attachment for their birth place than the Natives of the Plains. There is a degree of liberty here which you can hardly imagine at your side of the Equator. The whole country round, Mountains and Vallies, Rocks Glens, Rivers and Brooks seem to be their own domain; they shoot, ride, fish, bathe, go bivouacing in the woods — hunt O'possum and Kangaroos, catch and train parrots, Wombats, Kangaroo Rats etc. etc. They are in short as free as the Birds of the Air and the Aboriginal Natives of the Forests. They are also connoisseurs in horse, Cattle, Sheep, Pigs, Wool, Grain and leather — And they all understand before they can speak that two and two make four.

1822—1835

LACHLAN MACQUARIE, ILLAWARRA RANGE, NEW SOUTH WALES, 1822

Between 1788 and 1810, there had been a succession of nine governors and acting-governors (Paterson served two different terms) in New South Wales. Lachlan Macquarie served from 1810 until 1821, a term only one month short of 12 years. In this time, he transformed the Colony and gave thousands of convicts a chance in life that no one else would have allowed them. He was interested in what men and women could do for the new country, not what they had done in the old.

Macquarie was born on Ulva in the Scottish Hebrides on 31 January 1762. His mother was the sister of a clan chieftain, his father a poor farmer and cousin to the last chieftain of Clan Macquarie. He joined the army as a volunteer, serving with three different regiments in Canada, in the American War of Independence, then in India where he fought as lieutenant in several campaigns. He married Jane Jarvin in 1793, but she died of tuberculosis only three years later.

Macquarie served as chief-of-staff of the Indian Army in Egypt, and then went back to India in 1802 in command of the 86th Regiment. He had reached the rank of brigadier when he returned to England in 1807 to marry Elizabeth Campbell, the youngest daughter of his second cousin. She had waited two years for his term in India to end: he feared to take her to the unhealthy climate.

In 1809, Brigadier-General Miles Nightingale was appointed Governor of New South Wales; Lachlan Macquarie was to accompany him as Lieutenant Governor-elect and commander of the 73rd Regiment. Nightingale grew sick and resigned. Lachlan Macquarie took his place and Elizabeth accompanied him. He was sworn in as Governor on 1 January 1810. They had lost a baby daughter in London but in 1814, to their delight, a healthy son Lachlan was born.

Despite his humanitarian ideas, Macquarie retained a strict sexual bigotry. He thought the custom of living 'tally' (unmarried), 'a scandalous and perenicious custom so shamelessly adopted throughout the Territory'. However, it was an excellent arrangement for women. It ensured that they were treated as partners, rather than possessions. As well, it allowed them to keep possession of their own money.

Macquarie took an immense interest in the Colony. He made 10 major tours, often with Elizabeth and Lachlan, sometimes in carriages, usually on horseback or on foot, and kept a careful journal of each.

He built roads, put up impressive buildings for which he was criticised by the British Government. Working to imaginative ideas by Elizabeth, he designed Port Macquarie (named for him by John Oxley) as one of the world's loveliest towns. Buildings were sited to overlook the water, roads curved past them. The later imposition of a road grid and a long succession of predatory and ignorant officials have made the town ordinary and ugly.

Macquarie encouraged spending on education. He built a library and a savings bank; he appointed Michael Massey Robinson as 'poet laureate' with the valuable yearly stipend of two cows.

However, in encouraging farmers instead of stockbreeders, he overlooked the need for export income. Fresh food had no export possibilities, whereas wool offered an exciting future. His treatment of ex-convicts as worthy to share his table ran counter to the self-importance of soldiers and free settlers. So many complaints were made about Macquarie to the British Government that they sent John Bigge as Commissioner to look into the Colony's affairs. He spent 17 months listening too much to Macquarie's enemies and produced a devastating report. A great man was reduced by a man of no consequence. Macquarie left Australia on 15 February 1822 and died two years later.

I quote from his 'Tour to Illawarra 1822' made in January. The magnificent stand of timber that he describes was a rarity at that time. The rainforests of North Queensland and northern New South Wales had not then been discovered. Few of the names Macquarie gave to features on this trip have been maintained. Mount Regent is the mountain at Bulli Pass. His Mount Brisbane is probably Mount Kembla, but may be the top of the Illawarra Range west of Mount Keira. Where he refers to 'forest' he does not mean heavy timber; he means grassland dotted with big trees. The early colonists went back to an early meaning of 'forest' as the cleared land between the city wall and wood, where only those trees too big to cut down were left standing.

> Tuesday 15 Jany... At 10 mins. past 6 a.m. we set forward on our journey; and after passing Cataract River near it's source, we arrived at the summit of the great mountain that contains the pass to the low country of Illawarra, the top of this mountain being three miles from our last station. On our arrival on the summit of the mountain, we were gratified with a very grand magnificent bird's eye view of the ocean, the 5 Islands, and of the greater part of the low country

of Illawarra as far as Red Point. After feasting our eyes with this grand prospect, we commenced descending the mountain at 20 mins. after 8 o'clock. The descent was very rugged, rocky and slippery, and so many obstacles opposed themselves to our progress, that it was with great difficulty that the packhorses could get down this horrid steep descent. At length we effected it, but it took us an hour to descend altho' the descent is only one mile & a half long. The whole face of this mountain is clothed with the largest and finest forest trees I have seen in the colony. They consist chiefly of the black-butted gum, stringy bark, turpentine, mountain ash, fig, peppermint, box-wood, sassafras, and red cedar; but the latter is now very scarce, most of it having been already cut down and carried away to Sydney. There are also vast quantities of the cabbage palm, and fern trees growing in the face of the mountain, the former being very beautiful and of great height. Finding that this mountain has never yet received any particular name, I have christened it the Regent Mountain, as it was first descended by Mr. Throsby in the year 1815, when our present King was Regent of the United Kingdom.

We arrived at a creek containing a very pretty stream of fresh running water about 1½ miles from the foot of the mountain at a qr. past 9 o'clock, and here we halted to breakfast and to refresh our men and cattle [horses were then included in the description 'cattle', 'horned cattle' was used to differentiate]. I have named this stream of fresh water Throsby's Creek, in honour of Mr. Throsby who first crossed it on his descending the Regent Mountain.

Having breakfasted we pursued our journey at 11 a.m. along the sea shore towards Mr. Allan's farm at Red Point, riding chiefly on a soft beach for 12 miles, and through very barren unprofitable land. We crossed the entrance of Tom Thumb's Lagoon which was at this time dry, and soon afterwards arrived at Mr. Allan's lands, meeting there with about 100 natives, who had assembled at this place to meet and welcome me to Illawarra. They were of various tribes, and some of them had come all the way from Jervis's Bay, and they all appeared to be very intimate with Mr. O'Brien. They all knew who I was, and most of them pronounced my name (Govr. Macquarie) very distinctly. They were very civil, and I regretted exceedingly that I had no tobacco for them.

GODWIN, VAN DIEMEN'S LAND, c.1822

Godwin published a guide in London in 1823. It is so enthusiastic that anyone who was considering taking passage must surely have boarded the next ship. Its full title is, Godwin's Emigrant's Guide to Van Diemen's Land, more properly called Tasmania, containing a description of its climate, soil, and productions; A form of Application for Free Grants of Land; with a scale enabling persons in inland Towns, to estimate the expense of a passage for any given number of men, women, or children, a List of the most necessary Articles to take out, and other information useful to Emigrants.

The traveller in going from Hobart Town to Launceston, had better take the following route; cross the Derwent at Roseneath ferry, 10 miles from Hobart Town, from thence through the fertile plains of Bagdad to Stonyhut valley, at the back of which lies Cress marsh, a fine country; the next place is Fourteen-tree plain, which consists of a rich soil, and then the plains of Jericho, which are only thinly covered with timber: the pasturage is excellent, and the river Jordan flows through the centre of this delightful place.

The traveller will now arrive at Scantlin's and York plains; this quarter is one of Nature's master-pieces, nothing can exceed it in beauty; it is a perfect paradise. Tin-dish-holes is about twelve miles in extent, and is only surpassed by Scantlin's plains in the beauty of its scenery.

Salt-pan plains is a very extensive district; this place is not only famous for the salt which its lakes produce annually; but is said to resemble Salisbury-plain in Wiltshire, than which it is much more beautiful and picturesque; the pasturage is extremely rich, and interspersed with fine trefoil and cinquefoil.

Nor far from Salt-pan plains is a remarkable sugarloaf hill, called Mount Grimes, from the summit of which the eye wanders to the distance of thirty or forty miles, over extensive tracts of the richest land, *only requiring the grass to be burned to prepare it for the immediate reception of the plough.*

This leads to Macquarie River, which forms the Northern extremity of the county of Buckingham.

The *county of Cornwall* now presents itself on crossing this
river, which, taking a North-westerly course, falls into the Lake
River. Why it should be called Cornwall I am at a loss to guess,
for it surpasses the beautiful Buckingham in soil and productions;
the land also lays much lower, and is better watered. Proceeding
further on through Argyle plains, Ant-hill plains, and Macklaine's
plains, the traveller will arrive at Elizabeth River, (which runs due
West, and falls into Macquarie River,) and passing further on
through Macquarie plains is a place called Epping Forest, from its
being pretty thickly covered with wood, the easternmost end of
which borders on the South Esk, and extends North-westerly to
the Lake River. Henrietta plains lay a little further North, and
with New plains form a fine level fertile country...

Field Sports. — The coursing of the emu and kangaroo
furnishes sport and exercise equal to stag-hunting in Europe. The
meat of the latter is equal to venison, and the tail makes excellent
soup, superior to ox-tail soup. The general weight of the kangaroo
is from forty to one hundred pounds, but some have been killed
weighing one hundred and forty pounds; the flesh is brown and
full of gravy, but it has no fat: on which account some fat pork is
generally cooked along with it... The flesh of the emu is like
young beef, and is considered wholesome and nutritive: in form it
resembles the ostrich, and is nearly as large; when standing
upright, they are commonly seven feet high... Its weight is usually
from sixty to one hundred and twenty pounds, and though in
general the most gentle animal in nature, he will sometimes
defend himself with his beak and feet, and such is the force of his
motion, that a man cannot withstand the shock. They are,
however, easily tamed, and Mrs. Reiby, of Sydney, assured me that
she had a pair of emus that used to range her yard, protect her
premises, and perform the office usually alloted to a house-dog. If
a stranger intruded himself, the emu interposed, and if he did not
quickly retire, the emu never failed to throw him down by a push
with his foot against the head or breast, and continued to hold him
down with his foot until he was called off by some of the inmates
of the house, when he would quickly release his prisoner, and
allow him to pass.

THOMAS PAMPHLET, MORETON BAY, MOUTH OF THE BRISBANE RIVER, QUEENSLAND, 1823

Pamphlet sailed from Sydney on 21 March 1823 with three other ticket-of-leave men in a nine-metre open boat bound for the Five Islands (Lake Illawarra). They were sent out to trade for cedar and had flour, pork and rum on board as barter.

A violent storm caught them just short of their destination and carried them out of sight of land. The weather did not let up for five days and, in trying to keep the boat afloat, they lost all sense of direction and distance travelled. When they wrecked on Moreton Island, they thought they were still south of Sydney.

One of the party, John Thompson, died at sea. The other two, John Finnegan and Richard Parsons, were difficult companions. Finnegan refused to help with anything; Parsons tried to kill him several times.

All three lived with Aborigines around Moreton Bay for months. When John Oxley, sent out to pick a site for another penal colony, pulled into the Bay, Pamphlet met him in the company of Aborigines who had befriended him, and went aboard. The next day they found Finnegan, and the two castaways showed Oxley the rather hidden entrance to the beautiful Brisbane River. Parsons was up-river somewhere: the Aborigines sought the help of the whites in tribal squabbles, but never risked using all three together. Oxley left a note in a bottle for him, sailed back and collected him the next year.

John Uniacke, a young man with Oxley's expedition, took down Pamphlet's story. It was published in London in 1825 in a book edited by Barron Field, *Geographical Memoirs of New South Wales; by various hands*.

This extract is an unusually sympathetic account of Aboriginal Australians.

> We went on... towards the huts where we had lived with the natives. About half a mile before we reached them, we saw the natives fishing: they had been quite successful; and on seeing us they immediately put a quantity of whitings on the fire, nor would they allow us to proceed till we had filled ourselves with them. They then conducted us to our old quarters, and having kindled a fire,

they left us some fish, and went out again to catch more. We now set about making ourselves as comfortable as we could, when just at night-fall we were surprised by the return of Finnegan and two blacks with their nets. They had travelled the distance in one day, which it took us three days to perform, and had forced him to keep up with them. He was dreadfully fatigued; but his two companions, after leaving him, went out and procured fish and fern-root for him and themselves. We now became reconciled to him, and were all as friendly as ever, resting ourselves for the next three days in the hut, where the blacks regularly brought us fish and fern-root, which latter they called *dingowa*. We now consulted whether we had better take one of their canoes by night, or endeavour to make one ourselves; and having decided upon the latter, we made a choice of a tree, and immediately fell to work to cut it down and form a canoe. We worked from sunrise to sunset for nearly three weeks, having no other tool but the hatchet; and during the whole time the natives brought us food, where we were at work, and likewise left fish in our hut daily. During the whole of this time, Finnegan refused to work with us, which the blacks observing, frequently took the axe out of our hands and offered it to him, making signs that he should use it, and, on his continuing to refuse, they no longer brought him food, though to us they continued a liberal supply. He was consequently obliged to procure fern-root, &c. for himself. At the expiration of three weeks, our canoe being complete, the natives would not allow us to launch it, but did it themselves; and when they saw it afloat, with Parsons and me in it, their joy and admiration knew no bounds: they leaped, danced and roared, following us up and down the beach. Being now satisfied that it would answer our purpose, we landed, and the natives rolled the canoe up again on the beach, not allowing us to touch it. The remainder of the evening was spent in making preparations for our departure, Finnegan still refusing to go with us, notwithstanding our entreaties that he would. The natives having given us a quantity of fish, &c., Parsons and I set out the next afternoon with the flood-tide. We had not proceeded about a quarter of a mile, when the natives, perceiving that Finnegan did not accompany us, hastily launched a canoe, and two of them embarking, he was by the rest forced to follow, when they paddled quickly towards us; but we had gotten round a sandbank that lay some distance from the shore. They therefore pulled to the bank and made Finnegan land on it, where they left him, and went back to the huts. As he was unable to swim, he would have drowned when the tide rose, if we had not pulled back for him.

ALLAN CUNNINGHAM, LIVERPOOL RANGE, NEW SOUTH WALES, 1823

Sir Edward Parry, the Arctic explorer sent out to save the troubled Australian Agricultural Company, described Cunningham as 'a clear-headed, clever and scientific man, an excellent surveyor as well as a first-rate botanist'. Born at Wimbledon, Surrey, on 13 July 1791, Cunningham trained at first for the law but found it a dull life. In 1808, he accepted the position of clerk to the curator of the Royal Gardens at Kew where he developed a passionate interest in botany, especially after meeting Robert Brown, botanist with Flinders in Investigator *and then librarian to Sir Joseph Banks.*

On Banks's recommendation, Cunningham was appointed botanical collector. He spent two years collecting in Brazil, then the Gardens sent him to Australia. He arrived in Sydney on 20 December 1816, where Governor Macquarie suggested that he join John Oxley's attempt to find where the Lachlan River flowed. Renting a cottage at Parramatta, he collected in that district until the expedition left in April. Oxley could find no way around the wonderful Lachlan marshes – disastrously, they have now been drained – so he returned, but Cunningham came back with a collection of 450 specimens for Kew.

Thereafter Cunningham decided that he could combine plant collecting with exploration and devised his own 'botanizing tours'. These tours made him extremely important as an explorer, since he found a way over the difficult Liverpool Range onto the magnificent plains, and on a later tour found the Darling Downs. His energetic life was cut short by tuberculosis. He died in Sydney on 27 July 1839 at the age of 47.

Cunningham's 'Journal of a route from Bathurst to Liverpool Plains in New South Wales' is one of the chapters in Barron Fields *GEOGRAPHICAL MEMOIRS ON NEW SOUTH WALES*. There seems to be no other copy of this remarkable story in Australia. Many of Cunningham's papers are at Kew.

The Liverpool Range is difficult. Cunningham found himself confronted with

> ... a vast collection of bold lofty ranges, occasionally in series one behind the other, and again divided and terminating in steep precipitous heads, which overhung deep yawning glens and sharp rocky ravines.

So he turned west and found a pass he later called Pandora's because it 'had a Hope at the bottom'. If he had continued west for another 20 kilometres, the range gave out and the way north was easy.

5th [June 1823]. I accordingly conducted my party through a fine rich valley, watered by a creek, issuing from the ravine, and wooded with apple-tree, blue gum, and swamp oak, and having traced it about seven miles, it broke into small open plains perfectly clear of timber, which lying N.N.E. and S.S.W. appeared to extend between some rising grounds three or four miles. The steep range of forest hills that limited the valley on its western side, upon extending to this strip of plain, which I have named Duguid's, becoming exceedingly low and moderate, induced me to advance to the westward over it, through an open grazing forest, which soon brought me within sight of another heavy, bold, lateral range, constituting the boundary of a valley, much more ample at its entrance from the forest, and more promising, in its trending, to the object of my research, than any recess towards this belt of mountains that we had yet explored. The aggregate body of these mountainous ranges evidently inclined to the N.W., and their respective principal branches descended generally S.S.W. parallel to each other, forming valleys more or less spacious, through which the waters rising in the southern declivity of this belt escape to the interior, bearing S.W. and W.S.W. from us.

The difficulties with which we had to contend in every stage of our journey, more especially during our near approaches to these mountains, considered with the observations I have of late made on the arrangement of their main or aggregate body, and its respective parts, fully convinced me that the only practicable mode of continuing their examination, with a view towards discovering a passage through them to the northward, would be by travelling on the broad base, formed generally in the lower country at the southern extremities of their lateral branches, exploring at each stage those large valleys that open upon it, and which, by their general tendency, might afford the hope of ultimate success. Thus impressed, and deeming the valley south of us well worthy of our examination, I continued our journey to it over a fertile flat of apple-tree, the soil partly of a loose, rich, vegetable decomposition, and partly of a still alluvial nature, particularly along the margin of a fine brook, which ran through the vale from the N.E. Upon an inclining plane, we were enabled without difficulty to trace this valley to the N.N.E. about eight miles; when finding it became very contracted and sharp, by reason of a converging disposition of its boundary and other minor ranges, I was induced to halt and ascend a high point of the western range above us, being fully satisfied, from the northing we had made since we left Goulburn River, that we could not be many miles distant from the southern limit of Liverpool Plains. To my utmost gratification, upon tracing the line of mountain ranges, which continued very far to the N.W., a very considerable depression in the back of the main ridge, distant about three miles, afforded me a clear, although limited, view of a part of the open plains north of this extensive barrier; on which I immediately recognized and identified several detached round mounts, that had been previously seen from the summit of a lofty pinnacle (Mount M'Arthur) situate in these mountains to the eastward of us.

6th. Having again taken their bearings, as also those of several points around me, I descended to my people, and lost no time in shifting my encampment to an open valley immediately at the base of the mountains, and within two or three miles of this apparently practical passage to the northern country.

7th. Upon proceeding to examine it, I found that, from the level of the valley, the ascent through a close, lightly-timbered forest was exceedingly gentle and gradual to the highest part of the gap or pass, which was distant from our encampment about two miles; and the declivity on the northern side of the ridge, although less moderate (its face being grooved by small water-gulleys) was nevertheless found practicable, and not to exceed a mile to the open wooded country at its base. This was observed to be timbered with large stately box, and watered by a rivulet, which meandered through the forest northerly, forming in its progress the western boundary of a considerable extent of plain, about eight or nine miles north from the highest part of the pass, which on either side is overhung by bold, lofty heads of the mountain range. Having directed a line of trees to be marked from our encampment through the passage to the verge of the nearest plain, I climbed to the summit of the eminence on the east side of the pass, and thence had a most beautiful and extensive view of the country before me.

BARRON FIELD, SYDNEY, c.1824

Born in London in 1786, Barron Field was the son of a doctor. He was educated as a barrister and called to the Bar on 23 June 1814. He also wrote poetry and became well known in literary circles, being a good friend of Charles Lamb and known to both Wordsworth and Leigh Hunt. He was theatre critic for The Times.

Barron Field arrived in Sydney on 24 February 1817 as judge of the Supreme Court. His knowledge of the law impressed all who dealt with him, but he was not popular.

In 1825, John Murray of London published a second corrected edition of *GEOGRAPHICAL MEMOIRS ON NEW SOUTH WALES*: BY VARIOUS HANDS, the book that Field edited and for which he wrote at least one chapter.

ACROSTICHUM GRANDE [*Platycerium superbum*]
By Spittall in Macleay's garden at Elizabeth Bay from *Narrative of the United States Exploring Expedition during the years 1838, 1839, 1840, 1841, 1842* **by Charles Wilkes O.S.N. Commander, Mitchell Library, State Library of New South Wales**

At the back of the book, he republished his *First Fruits of Australian Poetry* first issued in 1819. It is not great poetry, though it is considerably better than the general view, especially that of a contemporary who wrote

> Thy poems, Barron Field, I've read
> And thus adjudge their meed —
> So poor a crop proclaims thy head
> A *barren field* indeed.

Lamb reviewed the book kindly in the *Examiner*. Shelley could rhyme 'spirit' and 'near it' with impunity, Field has never been forgiven for rhyming 'Australia' with 'failure'. *First Fruits* has great interest because it examines native plants and animals. In the following quote from a long poem, he celebrates Common Heath and Fringed Lilies, *Thysanotos juncifolious*.

Mountain heaths, especially the *Epacris* genus, hang long crimson tubes of flowers so densely together they weigh branches down. The plant that Field describes is now known as *Epacris impressa*. When he was admiring it in Australia, many English gardeners were cultivating it.

> When first I landed on Australia's shore,
> (I neither botanist nor poet truly,
> But less a seeker after facts than truth),
> A flower gladden'd me above the rest,
> Shap'd trumpet-like, which from a leafy stalk
> Hangs clust'ring, hyacinthine, crimson red
> Melting to white. Botanic science calls
> The plant *epacris grandiflora*, gives
> Its class, description, habitat, then draws
> A line. The bard of truth would moralize
> The flower's beauty, which caught first my eye:
> But, having lived the circle of the year,
> I found (and then he'd sing in Beauty's praise)
> That this sole plant that never ceas'd to bloom.
> Nor here would stop: - at length first love and fair,
> And fair and sweet, and sweet and constant, pall,
> (Alas, for poor Humanity!) and then
> The new, the pretty, and the unexpected,
> Ensnare the fancy. Thus it was with me,
> When first I spied the floweret in the grass,
> Which forms the subject of this humble song,
> And (treason to my wedded flower) cried:-

Th' Australian "fringed violet"
Shall henceforth be my pet!
Oh! had this flow'r been seen by him
Who call'd Europa's "violets dim
Sweeter than lids of Juno's eyes,"
He had not let this touch suffice,
But had pronounc'd it (I am certain)
Of Juno's eye the "fringed curtain" —
Pick'd phrase for eye-lid, which the poet
Has us'd elsewhere: and he will know it,
Who in his dramas is well vers'd:
Vide The Tempest, act the first. —
But I am wand'ring from my duty,
First to describe my fringe-ey'd beauty.
'Tis then a floss-edged lilac flower,
That opens only after rain,
Once, and never blows again;
Shuts too at early ev'ning's hour,
Soon as the sun has lost its power,
Like a fairy's parasol
(If fairies walk by day at all):
Or, it may quicker gain belief,
To call it her silk neckerchief,
Dropt before she blest the place
With her last night's dancing grace:
For surely fairies haunt a land,
Where they may have the free command
Of beetles, flowers, butterflies,
Of such enchanting tints and dyes:
Not beetles black (forbidden things),
But beetles of enamel'd wings,
Or, rather, coats of armour, boss'd,
And studded till the ground-work's lost.

HUME AND HOVELL, SNOWY MOUNTAINS,
NEW SOUTH WALES, 1824

Originally it was Hovell and Hume. After bitter quarrels between them lasting years
about who did what, it now seems that Hume was the leader in their journey from
Hume's farm near present Gunning to Corio Bay in the far southwest of Port Phillip
(Victoria). Unfortunately, they both thought that they had reached Westernport, the
big bay east of Port Phillip Bay, almost 100 kilometres away.

It was an extraordinary mistake for William Hovell to make because, until
then, his noted positions were far more accurate. Born in England in 1786,
he went to sea as a boy and 12 years later he was master of a trading vessel.
He migrated to Sydney in 1812 with £500 worth of merchandise and
a recommendation from the Colonial Office. He joined the ex-convict
merchant and manufacturer Simeon Lord and for five years commanded
Lord's vessels in trade along the New South Wales coast and down to New
Zealand. In 1819, Hovell settled on a land grant near Narellan, northeast
of Camden.

Hamilton Hume was a colonial, born at Parramatta in 1797 to Andrew
Hume, superintendent of convicts. He could find his way about on land. As
a youth, he explored the country to the southwest of Illawarra; with James
Meehan, ex-convict surveyor and explorer, he found Lake Bathurst and
Goulburn Plains. In 1821, on his own expedition, he found the Yass Plains
and later squatted on the best land that he found there.

When Sir Thomas Brisbane took over from Lachlan Macquarie as governor, he considered landing a party of prisoners under a responsible leader
at Cape Howe or Wilson's Promontory with instructions to work their way
overland back to Sydney. Brisbane thought it likely, as did Macquarie, that
a large navigable river disembogued on the southeast coast. Hume was
approached and he suggested that he lead a party from Lake George to
Westernport.

Brisbane dilly-dallied and eventually decided that he could not outfit the
expedition. Hovell heard of the proposal and joined Hume in fitting out
their own venture. When advised of the plans, Governor Brisbane arranged
for six pack saddles and gear, a tent, tarpaulins, a limited supply of arms
and ammunition, a few cooking utensils and slops for the six men who were
to accompany the explorers – three employees of Hume and three of

Hovell. Hovell had to borrow money to find his share of the rest of the expenses. Hume even had to sell a rare and valuable imported plough.

Both Hume and Hovell kept journals of the trip. Hume's cannot be found; Hovell's wondrously misspelt document is held by the Mitchell Library, Sydney. In 1831 Dr William Bland, who had access to both journals, published their story closely following Hovell's account.

On 8 November 1824, acccording to Hovell, 'a prospect came into View the most Magnificeant'. Bland told a fuller story.

> Monday, November 8. — At half past seven o'clock they had recommenced their progress, proceeding along the stream in a S. westerly direction, the stream becoming gradually broader and deeper as they advanced. [They were travelling down Burra Creek, southeast of present Tumbarumba]. At about five miles from their place of departure, it is broken by three several perpendicular falls, each from about ten to fifteen feet in height, and between twenty and thirty feet distant from each other. Two miles beyond these falls, their progress on the banks of this stream is arrested by the mountainous range forming the southern barrier of the valley, and which, on each side of it, rises precipitously out of the stream.
>
> Messrs. Hovell and Hume having ascended close to the stream, with some difficulty, about half the height of this range, in order to be the better enabled to decide as to their future operations, were suddenly surprised by a sight, to the utmost degree magnificent. Mountains, of a conoidal form, and of an apparently immense height, and some of them covered about one fourth of their height, with snow, were now seen extending semicircularly from the S.E. to S.S.W. at the supposed distance of about twenty miles. The sun was bright (it was about ten or eleven in the forenoon), and gave them an appearance the most brilliant.
>
> The mountains which they had hitherto seen, compared with these stupendous elevations, were no more than hillocks; from which, also their form, as well as their general characters, rendered them not the less dissimilar.
>
> The men no sooner heard of this unexpected and interesting scene than, catching the enthusiasm, they ran to the spot where the travellers were standing, and were not less than themselves surprised

and delighted at this pre-eminently grand and beautiful spectacle.
[They were looking southeast on to the western flank of Mount
Townsend and associated peaks in the Snowy Mountains north of
Mount Kosiuszko.]

Hovell was particularly impressed by the Goulburn River country in
Victoria, near present Yea.

... at the distance of 7 miles from the Goulburn we suddenly arrived
at the banks of another river, but although it was only a Small one
when compared with the other, yet it gave us nearly as much trouble
in getting our things across, which we did by Means of a tree lyeing
across it but we had much more trouble with our Cattle, as we had
every one to swim over Seperately accasioned by the deapth of water
broken trees, and a Mud bank to lend them upon on the opposite
side, after crossing it we loaded again and got to the edge of the
forest dist about 1 Mile, were we stoped for the night, it being Sun
down before we arrived here.

The Forest between the Goulburn and this river, Mr Hume
named Meehans Forest, in Compliment to his friend Mr Meehan,
who had kindly assisted him with many useful articles necessary for
the journey. In one Spot, in particular, which we passed through to
day, we observed a number of trees of the Wattle Kind (Mimosa)
were the branches had, not only the Leaf which is peculiar to that
tree, but it had also branches with leaves quite differant, I think the
leaf is more like that of the peach tree, only not so large, and it hang
Closeir upon the branch, some hang in bunches below the other
limbs, It was some time before I could be convinced of the reallity
of the thing till a Man Climbed up the tree and brought down a
branch, where those trees growe, the Honey Suckel growed also
very thick, the soil was very good near the last mentioned spot, was
a tree something of the Gumb, and the only one we had seen, full in
blosum, it had a very beautiful appearance — In all our travels, I have
seen no Country better adapted for feeding Sheep, the Hills,
adjoining the Goulburn river they being nearly Clear, of timber,
Grass to the top, and in the hollows below, an abundence of herbage
of a very excellent quality.

EDMUND LOCKYER, BRISBANE RIVER, 1825

Born in Devon in 1784, Lockyer came to Sydney with his wife and children in April 1825. He was a major with the 57th Regiment of Foot. Governor Brisbane immediately recognised his capabilities. Only five months after his arrival, he sent him to explore the Brisbane River that Oxley travelled a short way up in 1823.

Lockyer and his party navigated 195 kilometres of the river, a distance that took them near the headwaters of the winding stream. They had hauled the boats across rapids, sometimes negotiating a maze of logs and fallen trees, and climbed hills to see which way the river ran and what sort of country lay ahead.

The next year Brisbane sent Lockyer with a detachment of soldiers and a party of convicts to establish a settlement at Albany in Western Australia to forestall a feared French settlement. One of his first moves at the site was to establish friendly relations with the local indigenous people. Nevertheless, with a village established, Lockyer formally annexed the territory on 21 January 1827.

Lockyer returned to Sydney, sold his commission and became police magistrate at Parramatta. *Ermington*, the house he built to the east of the town, gave its name to the present suburb. He later took up a grant of land at Goulburn. In 1852, he was appointed Sergeant-at-Arms to the Legislative Council and Usher of the Black Rod in 1856.

His understanding of Aboriginal Australians and his humane treatment of them were rare qualities. I quote from the journal Lockyer kept on the Brisbane River exploration.

September 14th [well above tidal water and Oxley's highest point]. At 8.30 embarked and proceeded up the river. The hills beautifully covered with pine trees of large size, the banks as before with swamp oak, honey-suckle, blue gum, and ironbark. We this day for the first time saw some of the natives; ordered the boats to pull up to the shore on which they stood. After a little hesitation, and the sight of a looking-glass which I held up, they ventured down within a few yards; gave them some biscuit, shewed them two sheep we had in the

boat; at the sight of them their astonishment was great, as also at
two of the soldiers of the 40th Regiment, who had very red hair;
from their manner it was evident the colour of these soldiers' hair
was a matter of great curiosity to them as well as their red jackets.
They were perfectly naked, stout, clean-skinned, well made people,
and shewed no symptom whatever of hostility. From the short
intercourse I had with them, I do not think they had ever seen a
European before...

September 15th ... The natives we saw yesterday again made their
appearance; amongst them saw an old man a cripple, whom they
carried, also a little boy — gave them fish hooks and lines — they
kept constantly pointing to the boats and shouting, supposing them,
as I concluded, to be alive...

October 20th ... On rounding the point of one of the reaches we
came suddenly on the encampment of some natives, who on seeing
us, ran off, leaving their kangaroo skins, spears and tomahawks all
behind. We landed and examined their implements, giving strict
orders not to move a single article; sent to the boats for some
biscuit, and left it on the kangaroo skins. As I could not ascertain
the direction the natives had taken, or whether they would return,
we got into the boats, and proceeded about one mile, when two
natives were seen following us up the bank, and calling to us; we
returned to the shore, and after some difficulty induced them to
have sufficient confidence to allow us to approach close to them,
when they proved to be a woman and a lad about fourteen years of
age. The former had an infant in her arms; gave them looking-
glasses, beads, and fish-hooks; their surprise and apparent wonder at
seeing people so opposite to themselves in colour, as well as in other
respects, cannot well be described, but it is certain they had never
seen white people before, nor could they believe but that the boats
were living animals, as I could not induce them to go down to the
place where they were. On making signs to them to do so, the
woman shook her head and put her hand to her mouth, as if she was
afraid they would bite. While we were holding communication with
these natives, several women and children were seen at a distance,
but we could not induce them to come near; the men no doubt were

not far off though they did not appear. Finding we could not induce them to approach, we left our new acquaintances, after convincing them of our friendly intentions. The woman, in return for what I had given her, held out a neat basket made of plaited straw and a kangaroo skin. The former I took, but declined the latter as it was of considerable use and value to them.

JAMES ATKINSON. NEW SOUTH WALES. 1826

Atkinson came to Sydney in 1820 as a free settler. He was 25 years old. For two years he worked as principal clerk in the Colonial Secretary's office, then resigned to take up land grants in the Berrima district where he farmed successfully. In 1825, he visited England and in 1826 published, An Account of the State of Agriculture & Grazing in New South Wales, a very valuable overview. His friends had told him that despite numbers of books about the Colony, its rural and domestic economies were still comparatively unknown.

Atkinson married Charlotte Waring when he returned and they had four children. He died at the age of 39 unaware that, as Charlotte Barton, his wife would author *A Mother's Offering to her Children*, the first children's book to be written and published in Australia; and that their daughter, Louisa, two months old when he died, would still be known in the 21st century as a painter of watercolours, a writer of six novels, a naturalist and a botanist.

James Atkinson himself wrote well and was a sound observer.

The various descriptions of country in New South Wales may be classed under the following heads: viz. barren scrubs, brushes, forest lands, plains and alluvial lands; in describing which it will be necessary, in some cases, to make a further subdivision.

The barren scrubs almost every where border the sea coast, and extend to various distances inland; in some places two or three miles; in others, lands of a better description approach close to the water's edge. The soil in these scrubs is either sandstone rock or sterile sand or gravel, covered, however, with a profusion of beautiful shrubs and bushes, producing most elegant flowers, and affording a constant succession throughout the whole year, but most abundant in winter and spring; the shrubs and plants growing in these places furnish the Colonists with materials for brooms, but produce little else that can be converted to any useful purpose. — The grass tree, with its lofty flower stalk, is a conspicuous object in these wastes: of the hard and woody but light stalk of this plant, the natives make the shaft of their spears, and shooting or fish gigs. Very few trees grow in these places, except a few stunted gum trees, in situations sheltered from the sea winds ... Brushes may principally be divided into coppice, vine, willow, and indigo brushes. The first kind I have called coppice brushes, as they approach nearer to the nature of coppices in England than any other kind of woods in the Colony. They are not, however, known by that name in the Colony, but are distinguished into iron bark brush, stringy bark brush, &c. according to the kind of trees that predominates in them...

Vine brushes are mostly found on the sides and summits of steep mountains near the sea. It is here we may see the vegetable kingdom in its most magnificent form, lofty cedar and turpentine trees of the grandest dimensions, with large vines or parasitical plants of various kinds, thick as a man's leg, twining up to their very tops, catching hold of other trees in all directions, until an immense net-work is formed, impervious to the sun's rays...

Forest lands are variously designated according to the quality of the soil, or the nature and number of the trees growing thereon, such as good, poor, open or thick forest. It is, however, always to be understood, that forest means land more or less furnished with timber trees, and invariably covered with grass underneath, and destitute of underwood. Under the head of forest lands are included some of the best and most improvable soils in the Colony; they are generally either clay or loam, of various degrees of tenacity, with a layer of vegetable earth on the top, extremely well calculated for the growth of grain. In the county of Cumberland, one immense tract of forest land extends, with little interruption, from below Windsor, on the Hawkesbury, to Appin, a distance of 50 miles; large portions of this are cleared and under cultivation, and of the remainder that is still in a state of nature, a great part is capable of much improvement. The whole of this tract, and indeed all the forest in this county, was thick forest land, covered with very heavy timber, chiefly iron and stringy bark, box, blue and other gums, and mahogany...

The grasses and wild herbage form a most important part of the spontaneous productions of New South Wales; and, in this respect, the Colony justly claims precedence over many uncultivated countries; since by their aid alone, grazing and breeding live stock have been carried to an extent that is really astonishing.

The principal grasses are, the oat grass, kangaroo grass, two sorts of rye grass, a variety of the fiorin, timothy, &c. Of these the oat grass is the most generally diffused; it affords good pasturage, and is eaten by all kinds of stock, but does not stand the winter. The kangaroo grass is found in low and warm places near the coast; it grows with an upright stalk to the height of eighteen inches or two feet, has a few blades at the top, of a fine green, but is destitute of leaves at the bottom; it is relished by horned cattle, but does not feed horses or sheep well, being probably too succulent, and those animals delighting most in a short close bite. The other descriptions of grass above mentioned, are not found anywhere in very great plenty; the rye grass seems most to affect whinstone lands, and the timothy is found in sands and granitic soils. There are two or three varieties of rib grass; also chichory, trefoil, burnet, and some other herbs, which stand the winter, and in that season afford good food for sheep...

No person, to my knowledge, has yet tried any experiments to ascertain how far any of the native grasses might be improved, or made more useful by cultivation, or in what proportion they are nutritive, when compared with European grasses.

Fred Turner, imaginative Government Botanist, carried out experiments on native grasses at the Brisbane Botanic Gardens between 1874 and 1879 and found them generally superior to exotics. No one followed up his work. Native grasses were discounted until resourceful farmers and scientists began extensive work on them in the 1990s.

HENRY DANGAR. HUNTER RIVER.
NEW SOUTH WALES. 1827

Henry Dangar came to Australia in 1821, the first of a dozen or more brothers, sisters and relatives who followed. Most of them thrived on the land, in business and in parliament. Their children continued to thrive after them, as have their descendants to this day.

Although Henry Dangar came out as a settler, he was a trained surveyor and John Oxley persuaded him to join his staff. Dangar spent six months surveying in the Camden and County of Argyle areas, and then moved to the Hunter Valley.

Dangar was a hard worker, an outstanding bushman, and the first to find an easy track over the difficult Liverpool Range to the plains. For five years, he pegged out land grants along the Hunter and its tributaries for immigrants who were multiplying their fortunes by hundreds and thousands. Unsettled by their enthusiasm, he marked out good land that he had discovered for William, his brother, and himself. Peter McIntyre, an energetic Scot, disputed the Dangars' claim. An enquiry found Henry had used his office to further his own interests. It was probably an unjust decision. It was well accepted in Australia then that findings were keepings. But Governor Darling dismissed him.

Dangar returned to England in 1827 with petitions and protests that were unsuccessful in getting his job back. However, a book he began on the journey over was so successful when it was published in 1828 that it increased settlement in Australia.

He returned to explore and survey for the great Australian Agricultural Company, then began to build up his own enormous holdings. In 1838, there occurred the awful slaughter of a big group of friendly Aboriginal Australians on his Myall Creek run on the edge of the New England. His extremely energetic actions to save the seven murderers from hanging leave the suspicion that he might have ordered them to clear the run of Aborigines.

Dangar's time in parliament was a confusing experience. His slow Cornish wit could not match the clever self-interest of William Charles Wentworth or the ruthless ambition of the eccentric Robert Lowe.

Henry Dangar was happiest in the Hunter Valley. His short book has an extraordinarily long title. The style is factual and practical. In this passage, his enthusiasm for the Hunter breaks through.

INDEX AND DIRECTORY

TO

MAP OF THE COUNTRY BORDERING UPON

THE RIVER HUNTER;

THE

LANDS OF THE AUSTRALIAN-AGRICULTURAL COMPANY

WITH

THE GROUND-PLANS AND ALLOTMENTS

OF

KING'S TOWN

NEW SOUTH WALES:

CONTAINING

A DETAIL OF THE ANNUAL QUIT RENT, AND AMOUNT OF THE REDEMPTION OF THE SAME; ALSO, HISTORICAL NOTES UPON THE TENURE AND PRINCIPLE OF GRANTING LANDS IN THE COLONY SINCE 1810; ALSO,

FOR THE GUIDANCE OF EMIGRANT SETTLERS,

A DESCRIPTION OF THE UNLOCATED COUNTRY IN THE VICINITY OF HUNTER'S RIVER;

Useful Geographical Notes in Liverpool Plains;

THE PRESENT REGULATIONS AND CONDITIONS UPON WHICH GRANTS AND SALES

OF LAND ARE MADE BY GOVERNMENT, WITH OBSERVATIONS THEREON,

With a View of the Present

STATE OF AGRICULTURE IN THE COLONY,

PRICE OF LAND, ADVICE TO SETTLERS, &C.

THE WHOLE FORMING,

WITH REGARD TO LAND AFFAIRS IN THAT COLONY,

A COMPLETE

EMIGRANT'S GUIDE

The Hunter being formed by numberless drains and streams from the dividing range, first takes a south-west course, a considerable distance, through a rough and almost untenantable country, (except by its original proprietors,) being the lateral and other branching ridges of the dividing range, until it reaches within a few miles of Page's river, when it opens into a spacious, fertile, and beautifully picturesque valley; continuing from thence its south-west course about thirty-five miles, to its junction with the Goulburn, but in its windings about double that distance, in which it receives the waters of Page's river, Dart brook, Kingdon ponds, and some other small streams.

The rich alluvial lands on this part of the river, (St. Germain and Twickenham meadows,) are without parallel in the known parts of the colony; there being a chain, at alternate sides, the whole distance, varying in breadth from one-half to two miles. Some parts are without timber, and others have no more than enhances, rather than detracts from, their value, with an inexhaustible soil, and a natural herbage, but little inferior to the most improved English meadows.

HENRY HELLYER, SURREY HILLS, TASMANIA, 1827

Born in England in 1790, Henry Hellyer came to Tasmania in 1826 as architect and surveyor to the Van Diemen's Land Company. This company was newly formed by English midland woollen manufacturers to apply for land to grow fine wool. They raised capital of £1,000,000 and they applied to Earl Bathurst, Head of the Colonial Office, for a grant of 500,000 acres (200,000 hectares). It was such a colossal demand in little Tasmania that it led to three years of debate as to how much and where. Sensibly, Bathurst halved the area and stated that it had to be well away from areas already settled. Governor Arthur was concerned that the company would seize the best land in each district and restrict the growing number of free settlers, so important to the future of Tasmania.

Hellyer began looking for land immediately on his arrival. He was a good leader of men, he was superbly fit, he was enthusiastic, and he could sketch what he saw in words and pictures. Here he is getting out of the Mackintosh River country west of Cradle Mountain in 1828:

> We were obliged to descend from tree to tree nearly perpendicularly for at least one thousand feet and at last got safe down when we crossed a rapid roaring creek which I doubt not had in the course of time torn out the whole of this chasm or chine from the level of its issuing from the mountain. As I crossed it I looked up at the opposite side which we had to ascend and seeing the trees growing out of its side as though affixed to a wall, I thought some of us might revisit the creek before we wished to do so — it was awful... our only chance was by helping or rather fishing each other from one root to another.

After one such experience when his men began to question whether they would ever find a way out, Hellyer told them 'While ever you can crawl I'll get you home'.

After such country, we can understand his delight in finding the Hampshire and Surrey Hills. But Hellyer was not a farmer. The country was too high, too cold, too wet and the grass too rank for sheep or any European livestock. The company took up the land but abandoned it after a few years. Hellyer felt he had failed the company. Further harassed by a vicious convict who spread rumours that he was homosexual (a grievous accusation in those days), he committed suicide in 1832. With no more Aboriginal fires to keep them open, the Hills soon became eucalyptus forest, an aggressive invader always awaiting opportunity.

> At some short distance from the Don [Hellyer River] we ascended the most magnificent grass hill I have seen in this country, consisting of several level terraces, as if laid out by art, and crowned with a straight row of stately peppermint trees, beyond which there is not a tree for four miles along the grassy hills. I had now arrived at the grand opening seen from the Peak beyond the Brown Forest. Here the natives had been burning large tracts of grass. The morning being cloudy and wet, I was just able to discern, through the mist, that the Peak [St Valentine's Peak, 35 kilometres south of Burnie] bore from hence E.N.E.: the top was in the clouds. I congratulated myself on having had so fine a day yesterday, or I should have had a very imperfect idea of the extent of good country here. The plains, or rather hills, from the south foot of the Peak, I call, from their great extent and importance, the Surrey Hills, which name I here cut upon a large conspicuous tree, the country being about the same distance inland as that county in England. They resemble English enclosures in many respects, being bounded by brooks between each, with belts of beautiful shrubs in every vale, including blue-leaf tea-tree, box, sassafras, blackwood, woodpear, birch, sloe-leaf, musk-holly, celery-top pine, and myrtle. The whole country here is grassy. The grasses in the line of our walk are principally Timothy, fox-tail, and single kangaroo. The surface soil is dark vegetable mould, upon a rich brown open loam of various depths, and light in colour according to its depth; but on the tops of the hills there are rocks above the surface in several instances, and from what I could observe where trees had fallen torn up by the roots, the substratum is everywhere gravelly, which appears to render these hills perfectly dry. All the brooks have hard pebbly bottoms, free from mud, and the water is clear as crystal. The timber found on these hills is in general of fine growth, very tall and straight: some of it would measure more than 100 feet to the lowest branch. The trees are, in many places, 100 yards apart. They are principally peppermint and

stringy-bark, which having lately made their summer shoots, the whole country where they appeared from the Peak of a lively brownish hue, by which I was enabled to distinguish the large tract of country which I have marked Brown Forest on the map; and from what I have seen from the Brown Forest thus far, I do not think it at all too thickly timbered to afford a little shade from the summer heat. It will not in general average ten trees on an acre. There are many open plains of several square miles without a single tree. The kangaroo stood gazing at us like fawns, and in some instances came bounding towards us; and if we shouted, they ran like a flock of sheep. We never saw so many together. The plains or hills to the north of the Peak, being nearer the coast, I called the Hampshire Hills. They appear even more park-like than the Surrey Hills, and are handsomely clumped with trees.

ROGER OLDFIELD, SYDNEY, 1828

Roger Oldfield, a doctor of civil law, brought out the first issue of the South-Asian
Register *in October 1827. Until the 1880s, Australians considered themselves in Asia.*

The journal lasted four issues. Oldfield wrote most of it himself, intending
it to be 'an impartial register of colonial information'. It was to 'influence
men of a graver nature' who had 'no instinct of love for a country of adop-
tion only'. Some articles were to be of lighter tone suitable for a gentleman's
magazine.

Oldfield's style is prolix, purple and incohesive to the point of being
incoherent, though this passage gives a remarkable picture of Sydney streets
early in the morning. His reference to 'natives' is of girls born in the Colony.

The town begins to swarm. <u>Fish ho! Fine sand mullet. Snappers all
alive. Here's your fine large King-fish, sand mullet, whiting, fish-
ho! Oysters-ho! all fat. Fat and good oysters ho, all fat, all fat.</u> Hey!
What's the price of your oysters? "Six-pence a pint". Does that pay?
"Yes, Sir, but there's a deal of trouble to take them out of the shell,
and we have to fetch them five or six miles off and perhaps farther."
The cries of Sydney are all genuine cockney, perfect in tune from
the deep gutteral, to the shrill and plaintive cadence. Another is
approaching. <u>Fine Banbury cakes and mutton pies, all hot, all piping
hot, all hot and smoking, all piping hot.</u> This fellow was at one time
a banker and bill broker to a large amount, in dollar notes and
quarter dollars, but riches have wings, and grandeur as the poet says,
"is a dream, the man we celebrate must find a tomb".

Siste viator! That is to say stop! What cry is yond, like the
ruttling of a turkey-cock? We have heard it for years and often tried
to catch the odd syllable of interpretation, but were invariably
baffled, though we have a school of tongues in our stomach. Good
man! (filthy rather too) pray what have you for sale? "Caul,
bullock-head, and bullock-pluck". Hem! Besides these cries, there
are others changing with the seasons, as oranges, peaches, melons,
lemons, pumpkins, &c milk at 8d. per quart, 30 per cent under proof;
the proof is perhaps too strong for most constitutions in this

climate, though to say a land flowing with milk and honey, conveys a fine luxurious image of its richness and fatness...

This market is like a village fair. On the left we see maize and wheat for sale, on the right, green forage, pumpkins, melons, cabbages, turkies, ducks, geese, sucking pigs, fowls &c.; in front are rows of booths full of drapery and grocery; then there are pots, pans, and butter 3s. per lb. and potatoes 15s. per cwt. These girls with butter are somewhat sallow and sun-freckled, have sharp chins, wide foreheads, flat faces and are of majestic stature - natives, evidently. What a powerful effect this climate must have, to change as it does the contour and mould of our children all at once, without any reason assigned by the chymist.

JOHN DUNMORE LANG, HUNTER RIVER, NEW SOUTH WALES, c.1832

John Dunmore Lang was born in Greenock, Scotland, on 25 August 1799.
His preliminary education was at a parish school, and then he studied divinity at
Glasgow University, gaining both Master of Arts and a licence to preach in 1820.
He was ordained a minister in September 1822.

When his younger brother, George, who was established as a farmer in Australia, wrote to say that New South Wales was in a sad moral condition, John Dunmore decided to rectify the Colony with Presbyterianism. He arrived in May 1823 and soon gathered a congregation in a Sydney hall. There were already numbers of Presbyterians in New South Wales. A dozen families who had settled at a place they named Ebenezer on the Hawkesbury had built their own church by 1809, but they had no minister.

One of Lang's first moves was to establish the Scots Church. The foundation stone was laid in Crown Street, Surry Hills by 1 July 1824. Lang then went to England to interview Earl Bathurst, Secretary of State for the Colonies. It was an amazingly successful trip: Bathurst directed that Treasury should advance a third of the estimated cost of the church and that Lang be paid a salary of £300 a year, the equivalent now of $300,000. The church opened in July 1826 and Lang continued as minister until he died in 1878. It is now the Chinese Presbyterian Church.

Lang became enthusiastic about Australia's prospects. He travelled back to London in 1830 to secure money to build a Presbyterian high school in Sydney and to pay the immigration costs of 140 workmen, mostly mechanics (tradesmen) and their families. They were to refund these costs out of their earnings. It was a successful venture. On the way over Lang married his cousin, Wilhelmina Mackie, at the Cape of Good Hope.

Lang began a weekly newspaper, the *Colonist*, in 1835. In one of his early editorials, he attacked John Marshall as agent (and shipowner) for the Committee for Promoting the Emigration of Single Women. Too many prostitutes were arriving. Lang thought Marshall considered only the £16 he was paid per head to fill his ships, not the character of those he was recruiting.

His outspoken editorials caused him much trouble. In February 1851, a member of the Legislative Council sued him for criminal libel. Lang was found guilty, fined £100 (paid for by public subscription from his many supporters) and sent to gaol for four months.

Lang himself served periods in parliament: five years in three periods in the Legislative Council between 1843 and 1856 and 10 years in the Legislative Assembly from 1859 to 1869.

In 1848, Lang engaged in a disastrous venture. Incensed by the numbers of Roman Catholics coming in, he went to England to recruit good Protestant migrants. During that year and the next, Lang secured six shiploads with promises of land in Australia that he could not honour because he had made no arrangements with either government. As well, he left bills unpaid in England and Australia, borrowed money and never returned it. The immigrants – three shiploads of whom went to Brisbane in 1849 – not only missed out on land, they arrived in Australia to a shortage of work. Being Scots, most prospered nevertheless.

Lang lectured and wrote a great deal. I quote his estimate of the Hunter Valley from the second volume of his most important book, *An Historical and Statistical Account of New South Wales both as a penal settlement and as a British Colony*, published in London in 1834. Importantly, he records some Aboriginal Australian place names.

> The country along the course of the Hunter appears to have undergone considerable changes in its physical conformation from the inundations of the river. In some places the river has been entirely diverted from its former channel, leaving a line of long narrow lagoons to designate the place of the ancient rushing of its waters; in other parts its courses, lakes, whose existence cannot be doubted for a moment, have gradually disappeared, and been succeeded by grassy plains, islands, or peninsulas. This is particularly obvious at Patrick's Plains, a level trace of alluvial land of considerable extent, about thirty miles from the town of Maitland, as well as at the Green Hills at the head of the navigation. At the latter of these localities, the rivers Hunter and Patterson, or, as they are called by the black natives, the Coquun and the Yimmang, approach to within two hundred yards of each other, and, then diverging, inclose between their deep channels a peninsula of upwards of eleven hundred acres of alluvial land, forming almost a dead level. The peninsula, which the natives call Narragan, but which the late proprietor, Mr. Harris, a native of Dublin, called the *Phoenix Park*, is without exception the finest piece of land, both

for quality of soil and for beauty of scenery and situation, I have
ever seen, - being entirely of alluvial formation, and bounded on all
sides, with the exception of the narrow isthmus that connects it with
the main-land, by broad and deep rivers, the banks of which are
ornamented with a natural growth of the most beautiful shrubbery;
while over its whole extent patches of rich grassy plain, of thirty or
forty acres each, alternate with clumps of trees or narrow beltings of
forest, as if the whole had been tastefully laid out for a nobleman's
park by a skilful landscape-gardener. Mr. Harris has informed me,
however, that in digging a well, somewhere near the centre of the
peninsula, he found pieces of charred wood at a depth of nine feet
from the surface, or beneath the present level of the river. It cannot
be doubted, therefore, that the beautiful peninsula of Narragan was
formerly a lake, and that it owes its existence to successive deposits
of alluvium from the two rivers.

HENRY MELVILLE, VAN DIEMEN'S LAND, 1833

*Henry Saxelby Melville Wintle shortened his name when he arrived in Hobart early
in 1828 and bought the* Colonial Times *and later the* Tasmanian. *In 1830–31, he issued
the first novel to be written, printed and published in Australia in three volumes,*
Quintus Servington *by Henry Savery, a convict. Melville produced 18 issues of the
Hobart Town Magazine, Australia's first literary journal to which he contributed*
The Bushrangers: or Norwood Vale. *In May 1834, it became the first play with
an Australian theme to be written, published and staged in Australia.*

An incautious report on a cattle-stealing case in his newspaper caused Melville
to be gaoled for contempt of court in November 1835. Cattle stealing was a
sensitive issue since the practice was widespread among both the rustlers
and the respectability.

Melville's newspapers never recovered. By 1838 he was insolvent. He
sold what he still owned of his publishing business, farmed for a few years
at New Norfolk, and then returned to England.

Tasmania impressed him. I quote from the *Van Diemen's Land Almanack*
for the year 1833 which he edited and printed.

> MOUNTAINS.– With regard to mountains, there are several of
> great elevation. Mount Wellington, (or as it is sometimes called the
> Table Mountain, from its resemblance to that at the Cape,) rises
> four thousand feet above the level of the sea, immediately to the
> westward of Hobart Town. Its bold and rugged sides, with
> occasional spots of sombre foliage, have an imposing, or even
> magnificent appearance; and its top or surface, which is flat, and of
> considerable extent, seems like the landing place, as it were, of a
> long chain of progressive steps or elevations, those nearest the level
> of the sea being at a remote distance. To the naturalist, it amply
> repays researches in botany and mineralogy; and being only a few
> miles distant from Hobart Town, it has frequent visitors in the
> course of every summer, particularly as its ascent may be
> accomplished without difficulty. Eight of the twelve months its
> summit is covered with snow; but so pure and clear is the
> atmosphere of Van Diemen's Land, that it is very seldom indeed

that the clouds obscure even its highest points. Several small streams spring from it, and join the Derwent.

The southern mountains near Port Davey, are even higher than Mount Wellington, and a great part of the year are covered with snow. They form a long tier, which stretches inward for several miles, and in some places rise five thousand feet about the sea...

TREES AND SHRUBS. — It has been already said that Van Diemen's Land is thickly timbered. It may indeed be styled a land of forests, the woodlands being out of all proportion to ground that is even tolerably clear of timber; yet, in many places, there is no underwood, the ground being covered with tall, ungainly trees, standing at some distance from each other, and running up to a great height, before they shoot out their branches. Much of the timber of the Colony is extremely serviceable for every building purpose, particularly stringy bark, which has been not inaptly termed the oak of Van Diemen's Land, as well on account of the appearance and durability of the wood, as of the uses to which it is implied. Gum, of several sorts; almost equal to stringy bark. Peppermint, another wood of the same description, but particularly used where facility of splitting is required. Among the ornamental woods come light wood, she oak or beef tree, honeysuckle, myrtle, and the cherry tree. The woods that are most esteemed for the fitting up of houses, and for cabinet-makers and others, are Huon pine, black and silver mimosas, pencil cedar, and sassafras.

All the trees are evergreen, and some of them, particularly the mimosas, put forth very rich blossoms in spring; but the prevailing color of nearly all of this description, has been remarked to partake more or less of yellow. The foliage is generally of a dark or sombre green, and the eye wanders over the wide expanse of dense forest every where presented, searching in vain for the relief that is afforded by the many-varying hue of the deciduous family. The varieties of shrubs are many, and extremely beautiful; and several of them have very elegant flowers.

ABORIGINE CLIMBING A TREE BY CUTTING STEPS IN THE TRUNK
Joseph Lycett, c.1820, National Library of Australia R5673

VIEW ON THE WINGECARRIBEE [River, New South Wales]
Joseph Lycett, published 1824, Rex Nan Kivell Collection, National Library of Australia U636

VIEW OF THE CASCADE IN PRINCE REGENT'S RIVER
Phillip P. King, 1825, from *Narrative of a Survey of the Intertropical and Western Coasts of Australia*,
Rex Nan Kivell Collection, National Library of Australia U1422

PARTY PREPARING TO BIVOUAC
James Atkinson, 1826, from *An Account of the State of Agriculture & Grazing in New South Wales*, Mitchell Library, State Library of New South Wales

SITE OF ADELAIDE A view of the country and of the temporary erections near the site for the proposed town of Adelaide; in South Australia: forming the first of a series of views of that colony
Robert Havell, undated but probably late 1837, M.L. Crowther Library, State Library of Tasmania

A VIEW OF KOOMBANA BAY ON PORT LESCHENAULT, Australind, Western Australia
Thomas Colman Dibdin c.1840, (painted for the Western Australian Company), National Library of Australia S1113

THE FIRST PUNT [across the Yarra River, Melbourne]
W.F.E. Liardet, c.1840, La Trobe Picture Collection, State Library of Victoria

THOMAS BIRKBY, SYDNEY, 1834

Thomas Birkby emigrated to Sydney with his wife and three children in 1834.
Thomas Mitchell engaged him as an overseer for his farm on the Cataract and
Nepean Rivers for '£50 per year with a house and meat for myself and family'.

After nine weeks Birkby learnt from Mitchell that he could not pay him, so
he went to Sydney and

> ... engaged with my present master Alexander Brody Sport Esq.
> [Brodie Spark] to be overseer at his farm at Tempe Cooks River...
> he is one of the gentlemen of the Colony, he is an old Batchelor and
> makes gardening his Hobby... I have thirteen convict labourers.

The Australian National Library holds a long letter to Birkby's father
written for Birkby by William Hutchison on 3 September 1839. He told of
a storm that they encountered after leaving the Cape of Good Hope, of the
treatment of convicts, of wages, conditions of employment, cost of food and
clothing, of Aboriginal Australians and the appearance of the bush. He
ended the letter 'From your loving and affectionate son' but he was giving
five years news.

> On the 14th [September 1834] it came on a heavy gale of wind,
> which kept increasing in violence till the evening of the 15th when
> the sea ran mountains high and night so dark one could scarce see
> one half length of the ship, on the morning of the 16th about four
> o'clock, a sea struck the vessel amidships taking with it all Larboard
> [? Starboard] and Part of the Larboard bulworks, and everything of
> the deck fore and aft, that was not lashed down tearing away the
> cover and Battings of the main hatch, and filling the Guns Dock
> where the family slept in three of four feet depth of water, and as
> the vessel roled to and fro scors of them were washed out of their
> beds, then to here the screams and the oaths and curses uttered by
> many was shocking to here, but still a great deal of the [blank] in it
> some that passed off for single women calling out for their
> husbands and famylyes and wishing they had never left them, and
> others confessing to things that they never intended doing, but

death staring us all in the face, at the time, maid many Pray in
Ernest that seldom did, but still the storm kept increasing.

They were nearly wrecked again threading their way through the
islands in Bass Strait in a heavy sea, with the ship rolling 'till the main yards
touched the water'.

On the 23rd October we came in sight of the long wish for a
lighthouse, at the head of Port Jackson, and at 10 o'clock in the
night of the 24th we anchord in what is called the middle harbour,
the Pilot came on board the next morning, and at nine o'clock we
wheighed our anchor and sailed up the harbour to the town and
drops our anchor at the Bust of Daws Battery about 12 at noon. The
scenery on both sides of the harbour is I think the finest I ever saw,
being composed of Rocks, Trees and native shrubs, with here and
there a cultivated plot of Ground... in Botanical Production it may
vie with any Country in the World, Woods of never faiding green
and of Boundys Extent, the underwood of which is composed of
thousands of the finest species of Plants, sum of which are always
in flower.

JAMES BACKHOUSE, NORFOLK ISLAND, 1835

Born of a prominent Quaker business family in 1794, James Backhouse was educated at a Friends' School, then apprenticed to a chemist. After developing tuberculosis, he took on outdoor work while he regained health, and then trained for two years in a Norwich plant nursery. Backhouse was fascinated by Australian plants and bought his own nursery in Norwich with his brother as partner. He married in 1822 and had two children, but his wife died in 1827. He then began charity work in British prisons and among the poor, and joined Bible and Temperance Societies. The Friends encouraged him to extend his work to the Australian colonies and offered to pay for the trip.

Backhouse sailed for Australia in September 1831 leaving business and children to the care of friends. He was accompanied by George Washington Walker who held the same missionary zeal, 'with a view to promote the moral and religious welfare of its inhabitants'. They spent six years in the colonies, often visiting door to door.

Backhouse's deep interest in plants was elicited by a visit to Norfolk Island in 1835. I quote from his book, *Visit to the Australian Colonies*, published in London in 1843.

> In a few of the valleys, near the sea, in this direction *Euphorbia obliqua*, a remarkable shrub, forms copses, attaining, when shaded by trees, to 15 feet in height, and 2 feet in circumference. Here also, as well as in most of the other shady woods throughout the island, *Botryodendron latifolium* [Shade Tree, now *Meryta latifolia*] a shrub of singular form, allied to the Ivy, but of a very different appearance, prevails. Its figure may be compared to that of a long-leaved cabbage, mounted on a broom-stick. Its stem is about five feet high, and five inches round; its largest leaves are about two feet long, and one foot broad. The prisoners in the out-stations, wrap their bread in these leaves, and bake it in the ashes. The fruit is a dense cluster, of greenish, purple berries, not edible, produced in the centre of the crown of leaves.
>
> In company with Major Anderson, and the military surgeon, we ascended Mount Pitt. The vegetation is of the same general character, as on other parts of the north of the Island. Lemon trees

grow at the very top. On the northern ascent, a Pine was measured, 29½ feet [9 metres] in circumference, and a Norfolk Island Bread-fruit, *Cordyline australis* [now *C. obtecta*], 2 feet 9 inches [84 centimetres]. The last, sometimes attains 20 feet in height: it branches from within a few feet of the ground, and forms several heads, with flag-like leaves, and long, branched spikes of greenish, star flowers, succeeded by whitish, or bluish-purple berries, that are eaten by parrots. It often forms a striking object, where a woody valley runs out into grass, growing at the extreme margin of the wood.

Niphobolus serpens [*Pyrrosia confluens*, Robber Fern] and *Polypodium tenellum* [*Arthropteris tenella*], two climbing ferns, ascend the trunks of the trees, in the northern portion of the Island; and the Norfolk Island Pepper, *Piper psittacorum* [*Macropiper excelsum* subsp. *psittacorum*], which produces a yellow, pulpy, pendent, cylindrical fruit, of a spicy, sweetish taste, is every where plentiful, in the woods. It rises, with a few, jointed, cane-line, green stems, to from four to ten feet high, bearing large, heart-shaped leaves.

From the top of Mount Pitt, by ascending a tree, we could see the whole circuit of the Island, which approaches a triangle in form; it is rendered very beautiful, by the variety of hill and dale, wood and open land.

RICHARD BOWLER, BROADMARSH, TASMANIA, 1835

Richard Bowler arrived in Hobart Town in Malabar *on 11 June 1821 as a convict sentenced to life. He came from Brill, a village in Buckinghamshire. A farmer at Broadmarsh, on the Jordan River northwest of Hobart, received him on assignment. After eight years of good conduct, he got the ticket-of-leave that allowed him to work on his own account.*

The Australian National Library holds eight letters that Bowler wrote home to Brill between 1 June 1835 and 24 April 1843, seven of them to his brother John Bowler, a clockmaker, and one to Richard Smith, a watch and clock-maker. He received only four letters during the 22 years in Tasmania. But he did not write often, either: 'I was here Seven years and never touch a penn'. On his father's instructions, he had delayed writing until he could 'send good testimonials'. He also feared that his brother might 'have denied having any Kinsmen a exile'.

Both the Tasmanian farmer and, later, the Government must have worked Bowler fairly, since he considered that convicts were treated as they deserved: 'You will never frett about the Bad usage for it his entirely to your conduct whether Good or Bad'.

Bowler uses little punctuation and nearly always writes 'his' instead of 'is'. This quote is from the first letter, written after he had been 14 years in the Colony. A conditional pardon was granted him the next year.

Dear Brother,

I take this opportunity as it his unknown to me whether my dear Father or Mother his living if the are I send from their undutiful son my affectionate love to them hoping to find them in good health and crawn'd with Prosperity and everlasing happiness to myself eversince I left England I have enjoyed a very good state of health Dear Brother and your Wife and Family to my Sisters and my Relations and all inquiring friends I remember my kind love to you all hoping to find you as happy as I am at present I should have wrote before but it was my father's wish to bring or send good testimonials to which I can give you a very satisfactory account of this countrey in every particular way mentionable this island his

from England eighteen thousand miles distance we sailed from
Woolwich on the 11th of June 1821 and we left the English soil to see
no more on the 26th of June and we sailed for Vandiemens Land for
that his the name of the island the voyage was very pleasant and we
arrived at Hobart Town that his the capital town in the countrey on
the twenty-first of Octr. and we landed on the 26 of the same
month 1821 I was assigned to a farmer and lived with him seven years
and ten months and I then worked for Government till I got my
ticket of leave the sense of that his I can employ myself in any
employment the same as a free man... the countrey his very
prosperous the greater part of it his cultivated by farmers and
graziers the summer his a great deal warmer than england and the
winter is nothing so cold as home nor the days his never so long nor
yet so short as with you the prices of everything, whearing apparel
very reasonable and meat same flour same and every thing required
can be got hear same as at home there his but few wild animals and
none injurious there his the tiger she will destroy sheep but will run
away from any person there his the opposum kangaroo rat wharmbat
dog devils the snake his very venemous here where the bite if the
piece his not cut instantly it is almost sure death at sundown the
scorpion his venemous but not like the snake the Colony entirely is
beautiful and it is does daily flourish the alterations since I came his
quite surprising there his two towns in the Island and two countys
Hobart Town his the capital of the island and that his my own
county Buckinghamshire, Launceston his the other town and the
county Cornwall the two towns are one hundred and twenty miles
apart to which all shipping can land at either one or the other.

FRANCIS GREENWAY, SYDNEY, 1835

By 1835 the work of the brilliant, difficult, convict architect, Francis Greenway, was long over. He had quarrelled with Governor Macquarie for whom he designed superb buildings, and Governor Brisbane dismissed him as Civil Architect at the end of 1821. Thereafter he lived in near poverty on a marshy farm on the Hunter River until he died in 1837.

The following brief of ardent beliefs by an unnamed writer quoting Greenway is from an article, 'Colonial Architecture', in

AUSTRALIAN

ALMANACK

AND

GENERAL DIRECTORY

FOR THE YEAR OF OUR LORD

1835:

BEING THE THIRD AFTER LEAP YEAR: AND THE

FIFTH OF THE REIGN OF HIS MOST GRACIOUS

MAJESTY KING WILLIAM THE FOURTH

That definition of the year is strangely like Chinese dates. It was the last almanac in a series begun by George Howe, the convict printer, in 1806. Anne Howe, his daughter-in-law, printed it at the Gazette office.

Architecture, says Mr. Greenway, is an art which, in all ages, great princes and potentates have delighted to encourage, as one amongst those of the greatest importance to their subjects, and best calculated to convey to posterity the elegance, skill, and magnificence of the times in which they flourished. And so powerful has been the example, and such the influence diffused by so great and liberal a patronage among all classes of society, that men of inferior rank aspire to taste in this noble science; and by a liberality of sentiment endeavour to vie with each other in promoting its objects — improving the national taste — augmenting its splendour, and imparting an encreased value to its commercial and mercantile relations. When viewed in its proper light,

architecture will appear to have most influence on all the comforts
and luxuries of life. The advantages of erecting buildings, both
public and private, must be obvious to all who consider that they are
the first steps towards civilization — and that they exert the most
marked influence not only on the body but on the mind also. Men
secluded from each other — inhabiting woods, caves, and wretched
huts, and exposed to the vicissitudes and inclemencies of the
weather — are generally characterised by dull and indolent habits,
and as possessing views so limited to their immediate necessities,
that they seldom look beyond the present exigency. But when
societies are formed, and commodious buildings are erected,
wherein the occupants may breathe a temperate air, and combine
social intercourse with virtuous employment, men become
enterprising, ingenious, spirited and active — speculative in mind,
and vigourous in body. They progress in the agricultural and
mechanical arts; and the necessaries, conveniences, and even the
luxuries of life, soon become objects of desire and enjoyment.

This infant Colony, from its extent and the nature of its
situation on the face of the globe, will, in all probability, become, at
some future period, one of the most powerful nations in the world;
and indulging in such a pleasing anticipation it was, that our earliest
colonial architect, Mr. Greenway, projected the erection of many of
the most prominent public buildings.

1836 — 1850

JOHN H. NORCOCK, SYDNEY AND MELBOURNE, 1836

The son of a Royal Navy man, John Norcock entered the Service as a 12-year-old in 1821. He served as a midshipman in the Burmese war when he was 15 years old and was mentioned in despatches. Despite that honour and a three-year trip around the world in HMS Warspite, he was still only a gunner's mate when HMS Rattlesnake arrived in Sydney on 23 August 1836 under the command of Captain William Hobson. Norcock had spent three months in Sydney 'very pleasantly in 1826' when Warspite called in.

He kept a journal of the *Rattlesnake* voyage to India, Mauritius and Australia between 18 October 1835, when she left England, and 1 September 1836 when Norcock arrived home in command of the barque *Kinnear*. After so many years, his promotion was rapid.

The journal is unfailingly good humoured, but *Rattlesnake* was an unhappy ship with Hobson abusing his midshipmen and constantly quarrelling with his officers. Norcock declared him 'vile' and 'double faced' and usually referred to him as 'Sweet William'; the ship was *Rattler* or *Rattletrap*.

He greatly missed his Jenny, Jane Lawrey or Lowrey: 'Indulged myself in looking several times at my beloved Girl's miniature – kissed it & blessed the dear creature it represented'. Norcock married her on his return and they had seven children, but only three reached adulthood.

Years of service in India as a lieutenant cost him his health. Norcock later spent five years as Inspecting Commander of the Coastguard in County Cork, Ireland, but died in 1854 just as he was about to be relieved of duty.

From Sydney, which looked good to Norcock, *Rattlesnake* was directed to Port Phillip to land William Lonsdale and his family. Lonsdale had been appointed police magistrate and commandant of the new settlement. Norcock mentions nursing Mrs Lonsdale's baby aboard 'wishing all the time that I had one of my own to nurse'.

> **23rd.** [August 1836 anchored in Sydney Cove] At Daylight I could see that the place was, as formerly, exceedingly beautiful, much improved in size and cultivation — climate at this season delightfully salubrious — and everything around us calculated to charm the lovers of Nature, & to inspire them with feelings of gratitude to Nature's God. Finding a Brig on the point of sailing for

England, I closed and forwarded my letters to my dear Parents and my beloved Jane, and I trust they will receive them in due time. It was rather singular that the above Brig was scarcely out of sight when HMS Victor arrived from Madras and brought me all my stray letters from my dear Parents and my own sweet Jane, also several more, in all, up to Dec.r 24th. 1835 so that I have now got the 12 first letters my Jane has written — God bless her!...

27th. [September 1836] Arrived at Port Phillip and anchored about 2 miles inside the entrance to this beautiful and capacious Basin. In the afternoon I went on shore to look at the soil &c. and was quite "charmed" (as a lady would say) at its richness and beauty — the ground is like a beautiful Carpet, covered with grasses, herbs and flowers of various sorts — the scenery was that of an extensive Park — in short the whole Country only requires to be inhabited, and cultivated slightly to render it a most delightful region. The climate I need scarcely add is one of the most salubrious in the world, and as this was the commencement of Summer we all felt and duly appreciated its healthful influence...

29th. At Daylight we set sail again and after a day of the most lovely sailing we anchored at 6 in the evening at the place where the present settlement is situated, but which will be superseded soon by a spot better calculated for commercial purposes. [Although he preferred Williamstown, Lonsdale decided that the town that was to become Melbourne was already too entrenched to be moved.] The Country here is enchantingly beautiful. Extensive rich plains all around with gently sloping hills in the distance, all thinly wooded and having the appearance of an immense Park. The grasses, flowers & herbs that cover the plains are of every variety that can be imagined, and present a lovely picture of what is evidently intended by Nature to be one of the richest pastoral countries in the World.

RONALD CAMPBELL GUNN, PORT PHILLIP
AND WESTERN PORT, VICTORIA, 1836

Ronald Campbell Gunn came to Hobart Town in 1830 at the instigation of his brother,
William. He had been a clerk. In Tasmania he moved through positions as overseer of
a penitentiary under his brother, assistant superintendent of convicts at Launceston,
police magistrate, private secretary to the Governor, clerk of the Legislative and
Executive Councils, managing agent of big estates, Member of the Legislative Council
then of the House of Assembly, Deputy Commissioner of Crown Lands, Registrar of
Births, Deaths and Marriages, Clerk of the Peace and Coroner.

That series of jobs was his sustenance. Gunn's interests were exploration
and botany. He worked with John Gould and with members of many scientific expeditions. He sent a live Thylacine to the British Museum. But mostly
he sent plants, thousands of them, with detailed and knowledgeable descriptions. He made a worldwide name for himself as a botanist.

Explorers of Tasmania faced more difficult country than anyone anywhere. Here is how Gunn described part of a journey he made in northwest
Tasmania in 1860:

> From the summit of the Native-track tier in a north-easterly
> direction to the Leven, the country is uniformly poor and valueless,
> covered throughout with dense scrubs of various kinds. These scrubs
> I do not attempt to describe, as they baffle description; the greater
> portion of the country, however, being covered with the horizontal
> scrub (*Anodopetalum biglandulosum*), a small tree growing
> horizontally, or with an inclination down-hill, the trunks 50 to 70
> feet long, with a diameter of a few inches. From the horizontal
> trunks upright branches, having somewhat the aspect of young
> poplar trees, shoot up to a height of 30 or 40 feet. A forest of this
> plant can only be compared to a pile of drift wood washed up against
> some obstruction in a river, to a depth of 10 to 18 feet; the only
> means of progress being that of crawling on all-fours under the
> trunks, or walking many feet above the ground, cutting the smaller
> branches out of the way as you proceed. The wire scrub (*Bauera*
> *rubiodes*) is even more difficult to make progress through than the

horizontal. This plant grows 6 to 12 feet high, in one dense mass;
the stems like wire, tough and interlacing in every direction. I found
it usually associated with cutting grass.

Years earlier Gunn was in more gentle country. The following is from a
journal he kept of 'A Visit to the South Coast of New Holland in February
and March 1836'.

29th Feb.

Entered Port Phillip about 8 a.m. The entrance is narrow and rather
intricate without sailing directions. The Country on the West side
of the Entrance was very thinly wooded and looked beautifully
green — a correct idea of the land could not be obtained at my
distance. After entering I bore up for Arthur's Seat — being almost
due East. As the western side of Port Phillip has already been well
examined by several gentlemen from Indented Head to the River at
the extreme North — and had been to a certain extent taken
possession of by them I turned my attention to the Eastern side and
anchored there about ½ mile offshore Arthur's Seat. I found that
the country of the South West of Arthur's Seat Sandy but covered
with very fine Kangaroo Grass Centhestena Australis [now *Themeda
triandra*], indeed astonishingly fine quality — with a gentle
undulating surface — a little in from sea I found some lagoons of
rich soil — at least spots covered with water at certain seasons...

As the first part of New Holland on which I had ever landed I
was much pleased — the Grass surpassed my most sanguine
expectations and the ½ of a mile inland became richer and such as to
promise abundant crops when cultivated...

On the East Side of Western Port the land appeared very good
and the vegetation very superior to that portion of Port Phillip
visited by me...

I placed three days provisions in the whale boats to explore the
other parts of the Harbour as the vessel needed some repairs. I
proceeded up Basses River about 6 miles. It is considerably smaller
than the North Esk — about 6 miles being not above 40 feet wide.
The tides affect it at a greater distance up but the water beautifully
fresh. The land on both sides of the River was of richest quality
covered with Kangaroo Grass superior to anything I ever before saw.

The land was very heavily timbered and of the finest quality —
Basses River also would afford inexhaustible supply of fresh water.

On Basses River there were thousands of wild ducks which rose
before our boat in clouds. Black Swans and Pelicans were also
abundant about the Harbour — the former very abundant —
Kangaroos appeared scarce.

HENRY WILLIAM ST PIERRE BUNBURY, COLLIE RIVER, SOUTHWEST WESTERN AUSTRALIA, 1836

Lieutenant Bunbury, son of Sir Henry Bunbury who had been Under-Secretary for War and the Colonies, came to Australia in 1834 and served with the 21st Regiment in New South Wales, Tasmania and Western Australia.

Although he spent only 20 months in Western Australia, the town of Bunbury is named for him. He described that area in a diary he kept when the Governor, Sir James Stirling, sent him on an expedition to present Busselton to see if it was a suitable site for a military outpost. He was observant and capable and thoroughly enjoyed exploring. 'We have passed the night,' he wrote one morning, 'and a magnificently fine one it was. I know nothing that conveys such a pleasing sensation of thorough liberty and independence as a bush life in fine weather.'

Bunbury left Western Australia to become aide-de-camp to the Governor of the Cape of Good Hope, General Sir George Napier, and married his daughter in 1852. By then, Bunbury was continuing his military career, first in India, then in the Crimean War. Their youngest son also served in Australia. He established the School of Gunnery at Middle Head, Sydney.

This extract is from a part of Bunbury's diary, sub-titled 'From the Murray to the Vasse'. He was on the Collie River where it 'falls into the Estuary by two mouths, forming a low island covered with bushes'. The estuary is the Leschenault Inlet at Bunbury. Many features in that part of Western Australia are named for, or by, the French navigators d'Entrecasteaux and Baudin.

Higher up than this island the scenery becomes much more picturesque than anything else I know in this part of the Colony the river opening to a fine wide reach extending some distance to the northward with a high well wooded bank on the right the large flooded Gums & Casuarinae drooping elegantly over the dark still waters. In all the river scenery I know in this country there is a dull sombre hue occasioned by the dark foliage of the trees which makes it strikingly different from that of our Native country where the light green of the willows &c which fringe the banks & the bright colours of the meadows adjoining, with their herds of sleek fat

cattle give a life and animation to the scene unknown on the banks
of our Australian rivers, but still for my part I prefer the views of
the wilderness to those of a tame and civilized country as much as I
think black swans and Pelicans superior in appearance to Ducks and
Geese. By in appearance I mean in their wild & natural state, for in
appearance roasted at dinner I infinitely prefer the latter birds. After
ascending the long and wide reach to the northward for some miles
the banks narrow considerably and the stream comes from the
eastward about five miles from the mouth one crosses the mouth of
a tributary called the North Collie, or I believe now by the Govr.
the Brunswick; this also is said by the Natives to be navigable for
boats for some distance up but not as far as the Collie. It comes
from the hills between the latter river & the Harvey so that it
cannot be a very considerable stream, not being the drain of a great
tract of country but I have since heard from the Govr. that there is
much good land on its banks where it leaves the Hills & descends
into the open flat country, thro which the salt water evidently
ascends it for many miles. The Collie appears to abound with fish
of several kinds & one night near our camp about six miles from the
mouth we caught many large fish, both Jew Fish and Black and
Silver Snapper in about four to five fathom water where the banks
are rather high and steep principally of clay, with much firm timbers
of different sorts varying of course with the soil, red Gum,
Mahogany, Black and flooded Gums being the principled kinds the
two latter growing to a great size on the alluvial flats.

MARY THOMAS. ADELAIDE. 1836–39

Mary Thomas established a family that was associated with newspapers in Adelaide and Melbourne for more than 130 years. In conjunction with George Stevenson, formerly correspondent and perhaps joint editor of the well-known Globe, *her husband Robert published the first issue of the* South Australian Gazette and Colonial Register *in London on 18 June 1836. Stevenson had resigned from the* Globe *to take up an appointment as Private Secretary to Sir John Hindmarsh, the Governor of South Australia, with the additional duties of Clerk of the Council and Protector of Aborigines.*

Robert and Mary Thomas with two sons and three daughters, a female companion, two printers, a printing press and a fount of type arrived in South Australia in November 1836. The second issue of the newspaper came out on 3 June 1837.

The early settlement was a social and economic disaster. William Light arrived as Surveyor-General before Hindmarsh and had already marked out the present excellent site before the governor arrived. Hindmarsh immediately demanded that the site be moved to the unsuitable and impermanent mouth of the Murray. Tensions increased, Hindmarsh was recalled, Light resigned.

William Gawler, the next governor, faced the awful task of getting land surveyed for the 5000 prospective settlers who were loafing about the town because they had no land marked for sale. Food was short and had to be imported, Gawler spent all his own money on the settlement, and then drew bills on London authorities that refused to honour them.

There was much intrigue by those who, according to Mary Thomas, 'having lost both credit and character in their own country, have little more to lose here, and therefore hesitate at no means, however unlawful, to cover their own misdoings'.

By its outspokenness, the *South Australia Register*, as it was then named, infuriated Gawler. Tensions caused the partnership to split and the paper was sold. Robert and Mary's son, William Kyffin, maintained association with the newspaper, as did two of his sons and a grandson. All reached important positions.

Mary Thomas was upset by the social upheaval. As she wrote in a letter to her brother, 'What I have endured since I have been here is so far beyond all I had anticipated (and you well know it is not a little that will make me complain) that I would venture on a twelve months' journey to reach my own country again'.

She loved the appearance of Australia and kept a diary from 1836 to 1841, later extended as a journal concluding in 1866. Evan Kyffin Thomas, a grandson, edited *The Diary and Letters of Mary Thomas* in 1915. I quote from the third edition of 1925.

When their ship, *Africaine*, anchored in Rapid Bay in the southeast corner of the Gulf of St Vincent on 6 November 1836, Mary Thomas found the passengers

> ... in front of the most beautiful prospect imaginable... A party from the vessel went on shore, and on their return gave a most enchanting account of the country. which everywhere resembled a gentleman's park — grass growing in the greatest luxuriance, the most beautiful flowers in abundance, and the birds of splendid plumage.

The anchorage was no good in Rapid Bay. They moved north to Holdfast Bay, just south of Adelaide, which is little more than a slight indentation in the coastline but is good holding ground.

On the night of 13 November when they were establishing themselves in tents, there was an extraordinary late frost.

> A pewter jug had been accidentally left outside the tent in a tin dish containing some water, and on lifting up the jug to my surprise the dish came up with it, for the water had frozen to an eighth of an inch in thickness. This astonished me in a country where I did not expect to see such a thing, and yet the thermometer rose that day to 110 degrees.
>
> November 16.— As we had now obtained the poles belonging to the large tent from the ship, our men proceeded to put it up, and the children and I were busy all day in arranging our luggage and bedding. It was a marquee large enough to divide into two apartments, and gladly we took possession of our new habitation. It was situated near some large gumtrees about half a mile from the shore, and most of the settlers, both from the *Cygnet* and the *Africaine*, were within view. The country, as far as we could see, was certainly beautiful, and resembled an English park, with long grass in abundance and fine trees scattered about, but not so many as to

make it unpleasant, and no brushwood. We were about a hundred yards from the nearest lagoon, where at that time there was plenty of water and very clear. Nor was it bad-tasted, though not from a running stream. Far from being so good for washing as to get clothes clean without soap, as some accounts represented, it was harder even than the water in London.

The birds here were of beautiful plumage. White and black cockatoos were in abundance, the former with a large yellow or orange coloured crest, sometimes pink. Parrots, or rather parrakeets, as they would be called in England, for they were very small, were of every variety of colour. Also there were wild ducks and flocks of geese, with occasionally a black swan flying. Here was also the mocking-bird, and it was quite amusing to hear him imitate our cock crowing in the morning and the call of the guinea-fowls at a neighbouring tent, which he did with great exactness, but in a more musical tone, for it sounded like a barrel organ. But when he tried to imitate the laughing jackass it was so exceedingly droll that we could not forbear laughing heartily.

The next quote is from a letter Mary wrote to her brother on 7 April 1839.

Nature has provided an abundance of grass and trees, some of which are of amazing size (I myself measured one 10 feet in circumference) and extremely beautiful, especially the bluegum. This bears a kind of flower, something like those on a limetree, and when in blossom droops like a willow. The redgum is also a very fine tree. The wood of both is valuable. From the latter, I think, a crimson dye might be extracted. A person was boiling some clothes and accidentally left a stick of it in her copper. A short time afterwards she found a stain of a deep red colour wherever the stick had touched, and which nothing would eradicate. I also made a similar discovery while at Glenelg from having strewn the floor of the rush hut with some yellow flowers which grew there in abundance, somewhat resembling everlastings, and a handkerchief being on the ground, on which some of the water had been spilt, it was found to be stained with a yellow dye. Afterwards I tried the experiment by boiling some of the flowers, and found it to produce the same effect.

WILLIAM GRANT BROUGHTON,
POTTS POINT, SYDNEY, 1837

*William Broughton arrived in Sydney with his wife and daughters on 13 September 1829
as Archdeacon of New South Wales. He had been a clerk in the office of the East
India Company then, after study at Cambridge, a Church of England curate in
Hampshire. He had an influential friend in the Duke of Wellington and he had made a
name for himself by published studies on Greek ecclesiastical works. Governor Darling
appointed him to the Legislative Council and accepted his proposal for the King's
School, Parramatta. It opened under Governor Bourke in 1832.*

Broughton was consecrated Bishop of Australia in 1836. Although he walked
with a stick (he had been lame since youth), he worked hard and travelled
widely. Edward John Eyre who met him in Tasmania was impressed by his
energy.

He had not been keen to come to Australia and did not plan to stay long:
'There is no ground for congratulation on my appointment'. Nevertheless,
he stayed for the rest of his life. So did both his daughters who married
here.

Bishop Broughton opposed the Roman Catholic and Presbyterian
Churches. He was aloof, unbending and doctrinaire, though he wrote very
long letters to a few good friends.

The following quote is from a letter of 1 May 1837 to Dr Keate,
Headmaster of Eton. It was written from 'the neck of land between
Wollomolloo Bay & Rush Cutters Bay'. The house he rented there, *Tusculum*,
is in Manning Street, Potts Point where Broughton lived for 16 years. John
Verge, the renowned architect, designed it. He would not enjoy coming
back to that position now even though Clive Lucas, a fine modern architect,
rescued the house from dereliction in 1986. Life there was extraordinarily
gracious then. The fenced grounds extended from the waters of
Woolloomooloo Bay to Macleay Street.

> The spot on which our home stands is a ridge of land sloping down
> to the water on the North West, affording us the benefit of the Sea
> breeze, and a really superb view of the blue waters of the Port, as
> calm as a lake, and of the pretty Bays & Coves, Islands and
> Promontories that extend on all sides. From the position of the

house you will perceive we have no view into the open Ocean the South Head just shutting over the North and intercepting it. We see however every vessel that enters or leaves the harbour: indeed they pass almost under our windows; and the light-house tower with its revolving light, is a fine and interesting object on the other side. Towards the back we look to the Town across the quiet looking waters of Wollomolloo Bay by which we are bounded on the West. You would admire it, I think, very much: the water is so bright and the pretty native bush, as we call the thickets, growing within a few yards of the brink on one side, and on the other continual ledges of fine white sandstone rising one about the other like terraces, and the whole scene so undisturbed notwithstanding the nearness of the town makes this a very favourite resort of ours in which we continually find fresh beauties. The New Government House is just commencing to be built on the neck of land between Farm Cove & Sydney Cove. We shall have a full view of the principal front. It is to be a stone building in the taste of the Elizabethan age, and is really very correctly and tastefully designed in imitation of the Old English Mansion. It wants only a cloister along the front and North side to make it quite perfect. It is estimated to cost £25,000: but I think it will never be finished for double that sum. If we were Greeks I suppose all the promontories and headlands, which you perceive running out into the waters of the Port, would each have its shrine or temple for which they appear to be made on purpose.

GEORGE GREY. NEAR THE HEAD OF THE GLENELG RIVER. WESTERN AUSTRALIA. 1838

George Grey led an eminent but disordered life. He had sympathy for the poor and the harassed natives of several countries, yet his actions were too often autocratic and devious. He was born in Portugal in 1812, the son of an officer killed in the Peninsular War a week before he was born. He ran away from his first boarding school, but was eventually educated at the Royal Military College, Sandhurst. He joined the 83rd Regiment and served in Ireland until 1836 when he was appointed by Lord Glenelg to lead an expedition down the coast of Western Australia.

Grey had proposed the expedition to find out if a major river flowed out of central Australia and to search for land suitable for a settlement of Irish immigrants. Grey's idea was to move upwards from the Swan River. He was instructed to move downwards from the Prince Regent River.

Grey set out from England in HMS *Beagle*, which was to do much exploring under John Lort Stokes. They landed at Hanover Bay near the entrance to King George Sound, which receives the waters from the Prince Regent River. Aborigines attacked in the first few weeks and Grey was struck by three spears. He shot one assailant and escaped, and then he rested for a couple of weeks until he felt well enough to continue, although he had to be lifted on and off his horse.

Grey found and named the Glenelg River:

> There burst upon the sight a noble river, running through a beautiful country... I have since seen many Australian rivers, but none to equal this either in magnitude or beauty.

Eventually the country and his wound became too much. They retired to the waiting ship and he travelled to Mauritius to recuperate.

Grey made another attempt to complete his explorations in 1839 with even more disastrous consequences than the first. He was landed at Bernier Island off present Carnarvon intending to explore north in three whaleboats. He did not allow for the massive tides that were increased by gales. He lost his stores, then his boats and made a forced march back to Perth. One of his men died on the horrific journey.

His exploring days over, Grey became in succession resident magistrate at King George Sound, Governor of South Australia, Lieutenant-Governor of New Zealand, Governor of New Zealand for eight years, Governor of Cape Colony for over seven years, then again Governor of New Zealand for another term of eight years.

Although he tried to help native people, his ideas were not always sound. He wanted to save Aboriginal Australians by compulsory assimilation including compulsory christianising.

Grey was an efficient Governor, but his autocratic methods aroused continual protestation both from his subjects and the Colonial Office. His wife left him after a quarrel.

Eventually he settled in New Zealand and served in the House of Representatives for 20 years, once as premier in a disordered two-year term. By then Grey had been knighted. He died in England in 1898 and was buried in St Paul's Cathedral.

Grey's story of his explorations, *Journals of Two Expeditions of Discovery in North-west and Western Australia*, was published in two volumes in 1841.

I quote his finding of the remarkable Aboriginal paintings that have been named *Wandjina*. Grey sketched and painted the figures, the first European representations of Aboriginal paintings ever made.

SKETCH OF THE CAVE WITH PAINTINGS NEAR GLENELG RIVER
George Grey, 1838, from *Journals of Two Expeditions of Discovery...*, Mitchell Library, State Library of New South Wales

... on looking over some bushes, at the sandstone rocks which were above us, I suddenly saw from one of them a most extraordinary large figure peering down upon me. Upon examination, this proved to be a drawing at the entrance to a cave, which, on entering, I found to contain, besides, many remarkable paintings.

The cave appeared to be a natural hollow in the sandstone rocks; its floor was elevated about five feet from the ground, and numerous flat broken pieces of the same rock, which were scattered about, looked at a distance like steps leading up to the cave, which was thirty-five feet wide at the entrance, and sixteen feet deep; but beyond this, several small branches ran further back. Its height in front was rather more than eight feet, the roof being formed by a solid slab of sandstone, about nine feet thick, and which rapidly inclined towards the back of the cave, which was there not more than five feet high.

On this sloping roof, the principal figure which I have just alluded to, was drawn; in order to produce the greater effect, the rock about it was painted black, and the figure itself coloured with the most vivid red and white. It thus appeared to stand out from the rock; and I was cetainly rather surprised at the moment that I first saw this gigantic head and upper part of a body bending over and staring grimly down at me.

It would be impossible to convey in words an adequate idea of this uncouth and savage figure... Its head was circled by bright red rays, something like the rays which one sees proceeding from the sun, when depicted on the sign-board of a public house; inside of this came a broad stripe of very brilliant red, which was coped by lines of white, but both inside and outside of this red space, were narrow stripes of a still deeper red, intended probably to mark its boundaries; the face was painted vividly white, and the eyes black, being however surrounded by red and yellow lines; the body, hands, and arms were outlined in red, - the body being curiously painted with red stripes and bars.

Upon the rock which formed the left wall of this cave, and which partly faced you on entering, was a very singular painting, vividly coloured, representing four heads joined together. From the mild expression of the countenances, I imagined them to represent females, and they appeared to be drawn in such a manner, and in such a position, as to look up at the principal figure which I have before described; each had a very remarkable head-dress, coloured with a deep bright blue, and one had a necklace on. Both of the lower figures had a sort of dress, painted with red in the same manner as that of the principal figure, and one of them had a band round her waist. Each of the four faces was marked by a totally distinct expression of countenance, and although none of them had mouths, two, I thought, were otherwise good looking.

'A YOUNG COMMERCIAL GENTLEMAN'.
AUSTRALIA, 1838

In 1839, J.G. Johnston published The Truth: consisting of letters just received from Emigrants to the Australian Colonies *with an introduction and notes in Edinburgh and Aberdeen.*

In his introduction he stated:

> The excitement now prevailing in all parts of the country, on the subject of emigration to the Australian Colonies, has induced me to lay these letters before the public... It is not uncommon to find comparisons between Australia and America, which tend greatly to perplex intending emigrants... While it is freely granted that America presents many inducements to the emigrant, it ought to be clearly understood, that Australia holds out above all other countries the certain prospect of immediate and large returns from capital. A thousand pounds laid out in farming in the former country will not relieve him from the necessity of labouring daily with his servants for many years to come, probably at no period of his life; but in the latter, it will place him at once in the situation of a mere overseer of his own establishment, and enable him within a short time to delegate even this duty to another, if he chooses.

The 'young commercial gentleman' who wrote to 'My Dear Sir' on 11 August 1838 asked that his name not be published.

> My business has led me to visit all the principal settlements, with the single exception of Swan River, viz., Sydney, Hobart Town, Port Philip, and Adelaide, (South Australia.) At the former two, I travelled a considerable distance inland on business, shooting excursions, and visiting old country friends, most of whom, however, I had never seen *atween the e'en*, but here every countryman is a kinsman. At the latter, my travels were short there, being nothing beside the towns themselves but shepherds and flocks, and open plains. Well, then, in answer to your enquiry what I

think of the whole, there is of course considerable diversity, still there are general features in which all agree, and I must add my testimony to all I have heard and read, that as regards climate and productions, I have seen nothing to compare with it. One who has never travelled beyond the foggy atmosphere and ever-changing temperature of the great little island, can have no idea of the cloudless sky and balmy zephyrs of the Australian continent. The climate is reckoned superior even to the south of Italy, a comparison of which, I can say nothing, having never been in the latter country. At midsummer, away from the coast, the heat is sometimes oppressive at noon, (not however in my experience so much so as at home in 1826) but the mornings and evenings are delightfully genial. By the way, on this side of the globe, every thing is reversed: our winter is your summer, and our south wind the coldest, even the sun himself takes the wrong side of us. You may judge of the mildness of our winter, when I tell you that in Argyle county, New South Wales, I plucked ripe oranges of a morning before sun-rise, when the ground was slightly covered with snow, and that here in Van Dieman's, they have green peas at table eleven months in the year. When I am speaking of climate, I may as well anticipate your question about longevity. You must be aware that the colony itself is not of sufficient age to afford a satisfactory test on this point; but taking the salubrity of the climate, dryness of the soil, and my own experience for data, I do not see how it should be otherwise than favourable to long life.

A FRIEND TO TRUTH, AUSTRALIA, c.1838

*In 1839, an anonymous author calling himself 'A Friend to Truth' published
A True Picture of Australia its merits and demerits in Glasgow, Edinburgh, London
and Dublin. He was as enthusiastic about Illawarra, on the south coast of
New South Wales, as Lachlan Macquarie.*

The scenery at Illawarra is totally different from that of other parts
of the counties; vegetation springs up with a luxuriance that is
unrivalled, and the bright colours of the field, joined with the
splendid plumage of the feathered tribe, presents altogether a novel
and interesting appearance. The Shoalhaven river, which forms the
boundary of Illawarra, and distant nearly 190 miles from Sydney, is
navigable for small craft, for about 20 miles into the country. In the
neighbourhood of the river, the soil is of a rich mould. The long
narrow valley, called Barragotang, is in the same county, hemmed in
between the Merrigang range and the Blue Mountains, about 60
miles in the interior, with only one precipitous pass in it. The
county of Argyle is bounded on the north by the river Guinecoo,
and is sixty miles long by thirty broad. This county consists of
extensive ridges, and swelling hills, and is to be considered a
favoured country, by being watered by streams, that the heat of the
summer does not altogether dry up. Lake Bathurst is situated in this
county, 120 miles south-west of Sydney. It varies from 3 to 5 miles
in diameter, according as it is supplied by the mountain torrents.
Although 60 miles from the sea coast, it contains an animal,
resembling a seal, about three feet long, and rising every now and
then to the surface to breathe. There is a vast plain, called the
Goulbourn's plain, of 35,000 acres, without a tree; and though this
country cannot be said to be deficient in wood, yet it is more open
than the county of Cumberland.

He found the chief demerit of Australia in its 'Neglect of the Native
Tribe', an extraordinarily advanced view at that time.

The poor neglected Aborigines are to be met by the way, and our traveller could not help thinking, that if part of the expense incurred in bringing labourers out, was expended in trying some philanthropic and noble experiment to bring the original lords of the soil to act as labourers, it would be showing at least an equal degree of wisdom, and something too like an attempt to do justice. But our traveller was a simple man; he did not know that the recognised policy of Britain always was, and is up to this moment, in regard to the original inhabitants of her colonies — to take all — to confer in return nothing but her disgraceful vices and loathsome diseases. An author has lately had the daring impiety to write that it appears to be "the scrutable will of Providence that the Aborigines of New South Wales should disappear before the white man's face." Truly this is a convenient way of explaining how that race has dwindled down to little more than 5,000 throughout the whole of their native land! They are as intelligent and *well-clothed* as our forefathers were when they were conquered by the Romans — and they did not melt away before the face of their conquerors — or where would the writer of the "inscrutable will of Providence" have been at this time? This enlightened treatment of the conquered, distinguished the Romans, who were heathens. What characterises us who are christians?

HENRY WATSON, MOUNT BARKER, SOUTH AUSTRALIA, 1838

Henry Watson came to South Australia in 1838 with his family, consisting of his wife Charlotte Eliza, two daughters, Charlotte Emily about two years old and Louisa six months old when they sailed, and his mother and father. He kept a diary of the trip for the years 1838–39. It is written on old loose leaves machine numbered at random in the right hand corner as though the papers have been torn out of an unused office journal. The handwriting shows a good education, but it was possibly copied by John Sanderson Lloyd who married Charlotte Emily. His handwriting on the flyleaf closely matches the text. Rachel Mary Lloyd, granddaughter of Henry Watson, presented the diary to the Mitchell Library in 1965.

Watson writes of the Italian climate as though he knows it. The 'benevolent gentleman' was George Fife Angas, then taking an interest in South Australia from England. The town of Angaston records the great success of himself and his sons when they later came to Australia.

I quote Watson's story of a ride to Barton's stockyard. Barton was establishing himself as a grazier.

March 26 [1838] — Started before 6 in the morning with <u>Father &</u> <u>Barton</u> to see the special survey that they have got at Mount Barker. We rode over a fine rich plain from the town to the foot of the hills. We ascended the "tiers" with some difficulty, the road being very steep. The views down the different ravines became very grand, & much reminded me of the scenery of Wales & Cumberland, to which in this country is superadded the climate of Italy. On looking back we obtained a fine view of the Gulf with the vessels at anchor, the intervening wooded plain and the harbour, a beautiful sheet of water, 6 or 7 miles in extent. The road along this rocky region was extremely good & tolerably level; we passed through the stringy bark forest, many of them are very stately trees. We then entered a very superior country consisting of rich well watered vallies beautifully wooded, completely resembling a nobleman's park. The grass was dry from the long drought, but it was very deep. Flocks of different coloured <u>parakeets</u> flitted from tree to tree; we heard, but did not see, the "laughing jackass". Cockatoos occasionally screamed & scolded at us as we disturbed them, & took their flight deeper into the woods, conspicuous by their white plumage among the green leaves; but with these exceptions, nothing could exceed the silence and solitude of these wilds. We passed a little village of poor German emigrants, whom a benevolent gentleman has located in small allotments in a beautiful fertile situation. On approaching Barton's station, herds of cattle began to appear among the glades, & teams of working bullocks driven about announced our arrival near human habitations. On arriving at the stockyard we found Stephen (Hack) busy branding cattle; we joined him at his dinner of Pork and Damper, washed down with Tea made in an iron pot, & we did full justice to our fare after a 30 mile ride. The land in these vallies is of the richest description, consisting of a deep black soil. This region must be the garden & granary of the colony in future years. The substratum seems to be sandstone. The ranges near Mount Lofty are primitive. After resting about 3 hours we remounted our horses. The sun set as we entered the Mount Lofty ravines which looked very grand by moonlight. We got home about 9 having been out for 15 hours & in the saddle 12, having ridden about 64 miles, not bad work for people who have been five months on shipboard.

R.G. JAMESON, ADELAIDE 1838, SYDNEY 1841

R.G. Jameson arrived in Adelaide in October 1838 aboard Surrey as Surgeon
Superintendent of Emigrants. He then spent three years travelling in Australia, New
Zealand, Java, Singapore and Calcutta before returning to England. In 1842 he
published New Zealand, South Australia, and New South Wales: a record of recent travels
in these colonies with Especial Reference to Emigration and the Advantageous
Employment of Labour and Capital.

Jameson loved the country and noted the moonlight in the Mount Lofty
Ranges: 'Over this wild landscape reposed the radiance of a brilliant moon,
constituting such a scene of stillness and beauty as is not easily fogotten'.

He recorded examples of how quickly men could build themselves up
by well-planned businesses. He investigated farming, grazing, whaling, seal-
ing and general commerce.

Instead of Jameson's good impressions of landscape, I have quoted
passages on how Adelaide was developing in 1838 and an assessment of
Sydney society in 1841. He considered that Australians were maligned in
England. The fine house he visited was *Tempe House*, belonging to Alexander
Brodie Sparke, merchant and agent, to whom he dedicated the book. Built
about 1830, *Tempe House* was designed by John Verge who later designed
the town house, *Tusculum*, where Bishop Broughton lived. Both wonderful
houses still exist in compromised positions.

[Adelaide 1838] **Within the compass of a few roods stood, in**
strange contrast to each other, the blue or white painted wooden
cottage brought out from England, with Venetian blinds, and
perchance a brass knocker, and the mud-walled edifice, less elegant,
but not less comfortable than its neater and sprucer neighbour. Here
and there a substantial building of brick or stone, combining
neatness with durability, betokened that its owner, heedless of
expense, was resolved to possess that essential of English comfort, a
good house, whatsoever might be the fate of the colony. The gum
trees being left standing, except where they grow in a line of
thoroughfare, afforded to many of the dwellings a pleasant shade
from the noontide heats; and the background of evergreen foliage,

which extended on all sides, gave a fine pictorial effect to many of the buildings, especially to the church, on whose tapering spire few people could look for the first time without experiencing some retrospective emotion.

The town itself is pleasing and picturesque. It is divided into two portions, by an open valley, in which runs the chain of ponds called, rather incorrectly, the river Torrens. The intervening ground is reserved as a park or common, and during the nine months of the year in which South Australia is exempt from hot winds, the aspect of this undulating piece of land is susceptible of being rendered beautiful and ornamental. It demands no great effort of the imagination to picture in the mind's eye the North Terrace, overlooking a public garden in all its pride of hue and perfume.

[Sydney 1841] A few days after my arrival in Sydney, I received an invitation to an entertainment given on the occasion of consecrating the new church of St. Stephen; a handsome edifice built entirely by private subscription, for the convenience of numerous families who live in the heathy and retired neighbourhood of Cook's River. On this occasion I had an opportunity of seeing a specimen of the best society in the colony, and I looked in vain for any mark by which I could distinguish it from any refined or genteel company in England. The equipages were fashionable; the ladies were in general pretty, and elegantly attired; and the gentlemen were equally unexceptional in their dress and demeanour.

When the service was over, it being on a week-day, a portion of the company, to the number of two hundred, proceeded on horseback and in carriages, to the residence of a gentleman in the neighbourhood, where a collation was prepared. In front of the mansion, a lawn, tastefully and ornamentally laid out, sloped gently down to the edge of the river, across which the visitors were ferried in boats. The mansion itself, a large cottage orneé, with an exterior verandah and colonnade, and snow-white walls, constituted the chief ornament of a very pleasing landscape, and presented a lively contrast with the variegated and umbrageous foliage of a garden, rich in specimens of the rarest plants, native and exotic, which had been scientifically grouped according to their botanical characters.

Here I saw the beautiful <u>protea argentea</u>, the <u>araucaria excelsa</u>, or pine, of Norfolk Island; the <u>phormium tenax</u>, or flax plant, of New Zealand; and the gigantic lily, said to be the chief floral ornament of the Australian wilderness; while the orange, the citron, the pomegranate, and many varieties of the vine, flourished luxuriantly. Nor were these the only indications of the owner's cultivated taste that were to be seen on the domain of Tempe. The apartments were richly and elegantly furnished. There was a library and an aviary, and the walls were hung with Flemish and Italian paintings.

THOMAS TOURLE, SYDNEY, HUNTER RIVER, NEW ENGLAND AND SCONE, 1839, 1840

*Thomas Tourle arrived in Sydney on Lady Raffles on 12 September 1839
as a free settler with money to invest. He brought out labourers
whom he had hired in England.*

Tourle travelled about for several months getting 'a good insight to the whole management of a large Sheep Establishment', and then bought 850 ewes which he ran near Bathurst. He mustered his flock early in 1814, which had increased to 1218, and set out for New England with 7 men, 3 women and a child, 2 drays with 13 bullocks to pull them, and 11 dogs, where he went into partnership with George Morse on Balala, west of Uralla.

Tourle's early letters praise almost everything he saw, but the depression of the 1840s soured his opinions. He found Australia badly managed. Increasing prosperity changed his outlook again and, by 1847, he was urging settlers to emigrate.

Balala was eventually a great financial success and the partners developed it into a holding of about 40,000 hectares. They sold out in 1880. The Australian National Library holds a thick collection of his letters. I have made a selection from four that deal with city and country.

[14 September 1839, on board Lady Raffles] At about 5 pm we entered the Harbour and our Pilot came off to us in a Whale Boat rowed by 4 New Zealanders... and we in a few minutes began warking up the ship against a light breeze and anchored about 9 o'clock...

The scenery on either side most romantic, large craggy Rocks covered with green scrubby shrubs quite down to the water and deep water quite close to the Rocks and about every half mile there are small lakes stretching away in all shapes from the main Harbour and all again enclosed by the same sandstone Rock and trees forming the most beautiful scenery I ever beheld.

[Later the same day, Tourle wrote to his father after he had walked around Sydney]

The town is most beautifully situated on an eminence on a Sandy
Rocky soil several very good streets and excellent shops so very
English that were it not for the scenery you would think yourself
in England...

The streets are very broad and some of them at least a mile long
with many parts of them well paved. Shops well appointed and with
some as good an assortment as you will see at Atwoods. The villas
around the Town are beautiful most of them commanding a view of
the Harbour which is most romantic and always full of shipping.
17 ships came in at the same time your letter arrived.

Tell Mother she would delight in the Cactus, Geraniums and
aloes that grow here in profusion. I have seen a cactus hedge 4 feet
high and geraniums larger than gooseberry trees. The soil is black
and white sand covered with a sort of heath and green Broom with a
white flower...

[Exactly a year later, Tourle reported to his father from Scone on the
Hunter River and New England]

I am very much pleased with the Hunter River district many parts
being very beautiful and as it has been blessed with more good Rain
than any other part of the Country it is as you may imagine in a
flourishing state.

The New England country is very high table land, I believe
about 3000 feet above the Sea and about 60 miles off in a line in Lat.
31–33. It is abundantly watered having many swamps between
undulating Hills — the former Rich Black Land fit for grazing
cattle and in the driest parts of them for Wheat. The latter of a
sandy stone description with a large portion of Granite Rock from
which many Springs are constantly running...

[To his sister, Emma, 22 September 1840]

We had a pleasant Pic Nic party at Scone one day... After riding
about 2 miles the Ladies dismounted their steeds and proceeded on
Foot up a very steep and Rugged Mountain, commanding a very
beautiful view in the Distance with a few cleared Spots peeping
thro' the Bush showing the first Fruits of Man's labours with a
distant view of the Page River then Running at the Back of the

Range of Mountains a great many dwarf Mimosa in full bloom with several Mountain Flowers added much to the beauty of the Scenery as also to that of the Ladies who came home decked with wreaths of Wild Flowers by the light of a most lovely Moon that added much to the Romance of the Scene...

Some of the Country is very grand and picturesque — only wants for a few Pretty Girls to make it <u>Perfect</u>, for without that <u>Romantic Scenery</u> is nothing.

Tourle found his Pretty Girl. In 1846, he married Helen Morse, the sister of his partner.

PATRICK LESLIE, DARLING DOWNS, QUEENSLAND, 1840

Patrick Leslie's diary was preserved in The Genesis of Queensland *by Henry Stuart Russell, published in Sydney in 1888. Russell himself was a squatter. With a partner, he owned Cecil Plains on the Condamine 40 kilometres south of present Dalby. Leichhardt used it as a staging post. He stayed there in August 1847, when returning from his aborted second trip, and gave him an autographed sketch map of the Balonne River inscribed 'from his friend Ludwig Leichhardt'.*

Patrick Leslie was born in Scotland in 1815 and came to Australia in May 1835. He studied agriculture and stock management under the Macarthurs at Camden. He managed a run for his uncle at Cassilis, and then leased a farm in the upper Hunter and another near St Mary's on his own account.

When Leslie's brothers George and Walter arrived in Australia, they decided to explore the Darling Downs, of which Cunningham thought so much. They established a huge sheep run on the best land they found in that magnificent district. Initially they took up far more than they could stock, so they were forced to yield some areas to those following them.

Patrick Leslie married Catherine Macarthur, daughter of Hannibal Hawkins Macarthur, 'the prettiest girl in the world', who came with the substantial practical dowry of 2000 sheep. The economic calamity of the 1840s forced him to sell out of Canning Downs, the run that he established.

He had enough money to build *Newstead House* in Brisbane, a lovely home still standing, which he sold a few years later to buy another station on the Darling Downs. In 1848, Leslie bought the first block of land put up for auction in Warwick, the town built on the site of his brother George's sheep station. 'Come, Mr Patrick Leslie', he was urged, 'buy the bloody little lot for luck; you were the first man here, be the first to buy'.

Leslie spent a brief time in parliament campaigning for the secession of Queensland, and then settled in New South Wales for several years. After a visit to Scotland with his wife, he took up land in New Zealand but he came back to Sydney in 1878 and died there in 1881.

His diary is matter-of-fact – Leslie was a practical Scotsman. Nevertheless, it is fascinating to see how he could inspect such vast areas of land and recognise where unknown creeks and rivers flowed. He had hoped to get a copy of Cunningham's map.

Before leaving Sydney, I had heard from my old friend, Mr. Allan
Cunningham, the discoverer of Darling Downs, full particulars of
his journey out, and he most kindly offered me the use of his map
to assist me in my exploration, and wrote to my old friend, Admiral
King, who had such map, asking him to give it to me to copy, but
unfortunately Admiral King could not find it, and I had therefore
to manage as best I could.

On 2 March 1840, Patrick Leslie and Peter Murphy, a convict lifer and
'about the best plucked fellow I ever came across in my life', set out from a
station in the New England and made a three-week trip to blaze the best
trail to the Downs.

The squatting expedition set out for the same New England station on
14 April. It consisted of Patrick, his brother Walter, 22 ticket-of-leave
convicts ('as good and game a lot of men as ever existed, and who never
occasioned a moment's trouble; worth any forty men I have ever seen'),
2 teams of bullocks (a total of 24), 2 drays, a team of horses and a dray, 10
saddle horses, 4000 breeding ewes in lamb, 100 ewe hoggets, 1000 wedder
hoggets (it was common practice in those days to write, or pronounce, 'th'
as 'dd'), 100 rams and 500 wedders, 3 and 4 years old.

They arrived at the Condamine River on 4 June 'without the loss of a
single animal, or breaking a bullock chain'.

On the 6th of June, leaving all stock, drays &c., in charge of the
men, Walter Leslie, Peter Murphy and I left the Condamine camp,
and explored the country up the Condamine, by Canning Downs,
Killarney, Glengallan and Dalrymple creeks, returning to camp on
the 13th, and on the 14th moved up the river, arriving at the junction
of Sandy creek with the Condamine on the 20th. Here we made a
temporary camp, intended for our first sheep station, and for the
protection of the men and stock, made one station on the north bank
of the river and two others opposite — one on either side of Sandy
creek, thus giving mutual protection, and at the same time deep
water between each camp.

From this camp, on the 21st of June, Walter, Murphy and I struck
across the Downs to the northward, and crossing by (what is now)
Allora, Spring creek, King's creek, Hodgson's creek, and on to
Gowrie and One Tree Hill, and finding nothing we liked as much as
Canning Downs, we returned as far as Glengallan creek, and ran the

Middle Gap creek up to Cunningham's 'Gap', crossed it, following
a creek down to the Bremer river [flowing north into the Brisbane
River], intending to go on to Brisbane, but on second thoughts we
feared going without credentials, and re-crossing the 'Gap,' we
returned to our camp on the 1st July, and next day we left the sheep
at their stations, and moved down some four miles to Toolburra,
where we formed our head station. We afterwards sold Toolburra
to Gordon, and formed the Canning Downs head station. We took
up the country from the bottom of Toolburra to the head of the
Condamine, including all tributaries [40,000 hectares and
14 creeks]. Afterwards we gave up what was (afterwards) called
Glengallan creek to the Campbells, and Fred (Bracker) the
German's creek and Sandy creek to the Aberdeen Company.

JOHN LORT STOKES, PLAINS OF PROMISE,
QUEENSLAND, 1841

*Whether by land or by sea, Stokes found exploring a marvel of the imagination
and he had words to express his delight. At the mouth of the Fitzroy River,
which he named in northwest Western Australia in 1838, he wrote:*

**I prepared to enter upon the exciting task of exploring waters
unfurrowed by any preceding keel; and shores on which the advancing
step of civilization had not yet thrown the shadow of her advent.**

Born in 1812, Stokes entered the British Navy in *Prince Regent* as a 12-year-
old. The next year he was promoted to midshipman and transferred to
the brig *Beagle* on which he served 18 years, the last two as its commander.
He was a master marine surveyor. He drew hydrographic maps of the coast
of Australia between 1837 and 1843 which were still in use during World
War II.

In 1837, the Lords Commissioner of the Admiralty sent *Beagle*, under
Captain John Wickham, to 'explore and survey such portions of the
Australian coasts, as were wholly or in part unknown to Captains Flinders
and King'. Wickham had been first lieutenant on *Beagle* during its excursion with Charles Darwin.

The new job took six years, the last two under Stokes's command. At its
conclusion, he took *Beagle* home. He returned in 1847 to do four more
years of survey off New Zealand and New South Wales in *Acheron*, one of
the earliest steamers, and then he returned to England.

Stokes married twice. When he died in Wales in 1885, he had reached
the rank of admiral.

In 1846, Stokes published *Discoveries in Australia* in two volumes telling
the complete story of the work of *Beagle*. In this extract, he tells of the Plains
of Promise between the Albert and Leichhardt Rivers that flow into the Gulf
of Carpentaria. When A.C. Gregory walked across them in 1856, he was not
so impressed: 'The character of the country is inferior as the grass which
covers the plains is principally aristidia [*Aristida*, wiregrasses] and andropogon
[*Cymbopogon*, spectacular grasses but their strong lemon flavour makes them
unpalatable], anthisteria [now *Themeda triandra*] or Kangaroo grass only in
small patches. The soil is good brown loam'.

Following up a short woody valley, on reaching the summit of the level a view burst upon me, the nature of which the reader may learn from the accompanying plate. A vast boundless plain lay before us, here and there dotted over with woodland isles. Whilst taking the bearings of one of these to guide us in the direction we were to steer, I sent a man up a tree to have a further view; but nothing beyond an extension of the plain was to be seen. The river could be traced to the southward by a waving line of green trees; the latter were larger at this spot than in any other part, and consisted of tall palms, and three kinds of gums. No trace of the western branch could be discovered.

Time being, as I have before said, very precious, we moved off in a S.S.E. direction, at the rate of almost four miles an hour, in spite of the long coarse grass lying on the ground and entangling our legs. The soil was still a light-coloured mould of great depth, and according to one so well qualified to judge as Sir W. Hooker, who kindly examined some that I brought to England, is of a rich quality, confirming the opinion I entertained of it, which suggested for this part of the continent, the name of "The Plains of Promise."

FIRST VIEW OF THE PLAINS OF PROMISE ALBERT RIVER
John Lort Stokes, 1841, from *Discoveries in Australia*, Mitchell Library,
State Library of New South Wales

We were now once more stepping out over a terra incognita; and though no alpine features greeted our eyes as they wandered eagerly over the vast level, all was clothed with the charm of novelty. The feelings of delight which are naturally aroused in those whose feet for the first time press a new and rich country, and which I have so often before endeavoured in vain to express, burst forth on this occasion with renewed intensity.

LOUISA CLIFTON. AUSTRALIND. WESTERN AUSTRALIA. 1841

Louisa Clifton came to Australind by the sailing ship Parkfield in March 1841. It was a settlement marked out for the Western Australian Company on the Leschenault Inlet, country that Lieutenant Bunbury had described five years before. Already there was a whaling station and a depot for breeding horses for the Indian army.

Louisa was 25 years old and one of 14 children. Her father, Marshall Clifton, had been appointed Chief Commissioner of the company. He had retired early as Secretary of the Victualling Board of the British Admiralty, and he had been living with his big family in France for years because his pension stretched farther there than in England.

Marshall Clifton sailed with his wife, a fervent Quaker, 12 of their children and inexperienced prospective settlers who found that the farms they had paid for were uncleared and unfenced and that there was no labour to be hired in Western Australia.

A dozen or more great companies were proposed and several were formed to settle Australia and New Zealand. Most failed in a few years. Some, like the Western Australian Company, were badly organised; others were swindles. Even the great Australian Agricultural Company, which employed Henry Dangar as surveyor and explorer, made no big profits until the 1960s, some 140 years after its formation in 1824.

Louisa Clifton accompanied her family after an unhappy love affair. The year after she arrived, she married George Eliot of the 'little dwelling' that she describes seeing from the boat. He was Resident Magistrate. She sketched and painted, so she sees the colours of the shore as an artist.

17 March 1841 At noon today we were 115 miles from Cape Naturaliste and 96 from nearest land. About ½ past 5 the soul-reviving sound 'land in sight' rang from the mast-head. I soon after went and joined all the party on deck, and there in the far horizon, in the grey colouring of coming twilight, loomed the faint outline of our adopted land. At a distance of 30 or 40 miles it rose high. The moment any eyes first rested on that 'dim discovered scene' was one the remembrance of which the longest life can never obliterate; none who have not known what it is to sigh, to long with sickening

longing for land after a voyage of more than 3 months can fully
understand with what ecstasy of feeling the first view and scent of
land greets the weary senses.

18 March 1841 About 6 in the evening we found ourselves in
Leschenault Bay, within ½ mile of the shore, the sea perfectly
smooth, the temperature more warm and balmy than can be
described. We were all struck by the pretty aspect of the country at
the mouth of the inlet and in parts along the shore. Masses of
beautiful foliage grow down to the water's edge and in an opening of
it we descried Mr. Eliot's and Mr. Stirling's little dwelling. The
immediate coast rises in sandhills, but there is vegetation upon
them, trees everywhere seen beyond the hills in the distance and
reminding us forcibly of the Paris hill at Sauoer [?]. The colouring
as the sun began to decline became exquisitely soft and radiant, the
hills robed in the brightest lakes and blues, the sky reflecting every
colour in the rainbow, and yet so softly that every tint completely
melted into one another. I cannot easily cease to remember the first
Australian Sunset, nor the feelings with which I viewed its
promising coasts and the native fires burning along the country...

2 April 1841 [They are still sleeping aboard the barque].
We have been sitting on deck watching the fires on shore near
Shenton's store. The scene has been most beautiful, worthy the
pencil of a Claude Lorraine; the moon and sky dazzlingly bright;
the sea glistening and perfectly smooth; the out line of the shore
dark and clear; the livid flash and the curling grey and vermilion
smoke of the fires throwing a bright redness over the scene,
investing with a wildness congenial to the spot and exciting to
the imagination.

UNKNOWN WRITER, PORTLAND, VICTORIA, 1841

I own a second revised edition of Major T.L. Mitchell's Three Expeditions into the Interior of Eastern Australia: with descriptions of the recently explored regions of Australia Felix, and of the present colony of New South Wales, published in London in 1839. It is in two finely bound volumes with superb laid-in folded maps and reproductions of Mitchell's exquisite drawings. He was a more than competent artist.

The special value of the book is that it was bought by an English land-seeker in 1841. He marked the passage in Chapter VIII of the second volume where Mitchell, after crossing the Murray River, wrote that he was 'the first European intruder on the supreme solitude of these verdant plains'. Thereafter the land-seeker underlined words whenever good grass or good country was mentioned. He wrote all over the margins and the fading ink still reproduces his excitement.

Alas, he was too late for any of the land. Those who took it up did not wait to read the book. They followed Mitchell's tracks before he even reached the southern coast; they backtracked him from Portland Bay while he was travelling northeast on his return journey. Some men who arrived in the Western District of Victoria in 1840 found no land left. They bought from first-comers willing to take quick profits.

A PICNIC ON THE LOWER MURRAY

George French Angas, 1822–1886, S4691, National Library of Australia

I quote the longest passage of the land-seeker's notes to himself taken from the flyleaves at the back of the volume. Of part of the country he planned to ride over Mitchell wrote, 'Several small and very picturesque lakes, then as smooth as mirrors, adorned the valley immediately to the westward of the hill, I was upon. They were fringed with luxuriant shrubs, so that it was really painful to me to hurry, as I was then compelled to do, past spots like these, involving in their unexplored recesses so much of novelty amidst the romantic scenery'.

Charles Armytage bought this land from the squatters in 1858. He turned it into the marvellous Mount Sturgeon holding, running 30,000 sheep, 300 cattle and employing 130 permanent hands, as well as 150 or so seasonal carriers, contract fencers and thistle cutters. (The modern phrase is burr cutters).

Our hopeful land-seeker and Unknown Writer first considered Twofold Bay. He drew a rectangle in ink about 170 by 80 km stretching from Cape Howe to Moruya. Within it he wrote: 'Try this tract. Start from Goulburn, keeping by the bank of the Shoalhaven R. straight to Twofold Bay returning by Yass and the Murrumbidgee'. Then he made a note near Portland Bay: 'If Twofold Bay is not suited for settling, the most beautiful country will be found for pasture etc between the Wando and the Wannon'.

He expected a lot of Australian horses. They were, and are, of outstanding stamina, but 200 miles in 5 days (an average of just over 64 km a day) across creeks, rivers, ranges and plains of high grass is hard travelling. He must have read a lot about Australian exploration. He sounds experienced until he gets to the end of the instructions. Then he suddenly reveals that he knows nothing about the soils or pasture that grew on them.

> Proceed direct to the west of Mount Clay and passing close round the base of it, make the Fitzroy, where the two streams join distance about 10 miles. Then examine upstream for about five miles looking to the land on opposite bank as well as the southern bank, cross over to Mount Eckersley, and passing its base on the eastern side cross over the other branch of the Fitzroy following down its left or northern bank to the coast taking care to examine the ground on both sides of the stream then turning eastwards reach the bank of the Shaw distance travelled from Portland Bay about 45 miles. Next morning examine the banks of the Shaw up to the marsh or great swamp 3 miles north of Mount Eccles, cross the stream and rounding the swamp by its east side reach the Shaw again which

flows into it to the north. This part is spoken of as particularly
beautiful, like a park. Trace it to its source, and then 5 miles to the
north is Mount Pierrepoint. Skirting this on the eastern side you
see to the N.E. (or east) Lake Linlithgow and Grange Burn flowing
out of it. Cross this near the lake and then make straight to Mount
Sturgeon, the southern point of the Grampians, or rather Serra,
distance 2nd day about 50 miles. 3rd morning make the Wannon
pursuing the left bank N.E. till you come to a lake, about 10 miles,
cross to the right bank and make for Mount Abrupt (passing
through Serra range) due west close to its northern base. Proceed
for about 10 miles to the west inclining a little south, so as to make
the junction of a mountain stream with the Wannon, this stream
flowing south in the middle of the large valley situated between the
Serra and Victoria ranges, distance 30 miles.

   If not sufficient of this valley has been seen to form a correct
opinion of it — the following morning two should walk up the
tributary stream for about 7 miles, or ascend a hill which commands
a view of it, and examine it with a glass, the other man remaining
behind not too much exposed to meet the view of any passing
natives. So also in all the halting places, as little fire as possible
should be used, and before fixing on a spot some high ground
should be ascended to see if the smoke of any fires be near. The
necessary precautions should be taken against surprise at night but
the natives here are few and friendly. 4th morning cross to the south
of the Wannon, pursue its course for 10 miles westward or NW
which will bring you west of southern point of the Victoria range so
as to command a view of the Dundas Group, having in these 10 miles
ascertained the quality of the soil on the banks of the upper
Wannon, turn directly south and reach Grange Burn, about 15 or 20
miles, by skirting Mount Bainbrigge on its western side. Follow the
Burn down its right or north bank for 5 to 6 miles where its two
branches meet. Cross over and proceeding southwards reach the
Rifle Range, about 5 miles homeward. Reach on 5th morning Mount
Eckersly and Portland Bay. Distance travelled 4th day 40 miles and
last about 35. The things necessary for this journey would be one
man and myself with two good horses and one man with a led horse
and two hampers one pound of tea 3 of sugar 42 lb of cabin biscuits

and 21 lb of salt or preserved meat, a teapot saucepan and teakettle with a water jug or stone bottle holding 3 quarts (if the weather is dry) — a pistol each man, 3 picketting chains for horses, and my cloak and valise or two one for companion. I ought before starting to learn how to tell the different kinds of grass and soil. The distance about 200 miles in 5 days — average 40 miles a day. The led horse should be started very early.

J.F. BENNETT, ADELAIDE, 1843

Smith, Elder, & Co. in London and A. & C. Black in Edinburgh published in 1843
Bennett's Historical and Descriptive Account of SOUTH AUSTRALIA *Founded on*
the Experiences of a Three Years' Residence in that Colony. It was designed to attract
and inform immigrants. Little is known about Bennett. He must have had newspaper
experience since, when he arrived in Adelaide in March 1839, he edited the Chronicle.
When the depression forced the sale of that newspaper in April 1840 to the South
Australian Register, *Bennett, who must also have had seafaring experience, became*
mate on an Adelaide brig of 200 tons. Then he accepted the position of assistant
editor on the Register, *where he compiled and edited the* Royal South Australian
Almanack *for 1840 and the* Royal South Australian Almanack and General Directory
for both 1841 and 1842.

Bennett returned to London, and then came back a year or so later and
compiled the *South Australia Almanack and Town and Country Directory* for 1845.
He engaged in private mercantile dealings for a few years, then returned to
England, joined the army, and retired as major. Although Bennett made the
following statement:

> I can scarcely imagine a more interesting scene than to observe a
> country in the course of being rescued from a state of nature —
> than to see the trackless desert transformed into cattle runs and
> corn fields,

he had genuine admiration for the land in its original state.

> Beyond the range of mountains to the east of Adelaide, named the
> Mount Lofty Range, lies a district of fine undulating country, well
> watered, and generally covered with the most luxuriant verdure.
> This district takes its name from a hill situate in it, of moderate
> elevation, called Mount Barker, and has been pronounced by many
> travellers to be one of the finest tracks of country in Australia. The
> hills are of slight elevation, are intersected by fine vallies; and being
> partly wooded, partly clear, the country has been justly pronounced
> by many who have visited it, as well as the vallies already
> mentioned, to present more the appearance of an immense park than

anything that one would naturally expect to find in the wilds of an uncultivated land. The Mount Barker district being more elevated than the plains around Adelaide, there exists a marked difference in the climate; the heat never being so intense in summer, and slight frosts during the night being of frequent occurrence during winter. With slight variations, this description of country extends a great distance to the northward, portions of scrub and other inferior land intervening occasionally. To the eastward of Mount Barker, and on approaching Lake Alexandrina, the country falls towards the Lake, and spreads into extensive plains, in appearance and character similar to those at Adelaide.

It has been already stated, that the plain in which Adelaide is situate stretches to the north of the Town for many miles. The country then begins again to assume the character of hill and vale, which is retained through the greatest part of the northern portion of the Colony. In this quarter are found many of its most fertile districts. These stretch along from the Mount Barker districts, and include the sources of the Rivers Onkaparinga and of the Torrens — the beautiful plain named Lyndoch Valley — the very extensive and well watered lands in the neighbourhood of the heights of Barossa — the sources of the River Gawler, and the rich vallies on the banks, and in the neighbourhood of the Hutt, Light, and Wakefield rivers. The country around Lyndoch Valley and the Barossa Ranges, about 60 miles north-east from the Capital, is of a very superior description; consisting of fine alluvial vallies and flats, covered with a rich coating of grass, and surrounded by picturesque hills, which likewise yield good grazing for stock. Some of the vales, or meadows, are really beautiful, and the scenery in this quarter is more diversified than in most other places - the surrounding hills assuming many shapes and attitudes which strike the eye, while the rich verdure and evergreen trees with which the slopes are covered, give a pleasant and cheering aspect to the scene. To the west and the north-west, the country consists of open grassy table-land; to the east it falls into plains towards the Murray.

ANNABELLA BOSWELL. LAKE INNES. PORT MACQUARIE. NEW SOUTH WALES. 1843. 1844

Annabella Boswell left a delightful picture of herself husking corn in a big shed on the busy Lake Innes station. She was wearing:

... a muslin frock which had been quite clean a week before! By some mischance the skirt had been half torn from my body, and was now pushed up under my back, & half hidden by a green apron with torn pockets. a black shawl put on under a large collar. & a new handkerchief tied round my throat now picture to yourself a tall, thin, fair haired, dark complexioned young lady in the before mentioned dress, adding only a pr. of dirty gloves with torn out fingers. & allow me to introduce you to Miss Annabella Innes.

Annabella was 17 years old and was born near Bathurst. Her father, George Innes, had died and her uncle, Archibald Clunes Innes, invited his sister-in-law and her two daughters, Annabella and Margaret, to live with him at his fine home near Port Macquarie. It was then the biggest and most beautiful country home built in New South Wales. There were 22 furnished apartments, which did not include the bachelors' hall. Water from the roof was channeled into a deep, round brick well; there was a flush lavatory with a Wedgwood bowl; the extensive brick stables joined the homestead as an angled wing. The entire building is now little more than foundations.

The Innes brothers (they had 14 siblings) came to Sydney in the convict ship *Eliza* in 1822. Archibald was captain of the guard, George a paying passenger. Their father, Major James Innes, was a distinguished soldier living at Thrumster, in the far north of Scotland. In 1815, he was sent a blank commission for any member of his family. He filled in Archibald Clunes, brought the lad home from school in Aberdeen, got him measured for his uniform and hurried him off to London. Archibald arrived in Belgium as a 15-year-old soldier the day after the battle of Waterloo was fought and won. He fought in the Peninsular War as a commissioned officer.

A couple of years after Archibald's arrival in Sydney, he was sent to Van Diemen's Land where he made a great success of rounding-up escaped convicts. After serving as aide-de-camp to the Lieutenant-Governor of New

South Wales, he was appointed to the magistry and given the position of commandant of the penal colony at Port Macquarie. Archibald took over in December 1826. He resigned his commission in 1828 and became superintendent of police and magistrate at Parramatta.

In 1829, Archibald married Margaret McLeay, daughter of the colonial secretary, at a wedding described as the most magnificent that the Colony had seen. He went back to Port Macquarie as police magistrate with his new wife.

There he began a squatting career on a huge scale with Lake Innes as his headquarters. Archibald held runs on the Macleay River, the Manning, the Hastings and several in the New England – Glen Innes is named for him. He was responsible for building the road between Port Macquarie and Walcha. He transformed Port Macquarie from a penal settlement to a flourishing town. His hospitality was famous. Then came the depression and, by 1852, he was bankrupt. Archibald finished his days as magistrate and gold commissioner and died at the age of 57.

Annabella Innes, Archibald's neice, began a journal while she was at Lake Innes. In 1856, she married Patrick Charles Douglas-Boswell, an obscure relation of the famous diarist. He was a settler and a bank manager. They paid a visit to Scotland in 1864 and did not return. Annabella collected her diaries into a book, *Early Recollections and Gleanings from an Old Journal*. She also published other books that seem to be lost. She was a fine artist and many of her black and white sketches and her paintings of flowers are extant.

Hastings District Historical Society learnt of the journals in 1973 and sent a member to Scotland to buy them from a completely disinterested descendant. There are nine notebooks of about 120 pages each. Annabella loved Australia. In 1853 she wrote:

I am so thoroughly Australian in heart as well as by birth, that my mind often wanders from present scenes. so memory is busy with the primitive surroundings of my early life. the happy years of my childhood & the still happier years which followed — all clothed in sunshine, or decked with flowers.

Annabella went on one of her frequent walks on 13 March 1844.

When we met in the Library this morning, one & all Pronounced it to be 'a dreadfully cold day'... My Aunt proposed we should walk to Tacking Point to warm ourselves to which we heartily consented —

I do not think she quite expected such a ready acquiescence and can you believe it? — about an hour after breakfast we were all 'under way' — Gustavus and Gordy too — & Christy carrying a basket — [Gustavus was Archibald and Margaret Innes's son, Gordina their daughter. Christina Ross was a highland servant who came to Australia with Annabella's mother] — we walked to the beach very slowly, but once on the sands, with the wind in our favor, & ourselves quite in the Spirit of the thing, we got on fast & merrily. I helped Christy, & many a good race we had to try & overtake Margt & Dido [Dido was also Innes's daughter, three years older than Gordine and nearest in age to Margaret, Annabella's sister] who were far ahead — & then we gathered cockles which were lying in hundreds on the sand after the waves had receded — There is a large brown rock about a mile from the Point which for a long time puzzled us — first we thought it was a hut with bark on the roof — then we thought it a clump of small trees but as soon as I saw that it was a rock — away I ran & was standing in triumph on the top when Mamma & my Aunt came up — but they did not approve of my conduct as I was setting a bad example to the others. & that "Good

LAKE INNES
G.H. Bruhn, 1850s, by courtesy Port Macquarie Historical Society

Girl Margaret" declared that though she had arrived at the rock long before me, she had never thought of climbing to the top like she saw me do it! So we all walked — with admirable propriety till we reached a little creek very near the Point where I ran off again to explore the hills before luncheon — I do love mountains hills & dales, & am never tired climbing about them I had no idea Tacking Point was so pretty — I mean the green hills we first see — they are just now covered with soft green grass. it was delightful to run over them, & I was soon on the highest, thinking that from it I would see the Settlement — but I could only see a little on this Side of Point Plummer — I was delighted - & scrambling up the western side of the farthest hill — but in imagination travelling into cloud land when I was cruelly called back to lunch — It really is a pretty place We had luncheon under a shady bank — & with our sandwiches was a bottle of Port Wine!

DANIEL GEORGE BROCK, IN THE BARRIER RANGE
WITH STURT, SOUTH AUSTRALIA AND
NEW SOUTH WALES, 1844–45

Daniel George Brock was a member of a Dutch family of clockmakers who had
migrated to England and made a name for themselves as manufacturers of fireworks.
He came to South Australia early in 1838, joined a minor exploring party soon after
his arrival, and then took a job as stock inspector, which necessitated riding the newly
settled country south of Adelaide. He kept diaries of every trip.

Brock was married with a son when the inspector's work had cut out.
Captain Charles Sturt selected him from 300 applicants for his journey to
the inland sea. They took a boat to navigate it.

Instead of arriving by the seaside in mid-summer, they came on sandy
plains in the midst of a drought in one of the hottest years known. They
spent five terrible months by a dwindling waterhole waiting for rain to
furnish a way out.

It was an unhappy party. Officers and men kept strictly apart. Although
their lives depended on each other, they did not even eat together.

Despite Sturt's fame, he was not a strong leader or a good judge of men.
Louis Piesse as storeman was malicious, devious and sadistic, yet he was a
favourite of Sturt's. Sent back to Adelaide to bring up stores, he met the
returning party on the Darling and refused to issue the lime juice and
vinegar the men were desperate for. James Poole had died of scurvy. All,
including Sturt, were affected.

Brock was earnest, hypercritical and religious. John Browne, the surgeon,
was the only man he could get along with. 'I hear no voice which hath
learned to praise the Redeemer, I see no face that is turned Zionward – all
my familiars are enemies to the Cross'.

Brock kept a journal of the trip. Flowers and rock wallabies enthused him.

4th. [November 1844, in the Barrier Range]

About 2 p.m. the camp was broke up. After travelling some little
time we entererd among the ranges through which the creek flows.
As the day closed in, it was really delightful, the delight arising
from the fragrant odours produced from the multitude of flowers

and herbs which strewed our path. The scenery was so different from what we have been accustomed to since we left Adelaide, peak rising on peak either side of us, and in the distance vegetated to their very summits with shrubs. About sundown, we passed out of the gorge and entered upon more open country — and very soon came upon a hole in a branch creek containing 6 weeks supply of water, with abundance of feed for our cattle.

5th.

Skinned a bird of the parrot tribe, a very splendid specimen. About 9 a.m. the Captain and Doctor started upon which is known among us as a Scouting Expedition to find water &c beyond our present camp... The spot where we are now encamped is very pleasant; we are sat down in an Acacia shrubbery, some species of this shrub being now covered with delicate white flowers, and the soil seems pretty good.

15th. [December 1845, on the return journey]

This morning the Doctor with myself, instead of accompanying the drays, started, instead of going over the range, to follow the bed of the creek, through the range. It was terrific work, the Doctor having two horses, and I had the sheep. It was a continuous mass of broken rock in the creek, and the sides stood up as walls on either hand. It was wild scenery, wild as the wildest ever depicted by a writer of romance. What gave an interest to the scene, was the presence of that rare and beautiful animal known as the "Rock Wallaby". One jumped from before me, it appeared to have an iron grey back, black breast and a long sweeping tail. So rare are these animals, but few have ever yet been secured either dead or alive. We saw three who had become disturbed by us spring to the face of a precipice over-laying us, and how they could find a footing to spring as they did up its smooth face we could not account, but up they were, in less than no time, it was most astonishing. We at last broke through the range, and soon joined the drays, who were encamped on the creek which we had been running up. In this creek we found a native fruit, a small berry. I gathered a great quantity. They proved acceptable to Sturt, who is becoming hourly worse.

LOUISA ANNE MEREDITH, SPRING VALE, TASMANIA, 1840s

Louisa Anne Twamley published five books before she married and left England. She dedicated The Romance of Nature; or, The Flower Seasons Illustrated, *published in 1836 when she was 24 years old, to 'the poet Wordsworth'. It must have been something of an embarrassment to him. She illustrated long, romantic poems with bright, harsh paintings of English wildflowers. But the books were popular. Each ran through several printings or editions and there were re-issues by other publishers.*

Charles Meredith, Louisa's cousin, returned to England on a visit in 1838. He had gone to Tasmania as a 10-year-old in 1821 when his family migrated with settlers in a chartered vessel. His father, George, had set up as farmer and businessman with varying success.

Charles and Louisa married in 1839 and sailed for New South Wales where Charles was running sheep and cattle on the shares, a common arrangement when money was short. A landowner provided the pasture and an owner of cattle or sheep ran stock on the land paying with a share of what they produced. In 1840, Charles and Louisa bought Springvale, a farm on the Swan River that empties into Great Oyster Bay on the east coast of Tasmania.

The crash of the 1840s almost ruined them. Charles took a position as police magistrate and later spent over 20 years in the Tasmanian Parliament where he held important posts, Colonial Treasurer and Minister for Lands and Works among them.

Louisa continued to write and paint with great success. She published another 15 books and many articles. Bernard Smith in *European Vision and the South Pacific* lists her as an artist with John Skinner Prout and George French Angas.

Louisa is important, but her writing is like her art: too stiff, bright and harsh. She loses effect in striving. Nevertheless, she saw things as no one else has seen them and some short passages are wonderful.

As we neared Sydney [she wrote in 1839] the remarkable clearness of the atmosphere particularly struck me, in looking at distant houses or other objects, everything, however remote, seeming to have such a clean, distinct outline, so different to the diffused effect of an English landscape... The bright white villas seemed almost to cut into their surrounding trees, so sharp their corners appeared.

The quotes are from *My Home in Tasmania; or, Nine Years in Australia*, published in New York in 1853. The wattle Louisa likes so much is *Acacia dealbata*, the Silver Wattle. She brings the perhaps extinct Thylacine into everyday life.

I have never seen the lovely common wattles grow so luxuriantly or form such ornamental trees and groves, as at Spring Vale; and I often thought, if I could give a sly rub to Aladdin's glorious old lamp, and order the obedient Genii to transport some of the graceful golden-fringed trees into certain pretty gardens and shrubberies at home, how enraptured the beholders would be! Nothing can be more beautiful than some of them; tall and elegant, from twenty to forty feet high, thick with the delicate "sensitive plant" foliage, feathery and pendulous; and covered from the very summit to the branches that bend and sweep the ground, with the bright canary-coloured blossoms. Canopies and roofs of gold and jewels, such as dazzled our fancy in old fairy-tales, are no longer fables, when, pushing aside some heavy down-bending bough, we creep beneath...

The tiger is a large powerful animal about the size of the largest sheep-dog, but more muscular... The first opportunity I had of noticing the animal alive, was when a shepherd in the neighbourhood came to show us one about two-thirds grown which he had caught in a snare. Having killed the mother and caught the cub, he came to show his prize, and receive the usual tribute of money or tobacco, which is always given for a tiger killed or taken. He had the animal secured by a chain and collar, and when it was to be carried off, clipped a strong bag very adroitly over its head and shoulders, pushed the hind legs in, and fastened it. I pitied the unhappy beast most heartily, and would fain have begged for more gentle usage for him; but I was compelled to acknowledge some coercion necessary as, when I softly stroked his back (after taking the precaution of engaging his teeth in the discussion of a piece of meat), I was in danger of having my hand snapped off.

I obtained a place for this tiger in Sir Eardley Wilmot's collection; but its untamable ferocity and savageness resisted all endeavours to civilize and tame it, and, in consequence, the carefully-stuffed skin was eventually preserved, instead of the living form of my infantile protégé.

I believe the tigers are truly untamable, and in that respect if in no other, merit the name sometimes give them of Native Hyena; at least, I know several instances in which young ones have been kept and reared up kindly (chained, of necessity); but they never could be approached with safety, even by those who daily fed them; and so, on the whole, are perhaps ill adapted for pets.

Their colour is very light brown, handsomely marked across the hind-quarters with ten or twelve straight bands of black, the hindmost ones about an inch wide on the top of the back, and tapering off on either side. The stripes become narrower and less distinct as they approach the shoulders, where they cease entirely. The head is much like that of a dog, and would be far from ugly were its expression less savage. The ears are short, open, broad, and erect and look very soft; but I did not attempt to touch them, my previous attentions having been so rudely repulsed. The feet are like those of a dog, and the legs thick and muscular; but the tiger is by no means so swift as its appearance would indicate.

The common pace of the tiger is a measured steady canter, and, from various anecdotes I have heard, it appears that they pursue the object of their chase wholly by scent, and win (literally) "in the long run" by their endurance. On one occasion, Mr. Adam Amos, of Swan Port, had made his way, by a new track, to the top of the encompassing tier of mountains which separate the Swan Port district from the interior; after he had travelled for some time along the ridge of one of the numerous narrow steep "saddles" as they are termed, among the hills, the ground became so rocky that the fat cattle he was driving could not proceed any further, and he and his party encamped for the night. The next morning, about daybreak, they prepared to return, and were getting breakfast, when a brush kangaroo came along the ridge where they were and hopped past, within a few yards of their fire. In ten minutes after this, a female tiger came cantering along in the same line, with her nose to the ground, scenting out the kangaroo and passed round the fire exactly in the same track, not noticing the cattle-party, who were observing the chase with some curiosity. About twenty minutes now elapsed, when two young tiger-whelps appeared, holding the same course, and, passing round the fire, went on after their mother, who, with her steady pace, would finally run down the more swift but less enduring kangaroo, and the cubs, following on her track, if not actually "in at the death" were no doubt in excellent time for the dinner.

FRIEDRICH WILHELM LUDWIG LEICHHARDT.
LYND RIVER. NORTH QUEENSLAND. 1845

More than any explorer, Leichhardt went out in search of himself. He was born in Trebatsch (then in Prussia) southeast of Berlin on 23 October 1813, the sixth of nine children. A brilliant student, after high school he attended Berlin University, where he studied philology, especially Sanskrit and Indo-European languages.

He transferred to a university in Göttingen, southwest of Berlin, where he met John Nicholson. They became such good friends Leichhardt heeded his advice to switch from language to science. With William Nicholson, John's brother, Leichhardt later studied in England, then at a university in Paris. When natural science called for exploration in Australia, William paid Leichhardt's fare to Sydney and gave him £200 (equal now to $125,000). He had been supporting Leichhardt, who had no money, for years.

When he arrived in Sydney in February 1842, Leichhardt did not seek work. He sometimes acted as a private tutor, with a grounding in Greek, Latin, English, French, ancient languages, German language and literature, Hebrew, philosophy, religion, history, mathematics, physics, natural history, geography, political ecomony and medicine. He was probably the best-educated man in New South Wales, but mostly he wandered the bush in search of plants, insects and rocks. He quartered at the army barracks. Robert Lynd, in charge of the barracks, had scientific interests and he replaced William Nicholson as Leichhardt's benefactor.

Leichhardt took a boat to the Hunter River in September 1842, bought a horse and learnt bushcraft by making collecting trips. He wore a black top hat on which he pinned insects, leaves and flowers. He twisted vines around it, hooked specimens in his hair under it. When he doffed his hat, there was a shower of leaves and petals. He made his way up through New England, on to the Darling Downs and beyond. On the Downs, he met David Archer and stayed with him on one of his stations, an excellent companion for a prospective bushman. David was one of the adventurous Archer family who opened up the Burnett River and Peak Range country and established a chain of stations along the Fitzroy River.

From Archer's station, Leichhardt wrote to 'My Dearest Brother-in-law' on 2 February 1844, telling, among much more, of the variety of Australian timber:

I was asked some time ago by the French Museum to supply for Paris a collection of various timbers of the colony. I have tried to comply with this invitation and have collected about 130 pieces of wood, one foot long and an inch to 3 inches wide. If you consider how few varieties of trees compose our forests at home you will be astounded when I tell you that about 120 of these trees are to be found in a diameter of half a mile. Hundreds of these belong to the dense, fertile mountain and river districts, whereas 20 to 25 form the open forest. This forest cannot be classified like at home — Scotch fir — or pine, oak or beech forests, according to the tree most dominant in it, but these 25 different forest trees are equally mixed; some species being more frequent according to the components of the soil.

At that time, there was talk of an expedition to explore the country between Sydney and Port Essington, the site of the third attempt by Britain to establish a settlement in the far north. Sir Thomas Mitchell was to lead the party. Because of bad blood between Mitchell and Governor Gipps, Gipps found himself conveniently short of money to fund an expedition by Mitchell. Leichhardt hastened to Sydney and organised his own expedition. Private individuals supported him. The party set out from Jimba (Jimbour) Station in the north of the Darling Downs on 1 October 1844. They travelled north up the Comet River, on to the head of the Isaac, up the Burdekin, up the Lynd which Leichhardt named for the barracks master, to its junction with the Mitchell named for Sir Thomas. They turned south and then west across difficult rivers and creeks including the Nicholson named for William, the Roper named for John Roper, one of the party, and then to Port Essington where they arrived on 17 December 1845, many months after even the optimists had presumed them dead.

The journey took 14 months and 17 days. They lived off the land much of the time. Leichhardt drank coffee made from the beans of Kurrajong trees for several months. Those trees belong to the same family as the Cacao tree that produces cocoa beans. Their beans are higher in caffeine than true coffee. He could not eat the flesh of emus that had been feeding on the fruit of Native Apricots, *Pittosporum phillyreoides*. They are so extraordinarily bitter that if one merely brushes one's teeth with a piece of the hard flesh the taste lasts for hours. But they all ate much pigweed, *Portulaca oleraceae*, when they could find it.

On 30 December 1844, when they were on the Comet River south of where it joins the Mackenzie, J. Murphy, one of the party, noted in his

CATARACT GORGE, Launceston
T.E. Chapman, c. 1840, Allport Library and Museum of Fine Arts, State Library of Tasmania

THE DEPOT GLEN, MILPARINKA REGION, New South Wales
Original drawing by Charles Sturt, c.1844, from *Narrative of an Expedition into Central Australia*,
National Library of Australia R355

CURZON ALLPORT ESQ. FISHING IN HUMPHREY'S RIVULET 1844
Mary Morton Allport, Allport Library and Museum of Fine Arts, State Library of Tasmania

SHEOAKS ON THE PLAINS, Challicum, Victoria
Duncan Cooper, c.1850, National Library of Australia R323

MOUNT WELLINGTON, Tasmania
Knud Geelmuyden Bull, 1856, Allport Library and Museum of Fine Arts, State Library of Tasmania

WATERCOLOUR PAINTED FROM THE AUSTRIAN FRIGATE *NOVARA* ON 18 NOVEMBER 1858
Emily Macarthur [F. Selleny was master of the frigate], National Libarary of Australia R11334

TWOFOLD BAY, New South Wales
Lieutenant George Austin Woods, 1860s, Mitchell Library, State Library of New South Wales

journal 'Potolacca camp Here we find in great abundance potolacca, a plant having a fleshy leaf and which gives us an excellent salad eaten with Emu oil and mustard'.

Back in Sydney by sea on 25 March 1846, Leichhardt and his party were acclaimed as national heroes. Money flowed in from the government and a testimonial. It was certainly a deserved tribute: it was an amazing journey.

John Gilbert, the naturalist, did not share in the glory. He was speared to death in a night attack by Aborigines near the Gulf of Carpentaria. It was a revenge killing. The two blacks with the expedition had raped women.

Leichhardt used much of his share of the money in fitting out an expedition to cross Australia from east to west. Unaccountable finds of cattle in Western Australia that had not come from the Swan River settlement led to the belief that there was a watered route across the continent from the Darling to the Swan. Sturt's experiences in sandy wastes and genuine deserts upset the theory. But Leichhardt believed that by following the well-watered tablelands up into Queensland till he got above the central deserts, he could cut southwest across good country to Perth. Foolishly he set out from the Darling Downs with 108 sheep, 270 goats, 40 bullocks, 6 white

ONE TREE PLAIN, north of Hay in the Riverina
H.G.H. Sandeman, 1882, from *Gone out to Australia*, MS3628a, National Library of Australia

men, 2 Aborigines, one the troublemaker of the first trip, horses, mules and sheep dogs. They ran into heavy rain on the Mackenzie River and all contracted malaria. Leichhardt had not stocked a medicine chest and he had one small phial of quinine. They lay helpless beside the river for weeks while the livestock wandered away. They returned sick and defeated to Russell's Cecil Plains, their starting point. Of some 450 animals that they set out with, they returned with 10 horses and 9 mules.

After recovering his health, Leichhardt fitted out another party for the same east–west crossing. This time he took 5 Europeans, 2 Aborigines from the Newcastle area, 50 bullocks, 20 mules and several horses. They left Cecil Plains on 14 March 1848 bound for 'the setting sun' and disappeared.

In 1980, Gordon Connell published *The Mystery of Ludwig Leichhardt*, a thorough examination of all evidence. It seems certain that Leichhardt abandoned the trip and tried to come home through present Tennant Creek and down the rivers that supply Lake Eyre, before turning east. At Wantata Waterhole in southwest Queensland, filled when the Diamantina River floods, Aborigines killed seven of the party. Once again, the Aboriginal members had interfered with local women. According to Aboriginal stories, the eighth man, whom Connell identified as Kelly a station hand, had abandoned the party farther north. He lived with an Aboriginal group and fathered two or three children.

It is fortunate that Leichhardt submitted his story of the first journey to a London publisher between the first and second trips. *Journal of an Overland Expedition in Australia, from Moreton Bay to Port Essington, a distance of upward of 3000 miles, during the years 1844–1845* is an outstanding work. I quote a passage about his delight in the northern sky. They are on the Lynd River on the night of 3 June 1845.

> Sleeping in the open air at night, with a bright sky studded with its
> stars above us, we were naturally led to observe more closely the
> hourly changes of the heavens; and my companions became curious
> to know the names of those brilliant constellations, with which
> nightly observation had now, perhaps for the first time, made them
> familiar. We had reached a latitude which allowed us not only to see
> the brightest stars of the southern, but, also of the northern
> hemisphere, and I shall never forget the intense pleasure I
> experienced, and that evinced by my companions, when I first called
> them, about 4 o'clock in the morning, to see Ursa Major. The starry
> heaven is one of those great features of nature, which enter

unconsciously into the composition of our souls. The absence of stars gives us painful longings, the nature of which we frequently do not understand, but which we call home sickness: — and their sudden re-appeareance touches us like magic, and fills us with delight. Every new moon also was hailed with an almost superstitious devotion, and my Blackfellows vied with each other to discover its thin crescent, and would be almost angry with me when I strained my duller eyes in vain to catch a glimpse of its faint light in the brilliant sky which succeeds the setting of the sun. The questions: where were we at the last new moon? how far have we travelled since? and where shall we be at the next? — were invariably discussed amongst us; calculations were made as to the time that would be required to bring us to the end of our journey, and there was no lack of advice offered as to what should, and ought to be done.

GODFREY CHARLES MUNDY, SYDNEY, 1846

Godfrey Mundy was the eldest son of a major general; his mother was the daughter of the first Baron Rodney who defeated the French fleet off Domenica in the Windward Islands in 1782. So it was natural for Godfrey to enter the army as an ensign when he was about 17 years old in 1821 — it is not certain when he was born.

Mundy was decorated during service in India and rapidly gained rank. After service in Canada, he came to Sydney in June 1846 as deputy-adjutant-general of the military forces with the rank of lieutenant colonel. Returning to England in 1851, he served as under-secretary in the War Office during the Crimean War, and then he was appointed Lieutenant Governor of Jersey in the Channel Islands. He died in London in 1860.

Mundy wrote two books that ran through several editions and were translated into German and Swedish. He illustrated both with his own excellent sketches. The first, published in 1832, was *Pen and Pencil Sketches, being the Journal of a tour in India*. The second, published in three volumes in 1852, was *Our Antipodes: or Residence and Rambles in the Australasian Colonies*.

Mundy was a sound observer. I quote from his descriptions of June and July 1846.

> Sydney is, I think, more exclusively English in its population than either Liverpool or London. Were it not for an occasional orange-tree in full bloom, or fruit in the back yard of some of the older cottages, or a flock of little green parrots whistling as they alight for a moment on a housetop, one might fancy himself at Brighton or Plymouth...
>
> I dined this day with my respected chief, Lieutenant-General Sir Maurice O'Connell, at his beautiful villa of Tarmons [at Potts Point]; and I mention the circumstance merely to have an opportunity of remarking, that there were brisk coal fires burning in both dining and drawing-room, and that the general appliances of the household, the dress of the guests and the servants, were as entirely English as they could have been in London. The family likeness between an Australian and an Old Country dinner-party became, however, less striking when I found myself sipping

doubtfully, but soon swallowing with relish, a plate of wallabi-tail soup, followed by a slice of boiled schnapper, with oyster sauce. A haunch of kangaroo venison helped to convince me I was not in Belgravia. A delicate wing of wonga-wonga pigeon and bread sauce, with a dessert of plantains and loquots, guavas and mandarine oranges, pomegranates and cherimoyas, landed my imagination at length fairly at the Antipodes...

The drive along the southern shore of the harbour to the Heads or entrance to Port Jackson, and thence back to Sydney by the "old South Head Road," about thirteen miles, has hardly its equal anywhere for picturesque beauty.

The harbour itself rudely resembles, in its projections and indentations, the form of an oak leaf — or, to enlist a monstrous simile, it may be likened to the gaping mouth of some huge antidiluvian saurian, the bluffs and inlets representing the teeth and the interstices between them...

The road to the Heads, after passing over the neck of the peninsula on which Darlinghurst is built, dives into a small valley, crossing the head of Rushcutter's Bay; then rising again, and again falling, it traverses a series of these promontories and coves, alike, yet full of variety — the hills well clothed with timber though sandy, the valleys rich in alluvial soil, and covered with wild brush or reeds — or, more usefully, with the crops of the market-gardeners of the town.

The views of the harbour from the higher points of the road, over the tufted tops of the forest sloping down to its extreme brink, and the glimpses of its glittering waters between the boles of the enormous gum-trees, are truly beautiful. So completely is this great port shut in from the ocean, that I know of no spot a mile within its gates from which the stranger would even surmise the position of its mouth — were it not for the tall bluff of the North Head, which lifts a hundred feet of its sheer wall-like profile above any of the interior headlands. I cannot describe botanically the trees, plants, and shrubs among which the eye of the rider wanders, well pleased, on either side of the road. The Eucalyptus, and other gums of infinite variety, form the larger growth of "the bush". But there are trees, distantly resembling in aspect the European ash, the holly, larch, and myrtle, with a luxuriant undergrowth of ferns and lichens, and a multitude of flowering shrubs clad in spring and autumn with blossoms so lovely in form and hue as to justify the name of "Botany", conferred by Dr. Solander as a title of honour on the neighbouring bay.

HENRY TURNBULL, NORTH OF THE MACKENZIE RIVER, QUEENSLAND, 1847

Henry Turnbull was working as Assistant Superintendent of Horse Stock for the Australian Agricultural Company's holding at Scone (or as stable boy wrote someone who did not like him), when he applied to join Leichhardt's second expedition. Leichhardt refused his first application, but later, impressed by the young man, he agreed to take him if he could get release from the Company. Turnbull simply absconded and rode hard to catch up with the party, then about 300 kilometres north. The savage Master and Servant Act was then in force. The manager sent a man after Turnbull, but Leichhardt would not give him back.

After the grim weeks on the Mackenzie River with every man down with fever, perhaps malaria, perhaps dengue, perhaps something else, all made a brief recovery. They crossed the river and continued north, but the fever returned as diarrhoea and a strange general weakness. They turned back without even beginning the westward journey.

Turnbull did not keep a diary on the trip. The following quote is from a talk he gave in Launceston 11 years later. It refers to the country northeast of present Emerald in central Queensland where they were pleased to be on their way again after crossing the Mackenzie.

> I wish I could do justice to the beautiful country through which we now passed — my feeble description will fall very far short of what it really was. For upwards of 100 miles we passed through a most splendid, open country, consisting of plains and downs — plains stretching out as far as the eye could reach on one side, and beautiful grassy slopes running down from a long and high range of mountains on the other. With only a tree to be seen every 500 or 600 yards, the whole face of the country was covered with the finest grasses and richest herbage, with wildflowers of every tint and colour.
>
> Here for the first and almost only time we saw plenty of game. Kangaroos would bound by us in scores at a time, and frequently ten or a dozen emus would march up to within 30 yards of the party, stretching our their long necks towards us as if to ask us our reason for invading their wide and beautiful domains. Then at the least

movement of one of us toward them they would go "on the wings of
the wind" across the vast plain, never stopping in their onward flight
till they seemed but a speck upon the horizon.

This country was evidently well watered as we passed several fine
streams running down from the mountains and emptying the waters
into the vast plains beyond. We also saw numbers of wild fowl and
aquatic birds — the ibis, that sacred bird worshipped by the ancients
both black and white, the large pelican, black swans, geese of two
kinds. One of the geese is a very pretty little bird going in small
flocks of six or seven, the make having a most beautiful plumage,
the female of a dark-grey colour. They were not larger than an
ordinary black duck but much more plump-looking. Then there
were the teal, the black duck, the common wood duck or widgeon,
and also the whistling duck, a very pretty bird peculiar to the northwest coast of New Holland. They go in large flocks and make a
strange whistling noise. They roost on the trees and are delicious
eating. Then we had the partridge pigeon and the bronzewing, but as
we could seldom get more than three of four together we did not
kill many — they made in fact too expensive shooting. Then there
was the spendid bustard, mis-called 'turkey". We often shot these
and they were delicious eating — the emu too when not too old we
found very good and many a hearty meal we made from them. An
emu steak, especially when seasoned with that prince of sauces
"sharp hunger", is not to be despised.

We also saw the real turkey of New Holland, but only shot one.
This is a very strange bird about the size of a small domestic turkey,
of a black colour with a red wattle on the neck. The habits of these
birds are very singular. They collect together (how, has never been
correctly ascertained) an immense heap of dried leaves and wood and
then, depositing their eggs in holes, cover them up and leave them to
be hatched by the heat caused by the fermentation of such a large
body of vegetable matter. I am not in the least degree exaggerating
when I state that some of these heaps contained from 30 to 40 cart-
loads of rubbish. The eggs were of a dark-grey colour and about half
as large again as a goose's egg. They were not bad eating though
rather strong. It is evident that more than one bird lays in the same
nest, as I have known 150 eggs taken out of one heap.

JANE CAVERHILL, BERRYBANK, WESTERN DISTRICTS OF VICTORIA, c.1848

Jane Caverhill's unpublished reminiscences are in the State Library of Victoria. She was the daughter of Joseph Mack and Anna Austin. James Austin, Anna's uncle, a farm labourer in Somerset, was sentenced to transportation for seven years for stealing beehives and honey. A fellow labourer, John Earle, was sentenced with him.

Once they regained their freedom, still in partnership, Austin and Earle established a ferry across the Derwent River in Tasmania and built an inn near it. Austin went into farming and, by 1823, he claimed to have the biggest orchard in the colony as well as many cattle and sheep. His success earned him more grants of land.

Two of Austin's nephews went to Tasmania to join him. They liked the country so well that they induced their parents, three brothers, among them Thomas, notorious for his breeding of rabbits, and their sister Anna to emigrate. Thomas especially prospered and set up the grand Barwon Park near Geelong in Victoria. Then he lived the life of a sporting English gentleman. In 1859, he took delivery of 24 wild rabbits from England, cared for on the journey by his nephew named Mack. The rabbits so prospered that Austin was soon giving pairs to his friends. Anna Austin married Joseph Mack at New Norfolk, Tasmania in 1836. They too went to Victoria and bought a station at Berrybar in the Lismore Plain north of Lake Corangamite. They had 10 children.

Jane Caverhill tells what she and her sisters wore:

> Very thick lacing boots out of doors and substantial leather shoes indoors, white drawers almost to the tops of our boots, white stockings, round housemaids' skirts and very big holland pinafores with holes for the arms and falling straight down.

Every night the girls had to put their hair in curl papers. But they had fun when they could get away from the homestead and do things that Aboriginal children taught them:

> The orchids called by us "Parson & Pulpit" [probably a *Corybas* species] were what we deemed treasures to find and in the early spring many an hour was spent in digging for "murnongs" [Yam

Daisies, *Microseris lanceolata*]. It has a white tuberous root which we
used to prise as a great delicacy. It has an earthy taste and was very
sticky not any bigger than a hasel nut — I would like to taste one
now!!... From the wattle trees gum used to exude and every morning
those trees were visited to see what they brought forth in the night,
sometimes we used to try to enter into a compact and leave them
alone for a few days and get big pieces but found boys were not to
be trusted up to the last hour.

WILLIAM CARRON, CAPE YORK, 1848

William Carron came to Australia in 1844 bringing more plants for Alexander Macleay's 'botanists' paradise' at Elizabeth Bay. In 1848 Edmund Kennedy, the outstanding young explorer, selected him to go as botanist on an expedition up Cape York.

It was an impossible assignment. Kennedy was instructed to head up the coast from Rockingham Bay, replenish his stores from a ship waiting at the top of the Cape, explore the west coast to the southern end of the Gulf of Carpentaria, and then cut southeast to the Belyando River west of present Clermont (the northernmost point of Mitchell's 1845–46 expedition). From there, his exploration over, he was to bring his party home as best he could. They were expected to be out for 18 months.

Kennedy took riding horses, packhorses, drays and a mob of sheep to drive through vine-entangled rainforest in the wettest part of Australia. No one had any idea what the country was like. The few misleading descriptions had been made by sailors from their ships. The modern sugar town of Tully is on Rockingham Bay, the starting point. It measures its annual rainfall in metres, up to 7.8. The higher country is even wetter.

Because of sickness, Kennedy left seven men at Weymouth Bay, where there is still no settlement, in charge of Carron, and went on with Jacky Jacky, a young Aboriginal from the Hunter Valley, and three of the fittest whites, one of whom, William Costigan, shot himself in the shoulder loading a packhorse. Kennedy left him in the care of his two companions at Shelburne Bay and tried to make a dash for help with Jacky Jacky who was an amazing bushman, even by exceptional Aboriginal standards.

Aborigines attacked them and speared Kennedy. Jacky Jacky cut out the spears and nursed Kennedy in vain. After he died, Jacky Jacky dodged the Aborigines who chased him, put Kennedy's papers in a hollow stump and made his way to the meeting place where he cooeed to the *Ariel* in the shelter of Albany Island.

With absolute confidence, Jacky Jacky took the captain back to Shelburne Bay where no one could be found, then to Weymouth Bay where William Carron and William Goddard, a convict in search of his freedom, were barely alive. The others had died and they had no strength to bury them. Later, Jacky Jacky took a land party in to recover Kennedy's papers.

He had hidden them leaving no traces so that local Aborigines could not find them, yet he found them unerringly in hundreds of square kilometres of rainforest. The wet and the insects had destroyed most of them.

William Carron lost his samples and most of his records. He published *Narrative of an Expedition* in 1849. From that book I quote his reaction to some of the plants – he was the first white man to note them.

Of the plants Carron describes, *Calamus*, is one of the lawyer palms, possibly the well-known savage Wait-a-while, *Calamus muelleri*, though its fronds are usually yellowish, not dark green; the climbing plant like ivy is Climbing Pandanus, *Freycineta scandens*; the lactescent tree Milkwood, *Cerbera manghas*; the small tree with yellow flowers Golden Guinea Tree, *Dillenia alata*. The species of *loranthus* on acacia trees was probably *Amyema sanguineum*, a truly spectacular mistletoe usually growing on *Melaleuca*; the scarlet passion flower is now known as Red Passion Flower, *Passiflora aurantia*, and the water lily is the Giant Water Lily, *Nymphaea gigantea*, a favourite of modern American gardens. The little marsupial was a young Spotted Cuscus, plentiful in New Guinea, rare on Cape York.

> [25 May 1868] I proceeded along the edge of a mangrove swamp for a short distance, and entered a fresh water swamp about a mile from the beach, covered with very thick scrub, composed of large trees of the genus <u>melaleuca</u>, running for the most part from forty to fifty feet high. Here also I first found a strong growing climbing palm (<u>calamus</u>), throwing up a number of shoots from its roots, many of them 100 feet long, and about the thickness of a man's finger, with long pinnated leaves, covered with sharp spines, long tendrils growing out of the stem alternately with the leaves, many of them twenty feet long, covered with strong spines slightly curved downward, by which the shoots are supported in their rambling growth. They lay hold of the surrounding bushes and branches of trees, often covering the tops of the tallest, and turning in all directions...
>
> The leaves of this palm resemble those of the <u>livistona</u>, being about three feet long, of a dark green colour, and cut at regular spaces to the mid-rib. The shoots are remarkably tough, and I afterwards found were used by the natives in making their canoes. These canoes are small, and constructed of bark, with a small sapling on each side to strengthen them, the ends of which are tied together with these shoots. They are jointed, and resemble the common cane

used in basket-making, and when cut they exhibit the small pores in a similar manner...

On the beach, too, just above high water mark, was a beautiful spreading, lactescent tree, about twenty feet high, belonging to the natural order apocyneae, with alternate extipulate, broad lanceolate leaves, six to eight inches long, and producing terminal spikes of large, white, sweet-scented flowers, resembling those of the white nerium oleander, but much larger. I also met with a tree about twenty feet high belonging to the natural order dilleniaceae, with large spreading branches, producing at the axilla of the laves from three to five large yellow flowers, with a row of red appendages surrounding the carpels.

June 15... I found a beautiful species of loranthus, growing on acacia trees, and producing on its long pendulous shoots, abundance of beautiful scarlet flowers; the tube of the coralla was about two inches long, very short limbs, with long lanceolate glossy leaves. This most interesting parasite, covering the acacia trees, when in flower forms a most gorgeous sight; presenting a beautiful contrast to the dull foliage of the surrounding trees. I also found a scarlet passion flower, very beautiful, with three lobed glaneous leaves; and a nymphoea, (water lily), growing in the water holes and small creeks, producing large purple flowers, and pellate leaves; besides a number of other new and interesting plants.

Mr. Wall succeeded in obtaining a specimen of a beautiful little marsupial animal, resembling an opossum in form, but not larger than the common rat, the colour pure white, with very small black spots...

ENGELBERT HAHN AND JOHANN PETER FRAUENFELDER, NEW SOUTH WALES, 1849

*Numbers of German immigrants came to Melbourne and Sydney in the late 1840s,
encouraged by those who had gone to South Australia. A special group came to
Sydney in 1849, vintners and their families from the Rhine provinces: 170 aboard* Beulah
on 4 April, 160 on Parland *on 5 July and 30 on* Harmony *on 23 September.*

The German immigrants wrote enthusiastic letters home urging friends
and relatives to come. Apparently, they had good contracts and good masters.
Indian and Chinese labourers, recruited on exploitive rates of pay that
sounded good in their homelands, fell foul of the Master and Servant Act.
This bound a worker to a master under threat of gaol for a term fixed by a
signed document. Descriptions of absconders were circulated in newspapers
and on posters and they were hunted down like criminals.

Engelbert Hahn, a carpenter, came on *Parland* as a vinedresser. He went
to work for Thomas Icely, a member of the Legislative Council and a grazier,
at Carcoar. His magnificent Coombing Park of 10,000 hectares ran 25,000
merino ewes of a quality that influenced merino breeding in more than one
colony. It carried well-bred Hereford and Durham cattle and a thorough-
bred stud which bred Barb, the winner of the 1866 Melbourne Cup.

On 27 August 1849, Hahn wrote home to his wife's parents in Eltville
on the Rhein River southwest of Frankfurt.

> Compared to Germany, our work is child's play. Here are no
> masters who climb up hay stacks with spy-glasses to see whether the
> workers take a breather. No! Here we work as human beings, and
> not as beasts — as the poor man with you has to work if he wants
> enough bread for himself and his family. Here we eat no blackbread,
> our bread is made from wheat and resembles cake. Also, here is no
> official, who, if a poor man bakes cake once a year (and we eat it
> daily), has inquiries made lest he should by any chance receive poor
> relief. Not here! Anyone with a strong pair of arms can assure
> himself of an adequate living...
>
> Oh, there are very many Englishmen who arrived here poor, 12
> to 14 years ago and are now rich people... Come, all of you, who can

possibly arrange it. Leave Germany, for there you are and remain slaves; even if you broke the yoke of tyranny you would still be slaves of the aristocrats of money. There are too many in that narrow space to make a livelihood. Come hither, here you find ample space and means of making a living. What man of force and courage could hesitate between here and Germany? There, to be a witness to the grave death-struggle of old ideas, here, full freedom in the truest sense of the world. There, upheaval, religious hatred, partisan fury, revolution among all nations; here, peace, the plough, the sciences, the founding of new cities. There, you are under state despotism, oppression of faith and thought, oriental tyranny, castes and classes, war and mania for destruction; here man is enthroned in his eternal right, free in faith and opinion, as rich as his diligence and as great as his worth make him. Free thought is not suppressed by courts, ministers, priests and censorship. I ask everyone who can possibly come to bid farewell to Germany; not the pleasure-seeking lazy people, but industrious people with a desire and love for work. For the curse of perjury shall be on me, if I do not wish the best of you, my German brothers. Leave the tyrants to their piece of land and seek here a new home and hearth.

Johann Peter Frauenfelder came on Beulah with his seven children. He was from that part of Germany then known as Saxony with Leipzig as its capital. He wrote from the farm of William Walker, east of Mudgee, on 24 June 1849. William Walker prospered more as a merchant and ship owner than grazier, though he maintained an interest in the land he took up as a grant in 1825. Frauenfelder thought the farm was blessed. Aboriginal Australians would not have agreed with him.

Here is God's earth, the same as in Germany, but the soil is fertile and the climate healthy and God's blessing still lies in the earth. In Germany it has risen up in smoke, but here is still an innocent earth. Here have not yet been committed so many sins, not so much innocent blood has yet been shed as in Germany, nor have our fellow-creatures been robbed of their goods and chattels. Here, if you plough one furrow it is not one furrow too many for your neighbour. If emigrants come into this land with many children, no one says: he and his beggarly crew will soon be a burden to the

parish. Here is pleasure in the father of a family with many
children; when they are small they are easily fed, when big they can
work, be of use and have bread and good wages. The drudgery of
working many severe days and nights, as it is in Germany, is not the
custom here. Nature and climate themselves contribute; all the year
the woods and fields are green.

THE BUNYA PINE, Cooyar [north-west of Brisbane]
Conrad Martens, Feb. 13th 1852, Mitchell Library, State Library of New South Wales

NEHEMIA BARTLEY. TASMANIA. 1849. CLARENCE RIVER NSW. 1850s

Nehemia Bartley wrote two books, Opals and Agates: or, Scenes under the Southern Cross and the Magelhans, *published in Brisbane in 1892 and* Australian Pioneers and Reminiscences. *published in 1896 after his death.*

Bartley came to Hobart in 1849, a young Englishman with 'rich relatives settled in Australia'. For one of those relatives he travelled as supercargo on *Eudora* carrying Tasmanian timber, potatoes, onions and portable houses to the Californian goldfields. Bartley sold several of the houses off the wharf at Honolulu and was paid in a strange mixture of money: 'doubloons of Mexico, Spain, Bolivia, Columbia, Ecuador; dollars of Spain, Mexico, and United States; coins of Russia, France, and Germany'.

Bartley tried digging for gold on the Turon and, when that was unsuccessful, he built a bakery there and brought up a yellow cart from Sydney with sheaves of wheat painted on its sides to deliver the bread round the fields. He received a regular remittance from England, but it was from his deceased parents' estate. He was not a remittance man.

He tried banking, droving, and then became a successful agent and merchant with storerooms and wharf on the Brisbane River. Bartley married Sarah Barton, sister of Edmund Barton, Australia's first Prime Minister.

Bartley's prose is old-fashioned and sometimes purple. Both books peter out into disconnected notes, but there is much new observation and information in them.

I quote a description of Tasmania from *Opals and Agates*, and an unusual reference to settlers on the Clarence River from *Australian Pioneers and Reminiscences*.

[Tasmania, 1849] I was delighted, once more, to find myself amid the scenery and climate of Tasmania. Some people prefer New Zealand to it, but I do not. New Zealand is damper all over, and more "muggy" in the north part, than Tasmania, which has the climate of France, the clear sky of Italy, and a dry pure air beyond the utmost flights of either place. It is true that no mountain in Van Diemen's Land exceeds 5,000 feet in height, while New Zealand has them up to 13,000 feet: but what of that? Does anyone prefer the

gloomy grandeur of Norway's "fells" and fiords, to sunny France
and the sylvan beauty of Languedoc and Provence? Are not
Clermont, and the Auvergne mountains high enough for all
purposes of scenic beauty? I think so, and, therefore, I prefer
Tasmania, which, in lake and mountains, surpasses, for beauty,
anything in France, or Britain, save the vivid green hues, which are,
however, otherwise made up for. Nothing in England, in the way of
mountain and water, comes up to the bold outline of "St. Paul's
Dome", a rounded peak, of 3,370 feet, as it looks down on, and
contrasts with, the silvery surface of the South Esk. Tasmania has
its lake districts, 15 miles by five, but it is not the prettiest. Lake St.
Clair has an area of about 10,000 acres, and about nine miles long, by
two in width; its waters, blue as sapphire, are watched, at the head of
the volcanic gorge, which it fills, by the twin guardians Mounts Ida
and Olympus, as amethystine in their hue, as the lower hills are in
beryl tint, and with thin, fleecy clouds travelling over, and varying
the light and shade from time to time; no scene of greater
enchantment, outside the tropics, could be imagined.

[Clarence River, New South Wales, 1850s] In the fifties the
lower river was settled by a number of Highlanders imported by
Dr. Lang. They made excellent colonists, steady, shrewd, and
industrious. A large proportion of the first generation never learned
to speak English, and for years, even in the late seventies, Gaelic was
the most prevalent language of many neighbourhoods, especially the
islands of Shoal Bay. Many Germans, too, chiefly from the
Rheinland and Bavaria, settled on the river. These also formed a
valuable element. They introduced the cultivation of the vine, and if
the vineyards of the Clarence cannot pretend to vie in reputation
with those of Albury, the Hunter, and Inverell, they are certainly
neither less productive nor less profitable to their owners. The
mixture of Celtic and Teutonic blood ought, combined with the
warm Eastern Australian climate, to produce a race-type which, in
a century or so, will be worth the notice of ethnologists, and will
reward their study by supplying some new facts and inferences.

WILLIAM MOODIE, WANDO VALE,
WESTERN DISTRICTS OF VICTORIA, 1850

In his 'Reminiscences of Pioneering Days in Victoria', a manuscript held by the State Library of Victoria, William Moodie says 'I can claim to be one of Victoria's very oldest colonists'. He arrived in Melbourne on 1 January 1841: 'I have a distinct recollection of landing at Liardet's beach and seeing my mother carried on a sailor's back'.

Perhaps Moodie remembered his mother telling him about it; he was seven and a half months old when they arrived. His mother and father were Glaswegians ordered by a doctor to seek a milder climate when his father became ill.

Moodie's father's health improved in Melbourne where he opened an unstated business, and then in 1850 he decided to seek experience on the land. His mother's brother, John Robertson, who had landed in Hobart in 1841 with 'half a crown and sixpence', had saved enough money by 1843 to buy Wando Vale, one of the choice properties of the magnificent Western District where so many Scotsmen made so much money. So in May 1850 the Moodie family of mother, father, daughter and William set out from Melbourne in a spring cart drawn by Sam, a horse that had pulled a baker's cart. On the call 'Baker!' he stopped dead for the time taken to deliver a loaf. 'Us youngsters... just to break the monotony of the journey were prepared to convey the signal in a whisper loud enough for Sam to hear & he never failed to act'.

William was 10 years old when they arrived at Wando Vale, near Casterton on the Glenelg River.

> Wando Vale at last, to me who had been looking forward so long to the place so much talked about in our family my expectations were great, but the realizations were greater who could say otherwise looking from the snug site of the homestead nestling among the garden trees & a collection of native trees that my uncle was very proud of, and also a strip of stately red gums that fringed the edges of the little creek running through the garden, and such a garden, you would think that everything that could grow was there & though so late in the season there was still a fair quantity of fruit on some of the trees and plenty of grapes, I have eaten luscious grapes there in June, that for inside the garden fence, now step out to view Gods handiwork, look east & north and you get a picture in nature with the horizon for a

frame and the tableland with its forests of timber as though it were a battlement to protect the timberless though rich hills & hollows that make it so pretty. I loved Wando Vale in its native state...

The first work I got was the hand weeding of a native Grass plot that my uncle took great care of to preserve the Kangaroo & other good grasses. the work was not hard but tiresome. a table knife being the tool used...

I liked the look of Wando Vale with a sort of solemn grandeur in its density of timber and long rough grass made more picturesque by mobs of kangaroos from 8 ft high downwards. The most I ever counted in one mob was 88. from a dozen to 20 was about the usual size of mobs. always one & sometimes more old men in each mob these showed signs of being old Warriors with their ears split in half a dozen splits.

Eastern Quolls were about in extraordinary numbers for two or three years. William enjoyed trapping and poisoning them; after all he was saving the fruit, vegetables and poultry. One night he got 300 by strewing pieces of liver laced with strychnine in the garden and setting several types of traps outside the fence where the working dogs could have picked up baits.

On 11 September 1863, Moodie bought Wando Vale, 640 acres freehold (260 hectares), 19,000 acres Crown Land (7,700 hectares) with 18,000 sheep, 40 head of cattle and 12 horses. In a few years the selectors came, so he bought a station on the Bogan River in New South Wales and another in Queensland. On one trip from Hay to Booligal in the 1870s drought, they drove 'through 50 mile of wild turkies the season was bad out back and they were flocking in after feed on the old man plain'.

However, Moodie held Wando Vale for more than 50 years. He married in June 1866 and had 12 children. 'The Wando Vale garden grew to be famous under Mrs Moodie's care... the old house was added to occasionally & later on the Big House was built.'

For 40 years, William judged at merino sheep shows, four times at the Sydney Royal. He thought Wando Vale, as he improved it,

... is more nearly what God intended it for. the first race have gone as have the giant sheoaks on the two knolls near the station where their camp was. and where I got my first experience of a real live native camp... the grasses have very much changed for the better as far as increasing the carrying capability is concerned but the old time herbage used to grow fine healthy sheep and lambs. much bigger animals than now.

1851—1860

HENRY EDWIN WILLIAMS, CHANDLER FALLS,
NEW SOUTH WALES, 1851

*A journal that he kept from 14 September 1849 to 2 May 1853 seems to be all that
is known of Henry Williams. He was apparently a surgeon, though he did not practise
in Australia. He attended passengers on the way out, including a sick baby that died
despite his attentive care. However, at one time in Australia, disturbingly, he was
asked to attend a woman in childbirth but he refused:*

[18 June 1851] This morning a man came for me in a great hurry
to go to a labour 25 miles distant; however I got out of it, and as
I prophesied the woman was safely delivered before the messenger
returned. It is strange that I should have been for so many years
haunted by these cases; and by some chance I am constantly falling
in their way or they in mine and it is an affair I utterly detest!

After travelling to Melbourne and New Zealand, Williams spent some time
in Sydney where he met a grazier named Walker who held Aberfoyle, a big
run 40 kilometres northeast of Armidale. Walker offered him work. They
travelled by steamer to Morpeth on the Hunter River where Walker
engaged two drays, each drawn by 10 bullocks. He loaded the drays with
stores and rode on to his station, leaving Williams in charge of the drays and
drivers. It was a slow trip over difficult tracks. Williams was inexperienced,
the drivers careless. Just south of the Liverpool Range, they let the bullocks
go unhobbled one night and it took five days to find them.

Williams worked as storeman at Aberfoyle for three months, then William
Dangar offered him the job of storekeeper and bookkeeper at Kangaroo
Hills, a station 20 kilometres to the southeast and about 60 kilometres east
of Armidale. He stayed there for 18 months, and then tried his hand at
digging for gold at Bingara. His partner died, the product of eight months'
work was stolen from his tent, and so he left the diggings. As the diary ends,
Williams is working as a barman in the hotel at Scone waiting for word from
William Dangar who was trying to find him a job.

He was frequently unwell as well as unhappy in Australia, although he
wrote often of the flowers and magnificent scenery. On his own and in company, he made long walks in search of gold or to see spectacular views. Here
he tells of a visit to the Chandler Falls where the Chandler River drops into
the Wollomombi River:

[25 September 1851] Early next morning we breakfasted, charged our firearms and prepared for an excursion to the "Carbon Falls", as the black boy calls the place [In some languages a word sounding like 'carbon' or 'gawburn' meant 'big']. After walking and climbing over rocks and up ranges for a considerable time, we became enveloped in a cloud, which covered the top of the range and when we reached the edge of the precipice, much to our disappointment, we saw nothing but what might be conceived to be an enormous cauldron, reeking, the cloud being below us preventing our getting a glimpse of the lands below. We made a fire and sat down to rest after our ascent and soon our disappointment vanished, as an unexpected treat was afforded us. The thunder which had been rumbling around us at intervals for some time became louder and presently the lightning flashed and the thunder roared from the cloud beneath our feet which hung in the awful abyss before us! This was a scene so awfully grand that I cannot with my poor pen attempt a description. On our way back to the hut I killed a couple of "Wonga Wonga" pigeons and on our arrival were glad enough to lie down for the night...

[Next morning] I took a man with a musket, my own double gun and the black boy as guide and made another start. The valleys were delightfully warm and the air scented with the blossoms of numerous mimosas which were in full and luxuriant flower. The air however was considerably cold on the tops of the ranges; at length we arrived at the edge of the gulph and such a scene presented itself as beggars all description. Looking down immediately beneath the edge may be seen the tops of ranges of mountains undulating away into the far distance; another direction affords a view of dense masses of cedar and other trees, which appear like brush wood, and from another point, far distant may be seen plains bounded by the beach and sea. I could with my glass distinctly see the waves breaking on the beach. The mountains beneath appear like ranges of ant hills, although many hundreds of feet high. The height of this fearful precipice on the edge of which I was standing and whose side is almost perpendicular is 16,000 feet above the level of the sea. The grandeur and magnificence of Nature's works are here certainly exhibited in the most sublime manner. This natural wall extends for many miles on either side the point on which I stood.

ELIZA BROWN, YORK TO CHAMPION BAY, WESTERN AUSTRALIA, 1851

Eliza Brown, her husband Thomas and their two children arrived at Gages Roads, Fremantle, as settlers in March 1841. Thomas Brown, as a surveyor of roads, had made some money out of turnpike leases and he had borrowed £2000 from Elizabeth's wealthy father. They landed a Berkshire sow from their ship, Stirling, a cow that had kept them in milk for the whole voyage, and a sick horse. Five mares had their necks broken in a storm when their insubstantial boxes collapsed on them. The charterers had tried to economise.

A ship from Hobart was in port with 400 ewes for sale so the Browns bought them, although they still had to find land, and put them in the care of a shepherd they had brought out with them.

Instead of selecting new land, they bought Grass Dale of 11 square miles (2800 hectares) near York on the Avon River, one of the headwaters of the Swan.

Eliza wrote regularly to her father, William Bussey. The letters are extant and Peter Cowan, Eliza's grandson, edited them as *A Faithful Picture* published by Fremantle Arts Centre Press in 1977. They are newsy, formally loving and difficult to read. Short of paper, she sometimes turned pages side on and wrote across the lines of writing as many did in those days. Her crusty father complained that they were too long. He became increasingly upset that they had not paid him back. Based on wages payable, the amount is equal to $800,000 now. However, apart from the fact that the 1840s depression in New South Wales also depressed the west, there was scarcely any money in circulation. Business had to be arranged on the barter system. Thomas Brown took jobs as surveyor, magistrate and as government resident, but the family always struggled.

They let Grass Dale in 1851 and moved their stock to newly opened country at Champion Bay, now Geraldton. Eliza wrote of the move in the *Inquirer: Western Australian Journal of politics and literature*. I quote from that newspaper.

The extraordinary Cockleshell Gully is north of the Hill River. The second extract refers to the Irwin River country. The Irwin bird is probably the White-eared Honeyeater that has a restricted range in the west. The native food, 'warran', more correctly *warrany*, is *Diascorea hastifolia*, a yam so valuable Aborigines sometimes cultivated it.

[3 September 1851] A little farther on, an astonishing ravine, called the Cockleshell Gulley, forms a barrier to the progress of the traveller, who is obliged to go a considerable round to avoid the precipitous banks. It presents the appearance of an awful chasm or opening in the earth; the ground being flat to the edge of the chasm on both sides. It is not visible at any distance, and coming upon it almost suddenly, the effect is quite startling. Several trees are growing at the bottom of the ravine, which the beholder looks down upon, being far above the highest. After passing the head of this chasm, two or three miles of scrub are travelled over, and the spot for a night's rest is at hand in a sheltered hollow place, a narrow strip of rich soil much below the level of the scrub that surrounds it. Here was a plentiful supply of grass and water; the latter from permanent springs, making the ground moist all round. Mr Brown is of opinion that vines, orange trees, bananas, &c., might be cultivated here, and brought to perfection; and that it is very suitable for the potato. Being so pleased with the sparkling springs, we called them the Diamonds of the Desert. It is about five miles from the sea, which is discernible at the end of the scrub to the westward.

Here we rested, and next day got to the Logue, a very refreshing piece of water, presenting more the appearance of a river than anything I had yet seen, narrow and winding, filled to the brink with excellent tasting water. The place abounded with ducks, some of which fell a prey to our sportsmen. Groves of trees, much like the cypress, are in the vicinity; altogether it was a very pleasant place.

[10 September 1851] We first crossed an extensive flat, containing many thousand acres, upon which there is not a single tree or shrub, and considered by those who have seen it, to be first-rate land for the cultivation of wheat; it was at this time covered with blackened tufts, around which new grass was springing. We let our horses feed as they went slowly along; the way in which they stepped, shewed this to be a very different soil to any we had ridden over before. We could see that it was very deep, from the numerous holes that afford drainage for the water, or rather allow the rain to sink into the soil. There was no native warran on this land. After passing the flat, we came to some land of a different character, more crumbling, and the ground a good deal dug over by natives in procuring their warran. Hillocks and small valleys, with a few trees and shrubs, gave a pleasing variety to the scenery; birds were singing, and there was one with quite a new and peculiarly sweet note, which seems to take the lead in woodland harmony in these parts. We call it the Irwin bird. A little farther on we came to the banks of the river, and looked down upon the water which runs in several small streams along the bed and makes a rippling sound. The banks are steep and wooded, and in the bed of the river, which is very wide, there also some fine trees. After a little examination of the objects around us, we went on about four miles farther over the usual scrub, and as the sun was setting, rode up to a hill that looked a little green towards the top, which may be called Vine Hill, as we found upon it a soil suitable for the cultivation of the vine, dug over by the natives for warran and limestone scattered about, and what suited our purpose, plenty of grass amongst the trees.

WILLIAM HOWITT, VICTORIA, 1852

William Howitt, member of a prominent Quaker family and prolific author, came to Melbourne in September 1852 with his two sons. Two of his brothers had preceded him in 1839: Richard, who spent five years in Victoria, mostly in the bush, then went home to write Impressions of Australia Felix; *and Godfrey who stayed to become an outstanding physician and entomologist in Melbourne.*

William Howitt and his sons went digging for gold and made successful strikes at both Beechworth and Bendigo. He returned to England in 1854 and wrote *Land, Labour and Gold,* based on his Australian experiences, and *The History of Discovery in Australia, Tasmania and New Zealand.* He continued to write in England, then in Rome where he settled in 1870. One son, Alfred William Howitt, stayed on to become even more famous than his father. He bought a farm with his goldfield earnings and quickly made his name as a bushman. He led a party to Lake Eyre in an unsuccessful search for grazing land; he led a Government-sponsored prospecting party to Gippsland in a successful search for gold; and he made three trips to Coopers Creek, one of them to bring home the bodies of Burke and Wills. Little is known of him as an explorer since he was so singularly efficient that he went where he was sent and came home again. Of the country about Coopers Creek where Burke and Wills starved, he said it was so productive that he and his men could have lived there for any length of time.

Howitt spent about 40 years as a public servant, beginning as a magistrate and warden of the goldfields at Gippsland. He spent some years as Secretary for Mines and ended his career as Audit Commissioner and a member of the Public Service Board.

He produced a major study, *The Eucalypt of Gippsland,* and, after his retirement from the public service, he brought together years of work in *The Natives Tribes of South-east Australia* published in London in 1904, a major book still in print.

This quote is from William Howitt's *A Boy's Adventures in the Wilds of Australia,* published in London in 1866. He dedicated it to his son Herbert, stating 'the desire of the author has been to afford to Herbert's contemporaries a reflection, as it were, of his own great enjoyment'.

He certainly enjoyed Australian birds:

The laughing jackass, called the settler's clock, from his exactness in bursting forth with his peal of merriment at the dawning day, raised a loud cachinnation over their heads as they rode on; a score of warbling crows [magpies] woke up and tried again their melodious voices, of which neither themselves nor the hearer is ever tired. A thousand smaller birds took up their incessant chorus, which, though each uttered only some short and ever-repeated note, were so many and so different from the great number of performers, that they produced a very lively and delightful concert. Some of them, such as the thrush, which chirps "O teok, teok, O tuce," sent forth notes so rich, that even the nightingale could not rival them in melody, sometimes so varied as to resemble the song of our English thrush; and others, though not so musical, were full of the lustiness and delight of life, and gave a charm to the woods, that grows as it becomes more and more familiar. There were hundreds of small birds along the creek, crying, "Egypt! Egypt!" as if that were their native country, and soon their voices were so mingled with the pipings, tinklings, and whirrings of wood-crickets, grasshoppers, and cicadas, that the whole air was vibrating with this multiplicity of life and song...

Then there were numbers of that beautiful bird the magpie-lark, like a soft, gentle, and most delicate black and white dove. Oh! so gentle and lovely it seemed, and so tame, that it would sit upon the low boughs till you were close up to it, and come walking on the banks of the stream just by you without any fear, crying, ever and anon, "Chain! chain! chain!" in a ringing metallic tone, that could be heard very, very far off. I found a nest of these with fledged young ones, and had I been coming home I should have liked to try to rear them, and bring them over.

MARY BUNDOCK, WYANGERIE STATION, RICHMOND RIVER DISTRICT NEW SOUTH WALES, 1850s

Mary Bundock was born in the Hunter Valley of New South Wales in 1844. Her father, Wellington Bundock, and his brother Frederick had come in on a mail boat, the little packet Henry Turner, *in 1833:*

> Early in June the "Harry Turner" came near the coast of Australia, and the passengers, leaning over the taffrail, smelt a new scent in the air, which was blowing from the land, and knew later that their first welcome to Australia was the scent of Australia's special flower "the wattle".

Wellington Bundock had gifts from mutual friends for the well-known Ogilvie family, early settlers in the Hunter Valley and squatters in New England. He later married Ellen Ogilvie.

After several years in the Hunter Valley, the Bundock brothers moved to the north coast of New South Wales. The land was rich, they judged it with competent English eyes, and they were bewildered when their sheep died. Wellington Bundock rode in search of drier country and found Wyangarie, north of present Kyogle, a run of apparently superb pasture. In 1846, he moved the remnants of his sheep there and brought up Ellen and their two children. Mary, two years old, rode on the pommel of her father's saddle.

Sheep fared no better there. The country was still well out on the eastern falls. Stomach worms thrived in the long, wet grass. Even if stockowners had known what was the matter, no drugs existed then to drench sheep. They moved their sheep to the dry western slopes and plains. Cattle saved the north coast squatters. Thousands of big Shorthorn cattle carried B for Bundock branded on the nearside rump for more than 40 years.

Mary Bundock married T. M. Murray-Prior, eldest of the 11 sons of Thomas Lodge Murray-Prior, sailor, squatter, first Postmaster-General of Queensland and member of the Legislative Council. I quote from a typescript of her memoirs in the Australian National Library:

> He went up the river in search of dry open country, described by Edward Ogilvie. One afternoon he rode over the low gap to the

lovely Wyangarie Plain. He thought it the most beautiful spot he
had ever seen, a smooth open plain with one clump of heavy timber
and two or three small lagoons sparkling in the sun and backed by a
panorama of mountains at varying distance and the river fringed
with a scrub making a sweep round the back of the plain and holding
in its curve a low wooded hill that my father instantly decided
should be the site of his future home.

He moved his sheep up to these drier plains and living in a sort
of tent, made from bark and his men in another, went to work
energetically to build a wool shed ready for the shearing which had
to be done shortly.

The whole country was covered by a thick crop of Kangaroo
Grass, then in seed, and looking like a crop of Oats, beautiful to
look at but very easy to get alight and not easy to put out so that a
few weeks later, soon after the woolshed had been finished, a fire
started and the whole thing burnt to the ground...

In my childhood we were quite away by ourselves in the bush,
never seeing any other children and playing very happily at games of
our own invention and as we grew old enough, riding about and
fishing in the many creeks and the river.

The constant demand for water from both house and huts was a
great tax on bullocks and drivers. So, in fine weather the women
generally set up a pot beside the river and washed their clothes in
the running water, spreading them to dry on the grassy banks. The
Upper Richmond was then a beautiful stream of clear water, running
over clean sand and pebbles, an ideal of beauty and purity not to be
surpassed anywhere, with steeply shelving banks either of clean grass
or shaded by beautiful trees of many kinds, one of the most
beautiful being the Moreton Bay Chestnut with its deep glossy
leaves in spring, its clusters of red and yellow blossom and later the
big green pods, which we children spent many hours sailing as boats
on the river...

The term "Scrub" for the great forests, which, in the early days,
covered the banks of the Richmond, Tweed and Brunswick Rivers
and which stretched back unbroken over the ranges to the top of the
McPherson range, was a decided misnomer and gives no idea of the
beauty of what was really a semi-tropical jungle. It was a mass of

splendid trees, running up to 60 feet without a branch before forming a head and growing so closely that the sunshine was completely cut off. In some districts there was a great undergrowth of creepers and vines, especially the notorious "Lawyer Vine"... Upper Richmond was very free from vines. I have walked through it for miles and never seen the sun except where some great tree had fallen and made a gap in the green roof overhead. As you stood and looked around your view was bounded by the great brown tree stems which closed in around me.

BLANCHE MITCHELL, SYDNEY, 1858

Blanche was the youngest of 11 children of the great explorer, Sir Thomas Mitchell and his wife Mary. Her early childhood was extremely happy. She loved her father and life was special in the two fine homes that they lived in at Darling Point, first at Lindesay, now owned by the National Trust, and then at Carthona, which Mitchell had built. That magnificent house is also still standing.

When Blanche was 12 years old, her father died suddenly of pneumonia. Thereafter life changed. Sir Thomas had bought farmland and real estate, owning much of Darling Point, a big slab of what is now Kings Cross and about 3000 hectares of farms in the Camden and Georges River areas. He would have been extremely wealthy in another few years. But too much of the property was mortgaged and his widow, left no property and expected to live on what he thought would be substantial rent, was left in difficulties.

Mary moved from *Carthona* into a smaller house and did her best for her daughters, but rather coldly. In the diary that she kept from 1858 to 1861, Blanche wrote, speaking also of her sister Alice:

> Neither her nor Mamma ever show me the slightest degree of love. If they would only press my hand, care for me more, and love me, how different I would be! I cannot live without love, it is my whole existence.

It is a fascinating account of a lively young woman – it begins when she was 15 years old – fitting in with the strict conventions of the day. She may not go outdoors without a bonnet. She is rebuked for waving to a passing boat: 'I am very sorry it was very wrong I confess, but I only waved slightly!' Blanche also outraged a 'room full of company' by kissing a good friend whom she had not seen since her marriage: 'I, forgetting the presence of so many, kissed the former Julia James, a great breach of etiquette.'

Blanche did not marry. Although her father left her property, it did not bring in enough money to interest suitors in that acquisitive society. Tuberculosis killed her when she was only 26.

Here she is at the age of 15, with her sister Alice and her brother Campbell, enjoying a trip to stay with Mr Sparling, the rector of Appin, and his wife. Train travel was then a new event, though Blanche found the opportunity for unconventional behaviour much more exciting.

Wednesday 14th July [1858]

... we duly prepared ourselves for the coming journey on Monday night, our luggage consisted of two boxes, which were packed and corded all ready for starting next day. But the weather was not propitious to us, day came, but the rain poured in torrents, dark and gloomy was the morning, but we after having prepared ourselves, were not going to be put off our promised journey by any showers, so having procured a cab, Campbell packed us and himself in it, and having said adieu, we started on our expedition. When in the cab, Campbell deeply regretted having acceded to our wishes, for the mud was standing hillocks high, the cab literally tumbled to and fro, and certainly our prospects were not very bright. But a wilful man must have his own way, so on we went, and arrived safely at the Sydney Railway Station, where we got into a first class carriage, and were soon flying on our way to Campbelltown. As far as Parramatta, we enjoyed the company of Mr George Pinnock, who now and then made a few wise remarks, tending to some important fact about the weather, which were at least amusing, if not instructing. Oh, the dull monotony of a railway carriage! On, on you go, puffing, shaking, whistling, until you see the welcome station, which for one minute distracts the attention. The rain kept on pouring, and we were a little disheartened, at last reached the C. station, where we soon entered the ladies' saloon, and sat down wondering, what would become of us next. Mr Sparling had promised to send his carriage, neither he nor his carriage was there, and we were left to our own devices. Long we stayed there, undetermined whether we should go back or not. At last we decided on going to Campbell's Inn, cost what it might. So after tucking up our dresses we walked off to the hotel, where after having warmed our frozen limbs and wet clothes by the fire, we felt in a fit state to order in something to eat and make ourselves comfortable. Mrs Campbell came in and informed C. the amusing facts of how many servants she kept, what they did, their respective characters, and lastly how to make pork sausages. I am sorry to say the worthy lady was tipsy...

A fresh annoyance arrived. How were we to get to Appin? Go in the mail cart — it was preposterous, no lady we nt there before, the very idea absurd. Then stay in the inn, till tomorrow. The rooms

were comfortable, but the house was full of drunken men. So the
former idea was resolved upon. First we went to a room and
equipped ourselves in fit travelling dresses, and after tea, were all
ready to depart. At eight o'clock Campbell informed us the mail
was ready, and he led us to the door. It certainly was an affair. No
bigger than a small butcher's cart, drawn by two horses, and capable
of holding only four. Surrounded by a crowd of tipsy men, there it
stood. But all these difficulties must be surmounted, so consoling
ourselves with the very wise reflection 'What must be, must be',
Campbell placed us in the conveyance, and we started off. The
passengers beside ourselves were two. A woman (who knew us very
well) and young Tyson. Great respect was of course paid us. The
roads were fearful, Campbell and Tyson had to run nearly all the
way, the horses kicked, the cart rolled, they jobbed, they stopped.
Alice kept her head down, her tongue was chained by fear, now and
then an exclamation broke from her lips, but otherwise she was too
frightened to speak. Mrs Best kept calling out and crying, 'Oh what
would your Mamma say, if she saw ye here?' — 'Sorrow be to the
day I set my foot here. Oh when shall I see my babes again?' At
every inn we stopped, we were asked most kindly if we would not
take a nobbler, only a 'dhrop' just to warm us. Tyson had a rum
bottle, which he every now and then took a pull out of, handing it
to us, 'p'raps the ladies would like to take a little', but we most
respectfully declined. I liked it all! The danger gave a spicy feeling
and a zest to everything, the calm fresh bush, the lateness of the
hour, the dull moonlight, and quiet still trees, contrasted strongly
with the scene I was actor in. Heavy horses pulling, panting and
jostling up and down, now here, now there, men shouting 'Horses
steady! Up boys! Cheery up!' — C. and Tyson running like so many
brigands after the cart, wrapped up in thick buttoned coats and heavy
slouched hats, the wild scenery all around. The dull leaden
moonlight straggling through the clouds, with the dim haze all
around, all formed a picture so new and strange that I liked it
excessively and thoroughly enjoyed myself.

GEORGE BENNETT, OFF THE EAST COAST OF AUSTRALIA, c.1858

Born in Plymouth in 1804, Bennett was naturally attracted by the many ships in the harbour. He went to sea at the age of 15, but returned to England in 1821 to study medicine. In 1828, he obtained his diploma of membership of the Royal College of Surgeons. Sir Richard Owen, the great palaeontologist, interested him in natural history. Thereafter Bennett spent his life practising medicine, travelling and studying plant and animal life. He first came to Australia in 1829, then returned in 1832 when he was impressed by the 'beauties of the Kingdom of Flora, which are lavished so profusely on this colony'. He travelled inland, collecting fossils and extant specimens for Owen. In 1834, he published his first book, Wanderings in New South Wales, and in 1835 travelled to London to deliver a paper on the platypus to the Zoological Society of London.

Returning to Sydney in 1836, Bennett built a successful medical practice, but he did not relinquish his other interests. He was the first secretary of the Australian Museum and he was active in the Zoological Society. Unfortunately, he was also president of the Acclimitization Society of New South Wales with the object of 'spreading over the length and breadth of the land inestimable acquisitions to the wealth and comfort of the people'. These societies did enormous damage importing House Sparrows, Common Mynahs and Common Starlings – these birds are still increasing and still extending their range – other animals and plants, and in exporting plants and animals to Europe.

In 1860, Bennett published *Gatherings of a Naturalist in Australia being observations principally on the Animal and Vegetable Productions of New South Wales, New Zealand, and some of the Austral Islands*. Phosphorescence fascinated him:

> At some seasons of the year, that splended phenomenon, the
> phosphorescence of the ocean, is seen in all its beauty upon the
> Australian coasts, while at other periods there is scarcely a gleam
> visible over the whole surface of the ocean. The cause producing the
> luminosity of the sea, and its utility in the œconomy of Nature,
> have long been the subject of minute attention and patient
> investigation among many distinguished naturalists, and of the

AUSTRALIAN BAOBAB TREES
George Bennett, 1860, from *Gatherings of a Naturalist in Australia*, Mitchell Library,
State Library of Australia

admiration of those persons who have had opportunities of
observing it in various parts of the world, either during a calm in the
tranquil waters of a bay or harbour, or when the waves are breaking
and dashing about in livid masses of luminous matter. It has often
been stated to resemble "liquid fire;" but that expression can convey
no idea of the reality: it does not assume the glowing brightness of
that element; the effect of the light produced is the white, sickly
gleam of phosphorus, also displaying a similar deadly and livid
greenish hue. At sea, occasionally, the display of luminosity is very
great and extensively diffused: but at other times the gleaming of
the phosphorescent matter is in large and distinct patches, as if
occasioned by a congregation of the animals producing it; or it
becomes visible only in the broad luminous stream of phosphoric
splendour seen in the wake of the ship excited by the passage of the
vessel. During a dark night, the glowing of this peculiar pallid light,
illuminating the crests of the waves, and flashing as they break under
the influence of strong breezes, has a peculiar brilliancy of effect,
exciting the admiration of the spectators. We are now well aware
that the *living* phosphorescent matter is secreted and emitted at will,
or on excitement, by the animals possessing this singular property,
for purposes in their œconomy at present unknown to us. I say

luminous *living* matter, in contradistinction between that produced
by the decay of fish and other animal matter and that secreted by
the animals themselves during life. Such luminosity is not only
afforded by an infinite number of molluscous and crustaceous
animals with which the ocean abounds, but has been observed also to
obtain in a species of Shark, and among land-insects, as the Glow-
worm, Fire-flies, and, among the Myriapoda, is exhibited by the
Luminous Centipede (*Geophilus fulgens*). This luminous property
is also found existing in the vegetable kingdom among some of the
fungoid plants. There is one, a species of the genus *Agaricus*, which
has been observed to be vividly luminous. It is very common in the
Australia woods in the vicinity of Sydney, about the localities of
South-Head road, and among the scrubs and forests on the approach
to the headlands of Botany Bay, and emits a light sufficiently
powerful to enable the time on a watch to be seen by it. The effect
produced by it upon the traveller, when on a dark night he comes
suddenly upon it glowing in the woods, is startling.

ANNE BOWMAN, AUSTRALIAN BUSH, c.1858

In 1859, Anne Bowman published The Kangaroo Hunters; or Adventures in the
Bush, *in London and New York. The title page says she is 'Author of "Esperanza",
"The Castaway", "The Young Exiles", etc. etc.' British libraries hold copies of her books,
but nothing seems to be known about her. She certainly must have spent time
in Australia to write* The Kangaroo Hunters. *It is a romantic and impossible book,
but the information about plants and animals is authentic. She wrote it, as she says
in the preface, because 'The rapid spread of education creates a continual demand
for new books, of a character to gratify the taste of the young, and at the same
time to satisfy the scruples of their instructors'.*

The story is unrelentingly religious: God oversees every adventure of the
characters. Mr Mayburn, rector of Wendon and a naturalist who collects
the nests and eggs of birds, is mourning the death of his wife. He feels that
he has to get away from where she died, perhaps to northern India or
South Australia. When he was offered a mission to a remote part of India
his family were eager to go with him: Margaret, his 16-year-old daughter,
Arthur, his 15-year-old son, Hugh, not yet 13, Gerald, the son of a good
friend who had died recently and Jenny, an old nurse. An orphaned brother
and sister begged to go with them: Jack, particularly skilled with his hands,
and Ruth, lively, awkward and always getting into trouble.

So eight of them set sail for India via Melbourne. Also aboard the ship
were the Deverell family whom they had met in London. The Deverells
were on their way with sheep, cattle, horses, pigs, shepherds and stockmen
with their families to form a station of 50,000 acres as shown on their map
'on this great river that falls into the Darling'.

The Deverells set out from Melbourne with their livestock and a 'train of
waggons' to be guided to their squatting station by two ex-convicts; the
Mayburn entourage boarded a rather decrepit boat bound for Calcutta.
Somewhere north of the Swan River, in a latitude high enough for there to
be coral reefs around the islands, careless Ruth, trying by candlelight to
cage the chickens she mistakenly let out, trips over a rope set for her by a
nasty ex-convict and falls into the hold, dropping her candle.

When the ship catches fire, the rascally ex-convict crew take to the boats
leaving the passengers to their fate. Wilkins, a decent ex-convict, and Jack
quickly grab what rope and timber there is on deck and fashion a raft.

Wilkins is aware of extreme urgency. The crew had planned to mutiny and steal the boat. They had kegs of gunpowder aboard for sale; the main cargo was tallow.

They threw a keg of water, a box of potatoes, a couple of rifles aboard, whatever odds and ends were handy, Ruth grabbed her crate of chickens, all got on to the raft and paddled away as the ship exploded. They heard screams for help and rescued Black Peter, the worst of the crew and the only one left alive from one overturned boat.

They land on a coral-fringed island; Black Peter steals a rifle, food, most of their tools including the only axe and paddles away on the raft to the mainland. They kill a turtle, collect oysters, kill ducks, collect birds' eggs to eat and dig a well for fresh water. They find a rusty axe in a wrecked ship and Jack uses it to build a boat from the ship's timbers.

So they, too, reach the mainland and set off walking in a southeasterly direction. They fashion spears, bows and arrows because Black Peter left them little ammunition. They kill kangaroos and emus, birds of different kinds, find plants to eat, collect plenty of eggs. Black Peter has joined a group of Aborigines who make repeated attacks.

Eventually they come upon cattle tracks. A bull attacks them. It is an escaped beast of Edward Deverell. They find Edward looking for missing cattle and he takes them all to his established station where he has just finished building a church. He invites Mr Mayburn to be the first preacher.

Was Anne Bowman unaware of the distance and the dryness of the country between the Kimberley and the Darling River, or did she ignore it for the sake of her story? The part of the book that astonished me was this passage about the quality of a native grass:

> When they reached the hills, they found them steeper than they
> expected; but on ascending to the height, they were gratified to see
> before them a beautiful country. Lofty trees adorned the plain, and
> high grass rose even to their shoulders, as they passed through it.
> On several spots, vast fragments of the sandstone-rock, grown over
> with beautiful flowering creepers, lay in picturesque confusion, and
> the Eucalyptus, with its spicy flowers, the Pandanus, loaded with
> fragrant blossom, and the Cabbage-palm, were also encircled by the
> parasitic plants which add such a grace to tropical scenery. Wearied
> with forcing their way through the tall, sharp, wiry grass, they
> stopped before a high broken rock which overhung and flung a
> shade over the spot they had selected for their resting-place. Then

the boys cleared the ground, by laboriously cutting down the long grass, which they spread to form beds, a luxury to which they were unaccustomed...

Ruth usually released her unfortunate chickens at each resting-place, that they might have air, and seek food, and she had herself been running about for grubs, seeds, or anything they could eat, and she now returned with a perfect sheaf of some kind of bearded grain, suspended on the ear by slender filaments like the oat, but still unripe.

"This surely must be an edible grain," said Mr. Mayburn, "and will probably be ripe as early as November, in a climate which produces two harvests. How richly laden is each ear, and the straw cannot be less than six feet in length. I conclude it is an Anthistiria [now Themeda]. Feed your fowls, Ruth; the food is suitable, and happily abundant. Had we but a mill to grind it, we might hope in due season to enjoy once more the blessing of bread."

"There's not likely to be any mills handy hereabout," said Wilkins; "but when folks is put to it, it's queer what shifts they can make. Just hand us over a handful of that there corn, my lass."

Wilkins soon found two flat stones suited to his purpose, spread the shelled grains on the larger stone and bruised the soft corn into a paste, which he handed over to Jenny, saying, "Here's yer dough, mother! now see and bake us a damper, bush fashion; its poor clammy stuff yet a bit, but a bad loaf's better nor no bread."

Then Wilkins showed Jenny that slovenly mode of bread-making, common even among the civilized colonists of Australia, the product of which is a sort of pancake baked in the ashes. But this substitute for the staff of life was thankfully received by those who had been so long deprived of the genuine blessing; but the green paste was stringy and dry, and Jenny proposed to blend a boiled potato with the next damper, to make it more like bread.

JOHN McDOUALL STUART, WEST OF LAKE TORRENS, SOUTH AUSTRALIA, 1858

John McDouall Stuart was born in Fifeshire, Scotland, on 7 September 1815.
He must have studied surveying since he entered the South Australian Survey
Department on his arrival there in 1838.

In 1844–45, he was selected by Charles Sturt to join his expedition to central Australia as draughtsman. Daniel George Brock also accompanied them. The horrific five months by the dwindling waterhole cost James Poole his life and Sturt his health. He never recovered. Stuart's recovery was hampered by his drinking. It was jokingly said of him that on any return trip his face brightened when they got within 500 miles of a pub.

Stuart worked erratically for the next 12 years, and then began his life's work. In 1858, a group of pastoralists in search of new country employed him to investigate the country to the northwest of Lake Torrens. Setting out north from Port Augusta, Stuart turned west near the head of the lake, then south, coming home via Streaky Bay, a rough circle of about 1000 kilometres circumference.

One white man accompanied him and an Aboriginal lad who did not know the country and deserted when he became afraid of local Aborigines. Stuart did not take enough food with them. In the end stages, he wrote 'One meal per day, and a very small one we have been reduced to for five weeks.'

The next year he followed his northern tracks, then continued farther north and found the big creek that flows east into Lake Eyre, now called River Neales. A few months after his return, Stuart went back in November 1859 to institute a survey of the big plains of grass and saltbush that he had found.

Getting to the Centre that Sturt had failed to reach was a priority. At one good waterhole in a gum creek where he camped on 1 July 1858, he noted: 'What a capital position for a depôt to make the centre'. But crossing the continent was his passion.

On 2 March 1860, Stuart set out for the centre with the hope of making the crossing. He named the Finke River and the Macdonnell Range on the way and erected the Union Jack on a cairn of stones on Central Mount Stuart (he named it Sturt), which he calculated to be the geographic centre. He was not far out – the centre is only four kilometres southwest.

Stuart travelled north until scurvy, shortage of food and Aborigines who were hostile to his invasion of their country turned him back at Attack Creek. The next year he tried again and failed. Stuart tried yet again and, on 24 July 1862 near the mouth of the Adelaide River, 'I dipped my feet, and washed my face and hands in the sea'.

The Overland Telegraph Line follows his route. Stuart was a great explorer and he was honoured with money and awards, as he should have been. The last mighty effort ruined his health and he had no energy to stock his land grants. His eyesight failed, even his memory, and he died in England in 1866.

I quote from the little known journal of Stuart's first exploration, printed for the South Australian House of Assembly on 5 November 1858. On his return, he wrote to the South Australian Commissioner for Crown Lands saying that he had found 16,000 square miles (41,000 square kilometres) of good country. It was all soon taken up and is still good grazing country, but difficult to manage. The many creeks come down in sudden wide floods.

Saturday, June 26th. Edge of Plain. — Started at 9.30 a.m., on a bearing of 314°30', to the Tent Hill; at ten miles, sand-hills cease; at thirteen miles, point of stony table land; changed our bearing to 285°00'. There is apparently a gum creek to the north-north-west, distant about ten miles, and seemingly running north-east and south-west. At seven miles, we came upon a large gum creek, the one we saw from point of stony table land [Chamber or Stuart Creek running into Lake Eyre South]. This is as fine a creek of water as I have seen in the Colony, with long permanent reaches, with reeds and rushes around, and only a few yards of rocks dividing them for as far down as we could see; we noticed small fish about two inches long (no doubt there are larger.) From the top of the rise I could see about ten miles down; the country appears more open, and the gum-trees much larger. At this distance, I could see a large body of water in a bend of the creek. It is very rocky and stony where I struck it. An immense body of water comes down it at times; its breadth to where the drift has been lodged being upwards of 300 feet. The water at which we are camped is forty or fifty feet wide, and half a mile long, of first-rate quality. Its course from hence down is east-north-east. Were it near Adelaide, it would take its place as one of the South Australian rivers, and not the least by a long way. The first part of our journey was over an undulating plain; the sand-rises very low, and valleys wide, with plenty of grass and salt bush. The last part was decidedly bad, seven miles of a stony plain, thinly covered with salt bush and grass; stony table land still on our left, seven or eight tent hills to the east. In passing the first of these, there is a remarkable feature — it has the appearance as if a white tower had been built on the top of a conical hill; near the top it has a black ring round it; the top is white, coming to a point like a Chinaman's hat. Distance, twenty miles...

Monday, July 19th [northwest of Lake Gairdner]. *Dense scrubby plain.* - Started at a-quarter to 9 a.m., on a bearing of 120° to highest part of the range. Could only accomplish ten miles. Although very sorry to do so, I will be obliged to leave my favourite mare. The country passed over to-day is most splendidly grassed, with a light sandy soil — the mulga grows very tall here. Forster caught an opposum, the first we have met with, it will serve us for a good dinner. Found water a little distance down the valley, which I think will form into a large creek further to the south-west. We have again entered the country where kangaroo are plentiful...

Wednesday, July 21st. Grass and Salt-bush plain.- Left camp at 9 a.m., on a bearing of 97°; camped at some rain-water in a clay-pan. Distance, twenty miles. At twelve miles there is low rising ground, running north-west and south-east, which divides the two plains; no appearance of any creek. Dip of country south-west; good soil, covered with first-rate grass, with salt-bush thinly scattered over; clumps of mulga at intervals. It is the finest grass and salt-bush country I have passed over; but I did not fall in with permanent water. In some places there is a little ironstone to be seen.

FRANCIS THOMAS GREGORY, ON THE GASCOYNE, LYONS, FORTESCUE AND DE GREY RIVERS, WESTERN AUSTRALIA, 1858 AND 1861

Five Gregory brothers came to the Swan River as children in 1829. Their father, Joshua, a lieutenant in the 78th Highlanders, retired on half pay due to sickness, brought his family out as settlers.

Joshua and his wife, Frances, educated their sons. They became good bushmen by necessity; they had close contact with Aborigines and even learnt to use spears and fighting sticks. Joshua died in 1838 when he was only 47 years old. His eldest son, also Joshua, died soon after and ended a descending line of seven eldest sons to carry the same name. The other four brothers became surveyors and reached the top of their profession, although they were self-taught. All made outstanding explorations.

In 1856, Francis (Frank) Gregory was surveying farms on the lower Murchison when it came down in flood. The weather had been dry for months where he was working, so, realising that there would be water and horse feed on the upper reaches, he dropped his chain and headed up-river with one man, two horses and 16 pounds (7.25 kg) of flour. He found so much good land that settlers subscribed to send him out again. In 1858, he travelled up the Murchison for nearly 500 kilometres, and then he headed north and circled round the Gascoyne and its tributary, the Lyons, and added 400,000 hectares to the Colony's good land.

Gregory went to London in 1860 where cotton manufacturers, whose supplies had been cut off by the American Civil War, approached him with the wild scheme of leading ship-loads of settlers and thousands of Chinese and Indian coolies into northwest Western Australia to grow cotton. Persuaded that it would be safer to explore the country first, they induced the English and Colonial Governments to fit out an expedition.

Gregory set out from Nickel Bay, where Roeburne now stands, travelled south to the country he knew on the Gascoyne, then circled back northward to the Fortescue River and followed it and the coast back to the Bay where he refitted *Dolphin* that waited for them. Then he travelled due east to the Oakover River and continued past it through the southern edge of the Great Sandy Desert in the hope of coming on a great river. The belief of an inland sea had changed to a mighty waterway draining the Centre.

Gregory almost went too far:

> I cannot omit [he wrote] to remark the singular effects of excessive
> thirst upon the eyes of the horses; they absolutely sunk into their
> heads until there was a hollow of sufficient depth to entirely bury
> the thumb in, and there was an appearance as though the whole of
> the head had shrunk with them, producing a very unpleasant and
> ghastly expression.

They got back safely to the Oakover, followed it down to the De Grey, followed that river to the sea, and returned by the coast. He found a big area that he thought fit for cotton growing, but by then America was exporting again.

The next year Gregory went to live in Queensland and set up in Toowoomba as a surveyor. He later became Commissioner of Crown Lands and a long-serving member of the Legislative Council.

From his journal of the 1858 expedition, I quote his assessment of some of the good country; from the 1861 journal his descriptions of more good country and of the extraordinary tide that pours up the De Grey River:

2nd June [on the Lyons River near Mount Augustus]

> Nearly the whole of the country passed over this day was an alluvial
> flat extending on the south-west to the grassy range already
> described, while to the north and east it extended for many miles,
> branching out into the numerous valleys that drain the different
> ranges in that direction; the grass and vegetation on these flats is not
> so rank as that traversed the previous day, but more even, and the
> soil better adapted for agriculture; the amount of good land on this
> part of the Lyons River was estimated at 150 square miles [38,000
> hectares], while on the tributaries between Mount Thompson and
> Mount Augustus I have no doubt that there is as much more...
>
> The quantity of game seen in this part of the country was also a
> favourable indication. Turkeys, and a new variety of pigeon [Flock
> Bronzewing], having a brown back and slate-coloured breast, on the
> wing resembling a tame pigeon, congregate in flights sometimes of a
> thousand together; emus, cockatoos, quail, and parakeets are also
> very numerous, particularly the latter...

6th June [1861, on the Fortescue River]

Quitting the range, which had been named after one of the most
liberal promoters of the expedition, Hamersley Range, we took a
north-east course, crossing over twelve or fourteen miles of
beautiful open grassy plain, in many parts the kangaroo-grass
reaching above the horses' backs; the soil being of the richest clay-
loam, occasionally containing beds of singular fragments of opaline
rocks, resembling ancient lava. By 5.30 p.m. we reached the river
again, several miles above the deep glen that had checked our course
on the 5th. The valley having again opened out, gave us easy access
to its banks, which were here a rich black peat soil, containing
numerous springs. Here was first observed a very handsome fan-
palm, growing in topes, some of them attaining to the height of
forty feet and twenty inches diameter, the leaves measuring eight to
ten feet in length. The river had again opened into deep reaches of
water, and continued abundance of fish resembling cobblers,
weighing four and five pounds each...

26th September [at the mouth of the De Grey River]

For the first mile the river has a breadth of from 400 to 800 yards,
and would admit with the tide vessels of twelve or fourteen feet
draft of water with perfect safety up as far as Ripon Island, where
they could lie completely sheltered in all weathers quite close to the
shore, which here has steep banks twenty to thirty feet high; they
would however be left aground at low water, as we did not observe
any deep pools in this part of the river. I had only just time to
complete my observations when the roaring of the incoming tide
warned me that no time was to be lost in returning to the horses,
which were nearly a mile higher up the river. Although I ran part of
the way, the mud creeks filled up so rapidly, there was some risk of
my being cut off from the shore and having to take up a roost on the
top of the mangroves until the tide fell; I had time, however, to
observe that the head of the tide carried with it thousands of fish of
great variety, amongst them a very remarkable one from three to six
inches in length, in form resembling a mullet, but with fins like a

flying fish; it is amphibious, landing on the mud and running with the speed of a lizard, and when frightened, can jump five or six feet at a bound; I did not, however, succeed in catching one for a specimen. Swarms of beautiful bright-crimson crabs, about two inches diameter, were to be seen issuing from their holes to welcome the coming flood, on which was borne a great number of sea-fowl, who, it was evident, came in for an abundant feast in the general turmoil.

WILLIAM H. THOMAS. BOWEN HARBOUR. NORTH QUEENSLAND. 1859

On 5 November 1925, the Evening News *published this short piece about Bowen.*

'Bowen, scene of the latest strike sensation, has a wonderful harbor, and is 725 miles from Brisbane by water, and 120 miles by rail from Townsville. CAPTAIN HENRY DANIEL SINCLAIR discovered the Australian Naples on October 16, 1859, in the Santa Barbara, from which anchor was dropped opposite Stone Island. The official founding was in 1861. Sinclair was drowned in Cleveland Bay seven years later.

Bowen like Cairns, got its name from a King's representative, Sir George Ferguson Bowen, Queensland's first Governor. Fifty miles south-west of Bowen are its famous coal-fields. The Merinda meat works, which supplied the bulk of the meat ration to the Australians in the Great War, is seven miles by train from the harbor of many dreams and disappointments.

M'Kinlay, the explorer, rested his weary frame there after his long trip in search of Burke and Wills, in 1862.

SUCRE.'

Despite this attribution, Matthew Flinders had found and named the port in 'compliment to Captain James Bowen of the navy' on 21 August 1801. He did not elaborate on its quality, merely described it as 'a port of some extent, which had not only escaped the notice of Captain Cook, but by the shift of wind, was very nearly missed by us also'.

Santa Barbara was a small schooner of nine tons register. She set out from Rockhampton on 1 September 1859. It was a private venture. William H. Thomas and Captain Sinclair drew up an agreement signed by Thos. Metcalfe, Rockhampton:

This expedition for the discovery of a Safe Northern Port was fitted out by Captain H.D. Sinclair & William H. Thomas Capt. Sinclair finding the vessel and her outfit, provisions to be found

between them, & providing our Undertaking should prove successful
any compensation that might be awarded to be divided as follows
one third to W.H. Thomas.

James Gordon and Benjamin Poole, squatters in search of country,
accompanied them. Thomas kept a manuscript log of the journey. Here is
his description of finding the good harbour:

14 Oct. At 6 AM made sail and at Noon anchored between Gloster
Island and the Cape the Natives came of to us in Canoes & brought
us 2 Casks of Water for which we gave them 2 tomahawks and
sundry articles of Wearing Apparel they appeared very anxious for
us to go ashore & on our refusing they went ashore we lay at
Anchor in this passage all night. The passage has several coral reefs
& sand banks in it There is a good channel but narrow and intricate
and dangerous for parties <u>Unacquainted</u> with it.
   15 Oct. The Natives came on board early and as we would not go
ashore offered to bring us More Water we gave them the buckets
and they soon returned 2 of them jumped on deck one going
forward and the other aft they then call'd another Canoe alongside
when it was discovered the Men in the Canoe was armed. As well as
the 2 on board their arms being secreted beneath the shirts we had
given as soon as they found they was detected they was very eager
to get away & was allowed to go unmolested The Natives here
appear to be very strong & daring & more ingenious than any part
of the Coast we have Visited Their Canoes are formed of 3 pieces
of bark sewn together with grass tree very pretty Models & very
light & bouyant and capable of carrying 5 men at 8 we got
underweight and proceeded up the bay, & sailed well up towards
Mount Edgcombe beleiving there to be a passage through into
Repulse bay, & anchored for the Night in 3 Fathoms of water
under the high conical hill, sheltered in a bay from all winds
   Oct 16 At 6 AM commenced working round the bay at noon
passed 2 islands about 1 mile of the Main land passed inside of the
Northermost one carrying 1 Fathom of Water at 3 PM wind from
the N.E. & a heavy sea at 7 PM Anchored for the night in 4 Fathom
Water Midnight blowing hard from the N.W. water perfectly
smooth

Oct 17 Light winds to our astonishment we are laying in a fine capacious harbour well sheltered from all Winds We sounded the harbour. Within a cable length of shore there is from 3 to 4 fathoms while near the middle 7 to 10.

Oct 18 At 6 AM 3 hands went on shore to Examine the country at 8 PM returned stating the Country was very good and there was plenty of Fresh Water The Natives being so numerous and our party so small prevents us laying down a chart of the harbour... which we call Port Denison This port is very capacious having an Inner and outer harbor well sheltered from all Winds in entering from the South pass outside of Gloster Island & inside of Middle Island giving it a berth of 1 mile as there is a long shoal running off it then steer S.W. & by W. for The Inner Harbor you will scarcely perceive it to be an Harbour until you are into it In Entering at the South Entrance be careful not to go too near the Island as there is an extensive Coral bank running of & also a Sandspit In entering at the North Reefs near Mid Channel selecting a berth at discretion It is very good holding ground.

HUGH M. HULL, TASMANIA, 1859

*Formerly Police Magistrate and Chairman of Quarter Sessions for the County
of Cumberland, Hull came to Tasmania as coroner and clerk assistant of the House
of Assembly. On 23 June 1859, he delivered a lecture to the Mechanics Institute in
Hobart on the 'Capabilities of Tasmania'. Three thousand copies of this were
published in London as* The Experience of Forty Years in Tasmania:

In the firm hope and belief that the statements contained therein will
induce the emigration of numbers of industrious people, who *must*
better their condition by coming to Tasmania... It was suggested to
me that my personal experience of the abilities of the Colony would
enable me to prepare a small Pamphlet for circulation among the
Middle and Working Classes of Britain, from the pages of which
they might glean *reliable* information respecting Tasmania, the
GARDEN OF THE SOUTH — the SANITARIUM OF INDIA —
and to a certain extent, the GRANARY OF THE AUSTRALIAS.

Hull was impressed by Tasmanian shipbuilding:

...a pursuit for which the native born of Tasmania manifest a peculiar
aptitude. It is one for which there seems to be with them a national
predilection, and it is to be regretted that a larger amount of
encouragement has not been given, so that they might be induced to
follow a calling so inventive and so practically beneficial. Ship
building in Tasmania, ought above all other employments, to
command attention; for there are few colonies which possess so
many advantages for successfully embarking in this enterprise. The
timber is not only equal to any other in the world, but it is easily
obtained, and in scantlings, would startle and delight the English
ship builder; for the noblest oak of the English forests would be a
dwarf alongside some of the giant trees of Tasmania. Planking was
sent to England by Sir William Denison seventy feet long and four
feet wide. Timbers three feet [91.5 centimetres] square and 150 feet
long [45.7 metres] can readily be obtained; while whole forests
exist in various parts of noble pines, and graceful myrtles (beech, the

latter being 200 feet high and proportionately stout, while its timber is more close in grain, harder, and better veined than cedar.

These forest trees grow on the very banks of our rivers, and can be brought into active service without any considerable outlay, for it is the habit of sawyers to cut down the trees in summer, and roll the immense bolls to the water, to be carried down to deep water by the winter floods. During the last twenty years there have been built here, at an expense of about £8 a ton, a fleet of not less than 390 vessels, carring 23,200 tons, besides small craft, yachts, and boats innumerable...

In some of the southern parts of Tasmania, the blue gum grows to the height of 350 feet [106.7 metres], and 100 feet ' in girth. The Rev. T. J. Ewing mentions one of 102 feet round. One tree on my father's estate about five miles from Hobart Town, is 330 feet high and 86 feet round. This tree it is estimated would produce upwards of £200 worth of sawn timber. Sir W. Denison and General Wynyard measured it in the presence of Lady Denison and other ladies. Tasmania timbers received seven prizes and five certificates of honor at the Great Exhibition of 1851, and two silver medals, and two certificates of honor at the Paris Exhibition of 1855.

The value of the large gum trees may be estimated from the fact that a tree on Mr. John Abbott's farm at Long Bay was cut down and converted into building materials, the value of which was £245. A medium sized tree produces from fifty to sixth tons of firewood worth ten or twelve shillings a ton, and this is the coarsest timber.

Huon pine, myrtle, sassafras, bedfordia, and other cabinet woods are sold by the foot at considerable prices according to their veining and quality.

All our forest trees and shrubs are evergreen. The smaller shrubs are for the most part highly aromatic, and bear beautiful flowers, and in many instances berries.

The mimosa bears a sweet tasting gum in considerable quantities, which is eaten while soft by children. It resembles the gum arabic of commerce, and is equally useful. The gum trees of Eucalyptic bear gum kino, and the white species produces *manna*, both of which are medicinal. The grass tree, *Xanthorrœa*, produces a resinous gum of some value in the arts, and for the production of illuminating gas.

OUR CORRESPONDENT. THREDBO. SNOWY MOUNTAINS. NEW SOUTH WALES. 1860

On 28 December 1860, the Alpine Pioneer and Kiandra Advertiser *published 'Ascent of Mount Inchcliffe' by their correspondent writing under the pseudonym of Hammersed. There is now no mountain of that name. The highest point near Thredbo is west of the town and 7189 feet (2192 metres) above sea level.*

Both the goldfield and the newspaper were only a few months old. The easiest, but still very difficult, road to Kiandra came in from Twofold Bay. In July 1860, the track was too icy for horse teams, so the camels of Kiandra, as the Chinese carriers were called, brought up the type and presses for the newspaper on their backs. These men made many trips for stores during the winter. They walked to the coast in the morning and came back in the afternoon loaded with up to 65 kilograms per man. The first issue of the newspaper came out on 24 August. It was consistently anti-Chinese.

About 2000 men spent the winter of 1860 on these fields. Both the government and local graziers feared that few would survive. The fields were shallow and marvellously rich. The gold-diggers not only survived, many made £40 to £50 a week, a year's wages in a week; they also took time off to develop the sport of skiing. They cut planks, sharpened them on one end and curved them up a little, strapped them to their feet and made slides on which they raced one another downhill.

Thredbo, from which the party made the climb, is 80 kilometres south-southwest of Kiandra.

THE THREDBO RUSH
ASCENT OF MOUNT INCHCLIFFE
[From our Correspondent]

According to previous arrangement, a muster took place this morning amongst the most enterprising gentlemen on these diggings to make the ascent of the highest point in the mountain range encircling the valley of the Thredbo. The party consisted of nearly twenty gentlemen, amongst whom were Mr. Inchcliffe (an American), D.C.H. Thomas, Mr. Millar &c. The ascent took upwards of three hours. The height is 4000 feet above the Thredbo.

The party found the lower part very scrubby and rugged, and with difficulty made their way; at an elevation of 1000 feet they found gullies and immense beds of quartz. Two snakes were killed by them, and the mountain was infested with them. The gullies about half-way up were literally lined with birds' nests of every variety, and the banks bloomed with the choicest and most brilliant wild flowers.

On ascending the tableland, immense herds of wild horses were seen, which it would be impossible to drive in. Here they found the cold extreme, and lighted fires. Beautiful streams flowed from the summit — their beds glistening with mica and quartz. Immense beds of snow frozen as hard as ice, about three feet in thickness, - a solid mass of which Mr. Inchcliffe brought (and which enabled us to enjoy our sherry cobbler, the day being extremely hot.) On reaching the highest point their toil and enterprise was richly rewarded by a view surpassingly grand. To the south were seen mountains covered with snow, - and to the west [east] the plains of Monaro. Having feasted their eyes with this splendid scene, they turned their attention to something in the shape of cold ham, &c.; and, planting a flag, with a bottle of champagne and brandy, christened the peak "Cook's Mount," in honour of Captain Cook, the discoverer of Australia; but it is now known as Inchcliffe Mount, in commemoration of the first ascent.

The party descended in safety, bringing down ice, flowers, and specimens of quartz; also, part of crayfish found at the summit.

HAMMERSED.

Great Thredbo, Dec. 23.

JOSEPH ELLIOTT, ADELAIDE, 1860*

Joseph Elliott and his brother, James, came to Adelaide in December 1851 and went to work for the Register News-Pictorial. A few months later Joseph married Eliza a'Court, an 18-year-old emigrant by the same ship. He was only 17, but he added three years when he signed the marriage register.

Both brothers left with the first big batch of excited Adelaide diggers who did better than most on the Victorian goldfields. Experienced Cornish miners from the Burra copper mine dropped tools and went with them.

Joseph did not have long enough there to make any money. He got word from his young wife that she was pregnant and sick, so he came back to the newspaper. She died giving birth to a son who also died a few months later.

Rebecca Kearns, a friend of Eliza, married him the next year. They had ten children, seven of whom lived. Joseph eventually became owner-editor of the *Southern Argus* at Strathalbyn, south of Adelaide.

In August 1860 when he and Rebecca were living in Jeffcott Street, North Adelaide, and while he was still with the *Register*, Joseph wrote an illustrated letter home to his mother 'on strong though thin paper' that he bound into a book now in the South Australian Archives. Brian Elliott, Joseph's grandson, edited it as *Our Home in Australia* and published it in 1984.

It reveals the life of conventional immigrants of very moderate means, keeping up English ways in a developing Australian city. The family baths each Saturday night:

> ...there is not a great deal of washing required on Sunday. [At breakfast each Sunday] ... my dearest Becky cuts a slice of our leg of mutton & grills it for me, & she and the children generally have some thing left from dinner on Saturday evening. [On Sunday] ... come when you will, you will always find the same dinner! We consume 52 legs of mutton a year! Baked in the oven & also a few baked potatoes. I can tell you we would not change this dinner for any other. [And there was always enough left for Monday dinner] ...cold mutton & warm potatoes with mint sauce, of which I am very fond.

* Item courtesy of the State Library of South Australia

First then, suppose me at work at my office, & you had arrived in South Australia. You would enquire naturally for the "Register" Newspaper office and you would find us about 10 minutes walk from the Railway Station in Grenfell Street ... It is a very extensive

Concern — the largest Printing & Newspaper office in the Colony, and a very rich proprietary of property. Freehold, & built after their own designs. It consists of large rooms or Cellars under ground for the Machines, Engine, & Presses — rooms & offices on the ground floor & large & commodious & comfortable rooms upstairs for the Editorial department & news composing room.

The department over which I have charge is the General Printing dept. on the right hand ground floor, with the cellar or large room underneath (where I have put up a few stars). Here Printing of every description & kind is done on the cheapest, neatest & promptest terms &c &c &c. On the top of the building is erected an observatory on the top of which a good view (the best view in fact that can be had in Adelaide) of Adelaide & surrounding country. The office faces the north. So we see to the North — North Adelaide. I can see my house quite plain (about a mile & half walk but about a mile by the crow); to the West we have the Gulf & Port Adelaide; to the South and East the beautiful & glorious hills as they are called but more like Mountains. The highest of these visible in Adelaide is called Mount Lofty and is 2400 feet above the level of the sea. I will suppose you have found the office, & of course found me - & I will now take you northward - to North Adelaide. North Adelaide is about a mile from South Adelaide - being separated by a river (which is nearly dry in summer weather!) and on either side of that are park Lands. Some parts of which are enclosed and planted with trees — the original gum & other trees

having been cut down years ago. We leave town - cross the park lands
by a road & across the bridge over the Torrens, then across more
park lands, up the Hill (N.A. is on a hill & so is S.A. but the land
lies low between the two) and up one wide street - & exactly
opposite Christ Church is -- our house - or rather two cottages
attached & belonging to Mr. Downs, one on the right hand occupied
by himself & the other on the left occupied by us. It is built of

Stone and Brick Quoins. (I shall speak of
our house only). We will now open the
gate (by the bye the railing in front of
the garden is white or rather of a light
colour & step into the garden & then on
to the Verandah floor (concrete) and
Knock at the door; but while the door is

being opened just let us turn our back to the house & look at the
garden. Suppose we are standing just in front of the door and
looking towards the gate... the beds are all enclosed by Soda water
bottles turned upside down in the ground. There are not many trees,
but a good many plants. On the left hand we have a creeping plant
which shelters the bed-room window... You must excuse my
Keeping you under the Verandah so long, but even if it were raining
we should not have got wet. The path under the Verandah is about 3
or 4 feet wide - & if you are tired standing there is a form under
each of the windows - so you can sit down - providing your crinoline
will allow you room enough on a form five feet long X 9 inches

wide! As perhaps our knocking at the door was
not heard before (there are children inside!) we
will Knock again & look at the door a minute.
It is painted a light colour, has a white pot
handle in the middle, & a brass Knocker on
which is engraved ELLIOTT.

1861–1879

OSCAR DE SATGÉ, PEAK RANGE, QUEENSLAND, 1861

Of noble Catalan origins, de Satgé was born in England because his father, a created French vicomte, had been exiled for taking part in a royalist revolt. He came to Melbourne as a 17-year-old in 1853. An introduction to Governor La Trobe earned him a position as a clerk in the Goldfields Commission. He later served as a parliamentary clerk.

De Satgé's brother owned stations in the Darling Downs and Oscar decided that the life of a pastoralist was more exciting than that of a clerk. In December 1854, he joined his brother to get experience, taking part in a 1600-kilometre drive of cattle for sale in Victoria, then worked on other stations for several years.

In 1861, in partnership with Gordon Sandeman, who became his brother-in-law, he bought stations in the Peak Range district 200 kilometres northwest of Rockhampton. De Satgé bought numbers of stations in different districts, stocking them heavily and improving them with fences and wells for water, then selling at high prices. He spent 13 years in the Queensland Legislative Assembly and had a powerful influence on pastoral land policies.

De Satgé retired to England in 1882 and married, but made visits to Australia to inspect his properties. His policy of heavy stocking failed him in the long drought of the 1890s. He lost 90,000 sheep and 10,000 cattle and the Bank of New South Wales took over. When he died in 1906, he left an estate worth little more than £400.

De Satgé published *Pages from a Journal of a Queensland Squatter* in 1901. This passage tells of his excitement at first seeing the Peak Range country. The Archers that he mentions were the adventurous brothers known to Leichhardt.

August, 1881, was a glorious season for the country we came to explore; abundant and unusual rains had fallen early in the month, filling the many little creeks that headed from Peak Range. The country, which chiefly consisted of black and chocolate-coloured loam, had evidently been burnt before this late rain by the blacks, and the undulating plains that lay under the picturesque peaks that formed the so-called range were clothed with a carpet of burnt feed, forming a vivid green dotted with a variety of wild flowers, also many kinds of wild peas and vetches, wild cucumbers, and other trailing plants I did not then know. Never after, during my long experience of the district, did I see it in such splended condition — I might, indeed, say glory — as when our little party, after some buck-jumping at the start on the part of Thorne's young horses (which only damaged the packs), started from Thorne's camp, ascended this low range, and dropped on the rolling downs the other side, the most of which country we knew to be included in the tenders that had been transferred by the Archers to Sandeman.

We ascended one of the twin peaks called by Leichhardt "Brown & Charlie's Peak," which rose 700 or 800 feet from the high downs at its base, and from that point the country lay before us like a map, enabling us to identify with more or less accuracy the site of the creeks and the position of the various blocks on Archer's tracing, which we carried with us. It seemed all open country before us and on both sides, and we could not look upon this vast stretch of open land, clothed with the richest herbage and grasses, without forming dreams of future success and its accompanying fortune.

As we descended from that preliminary survey of our realms to be, and followed the biggest watershed we could make out and trace with our glasses, our spirits rose, and mutual exclamations of interest were the order of the day. The spare horses could hardly be driven along, so anxious were they to crop the sweet burnt feed. Huge kangaroo lazily turned round to gaze at the new intruders before hopping majestically away; bronzed-winged pigeons sprang up on every side with the strong whirr of perfect condition; the grey-headed wild turkey or bustard stalked about in robust alarm; whilst occasional mobs of the statelier emu trotted round us with their usual curiosity. Nature, in fact, both as regards season and time, was at its fill, before the hand of the white man had been able to set its riches to good account. To my last day will I remember with gratification that first impression of the Peak Downs, with its many glories of anticipation.

CAPTAIN KIRBY, BOUNTIFUL AND SWEER'S ISLANDS, GULF OF CARPENTARIA, 1861

Kirby was captain of the sailing ship Firefly *chartered by the Government of Victoria to take on William Landsborough and his party at Brisbane and convey them to the Albert River in the Gulf of Carpentaria. Landsborough was in charge of a party sent out to search for Burke and Wills.*

After delivering the explorers, Kirby was instructed to sail on to Surabaya to deliver a load of spirits and mixed goods. The steamship *Victoria* under Captain Norman was to accompany them on the Australian leg. Norman was in charge.

Kirby left a published monograph of the trip, *Narrative of a Voyage from Melbourne to the Gulf of Carpentaria*. They ran into heavy weather a couple of days out from Melbourne and it took 12 days to sail to Brisbane.

In the company of *Victoria*, they made Torres Strait in eight days of 'tolerably fine' weather. Then a gale set in:

> Reefed fore and aft canvas, and stood south-east, the gale still increasing, until at last it became such a hurricane that we could no longer keep sail on the vessel... the pumps continually working, and an immense volume of water on deck.

Currents up to five knots threatened to run them on to reefs: 'We were in great danger... the explorers bewailed their fate to such an extent... I feared their terrors might affect the crew.'

Victoria sought her own safe water and abandoned them. Kirby ran southeast to the Raine Island beacon on the Barrier Reef hoping for calmer water through the passage. He weathered the beacon, and then anchored in safe water. Severely short of water for horses and men, he was forced to turn southwest for Sir Charles Hardy's Island through wild seas. It is one of a group of islands about 200 kilometres south of the Cape. When he anchored off the island, both port and starboard chains broke. While he was setting sails to get steerage way, *Firefly* ran aground: 'The sea was at the time running mountains high, breaking clean over the decks'. He lowered the quarter boat to get the explorers ashore. She stove in immediately. Luckily, the long boat survived to save explorers and stores.

At low tide, the crew could walk to the vessel to collect tents and the rest of the stores. When Kirby got ashore, he 'found the explorers, who seemed to know nothing about rigging tents or lighting fires... in a most deplorable condition'. Back on the vessel, the horses were up to their bellies in water so they cut a hole in the ship's side and got 26 of them safely on land. On the island's good grass and good water, they soon recovered and put on condition.

Victoria put in an appearance at last. Her crew plundered the stores bound for Surabaya and got drunk for days on the spirits. Kirby got them sober by throwing the rest of the bottles overboard.

There was no room for the horses on *Victoria*, so they repaired *Firefly* as a barge to be towed by *Victoria*, loaded the horses and steamed for the Albert River. Near the bottom of the Gulf, they collected turtles from Bountiful Island, fish and fresh water at Sweer's Island, both named by Flinders.

The Gulf seas are frequently confused with short, bouncy waves rocking the ship and sometimes irregularly slapping against the bow and sending spray over. In 1992, I sailed down it on *One and All*, the beautiful South Australian sailing ship built to the design of the late 18th century. Our course lay along the meeting of two tides carrying a stream of food. Surface-feeding sea snakes followed it in extraordinary numbers. With the help of all the passengers, Colin Limpus, a scientist studying turtles, counted about 100 snakes of four species in an hour.

I watched the sun sink into the Gulf. It seemed to be only a few kilometres away and the great glowing globe sank so quickly, I expected the sea to erupt.

Bountiful Island is still bountiful. It is one of the world's premier breeding grounds for Green Turtles. Five thousand lay their eggs there each year. As the tide goes out, they congregate in shallow pools and bask until the next tide. I counted 165 in one pool. The snakes that Kirby refers to are non-poisonous Water Pythons. They sense the slight lift in temperature of the sand when turtles are hatching 45 centimetres down. They wait for a day or two for them to claw their way to the surface, then gulp them as they emerge.

Sweer's Island became a sanatorium when a ship brought yellow fever to Burketown in 1866. Thereafter, for many years, it became a beautiful suburb of Burketown. Now it is a superb fishing resort. Because the surrounding waters are shallow and rocky with patches of coral, commercial trawlers cannot get in there. A well sunk by John Lort Stokes in 1841 still supplies the island with all its fresh water.

Petrogale penicillata

BRUSH-TAILED ROCK WALLABY
Louisa Atkinson, 1860s, Mitchell Library, State Library of New South Wales

CLARENDON [Cox family home in Tasmania]
Eliza Cox, c. 1860, Allport Library and Museum of Fine Arts, State Library of Tasmania

BEAUFRONT, Tasmania
Henry Gritten, 1861, National Library of Australia R9925

Blandfordia.
Grandiflora.

CHRISTMAS BELLS, painted at Lake Macquarie near
Newcastle, New South Wales
Annabella Boswell, 1861, by courtesy Port Macquarie Historical
Society

SASSAFRAS GULLY, Dandenong, Victoria
Isaac Whitehead, c.1870, Rex Nan Kivell Collection, National Library of Australia T347

SOUTH AUSTRALIAN BOTANY
George French Angas [1882–1886], Plate LV in South Australia
illustrated, Rex Nan Kivell Collection,
National Library of Australia U1267-U1333

MALLEE SCRUB, Murray River
Nicholas Chevalier, 1871, National Library of Australia R3927; the Aboriginal Australians are taking
eggs from a Malleefowl's mound

... we then proceeded up the Gulf to Bountiful Island, which is some six miles in circumference, and in some places one hundred and fifty feet in height. This Island ought to have a corporation and aldermen of the old school, as the finest turtles I have ever seen were to be had in the greatest abundance for the trouble of catching them; to people who had been on salt provisions for months, they proved a most acceptable treat. We saw no animals on this Island, if we except snakes of a large size, which were most disagreeably abundant, in fact, it was impossible to walk twenty yards in any direction without meeting some of those reptiles; birds were, however, abundant, more especially cockatoos and buzzards, which were to be seen in all directions. Bountiful Island does not seem at all adapted for settlement, and is merely a place for ships to touch at to obtain turtles.

From Bountiful Island we proceeded to Sweer's Island, where we arrived in about twelve hours. I was rejoiced at last to find a spot admirably suited for European settlement; the harbour is excellent and affords shelter at all seasons, and from all winds; the Island is about twelve miles in length by about six miles in width; it is for the most part composed of flat land, with trifling undulations; there is an abundant and never failing supply of good water from springs, and, indeed, the pure element can be obtained by sinking a few feet on any part of it. The temperature when we were there was from 90° to 100° [32 to 38 degrees Celsius], and the climate seemed to be remarkably salubrious. There are no large trees, those we saw being stunted in their growth, and of small size; we saw neither plants nor fruits. The soil is a dark loam of considerable depth, and, except on the beach, there is little or no sand; no animals were seen, but birds of the cockatoo, pheasant, and parrot tribe are abundant. There can be no doubt but that tropical fruits would grow most luxuriantly; and if the Albert River became ere long an important settlement, Sweer's Island must also be a place of much consequence. Fish are to be had in the greatest abundance, more especially codfish, weighing from seven to twenty pounds, and I see no good reason why a fishery of a remunerative character might not be established there.

WILLIAM LANDSBOROUGH, FLINDERS RIVER, NORTH QUEENSLAND, 1862

It is difficult to know why Captain Kirby thought so little of William Landsborough and his party. Kirby's comments do not tally with anything known of him. In 1859 and 1860, Landsborough made two expeditions with Nat Buchanan, a supreme bushman who had no tolerance for the incompetent. A couple of years later, in partnership with Buchanan and others, he took up land they discovered on the headwaters of the Thomson River which flows south past Longreach and Windorah into Cooper Creek.

Landsborough was born in Ayrshire, Scotland, in 1825 and came to Sydney in 1841 to join his elder brothers who were established on stations in the New England district of New South Wales. In 1850, he leased a run of his own and, in 1852, joined the gold rush to Bathurst with success. Then he moved to Queensland where his brother had a station on the Kolan River west of Bundaberg. He took up leases of his own with various partners.

Now an experienced bushman, Landsborough made private explorations into the many watersheds of the Fitzroy River, which flows out to sea through Rockhampton.

After the terrifying journey on the *Firefly*, the expedition to find Burke and Wills finally got under way. The *Victoria* took Landsborough and his party 30 kilometres up the Albert River and the horses walked ashore from the *Firefly* barge. The party found traces of Burke and Wills on the Flinders River; they also found a notable extent of good country, all of which was quickly settled. They found and named the Gregory River, its headwaters the Georgina (they called it the Herbert) and the Barkly Tableland.

They returned to camp on the Albert and set off southward via the Flinders and Thomson Rivers, finding much more good land on the way. By the time they reached a station on the Warrego, they were reduced to eating boiled greenhide. After a good rest, they set out for Melbourne with bulging tucker bags and delivered their horses and gear to the authorities.

After buying his properties on the Thomson, Landsborough married Caroline Raine and they spent two years travelling through India and Europe. He then returned to become government resident for the district of Burke for four years during which time he lived on Sweer's Island. The position did not stop his exploring. He investigated the headwaters of the Diamantina River and its tributary, the Western, a trip there and back of about 1700 kilometres.

Soon after Landsborough returned to Melbourne, he gave an address to the Royal Society. Two of the three Aboriginal lads who had accompanied the party from Brisbane were present at the meeting. His journal, published in Melbourne in 1862, shows him extraordinarily meticulous about time.

March 4. [1862, approaching the Flinders River] — We started this morning at 8.20. Came E. three-quarters of a mile over rich level ground, with a few trees upon it. The ground was so soft from the rain that the horses were with difficulty driven along. From following each other in single file and sinking at every step to their fetlocks, the track they made was so deep that it will not be easily effaced. At 10.50 came S.E. for five miles and a half across rich plains, with the greenest herbage; the plains separated from each other by wooded land, with shallow streams flowing to the northward. At 11.35 came S.S.E. two and a quarter miles, up along a shallow stream, with slightly wooden plains on its banks. Here Jemmy and I stayed behind the party, and got the following observation, viz., meridian altitude of the sun 76 deg. 3 min., lat. 20 deg. 19 min. 12.45 came across the plain on the tracks of the party, two and a quarter miles. At 2.35 came at a quicker pace, as the ground was harder, for two and a half miles S.E. and by E., and crossed a shallow water-course, with box trees along its margin, coming from the south. At 3.30 travelled over rich plains, separated from each other by wooded land, with water-courses from the south, for one and a half miles S.E. and by S. At 4 came half a mile S.E. and by S. over thickly wooded land, and overtook our party where they had formed their encampment. Jemmy, Jackey, and Fisherman were very successful in collecting food for their supper. On the plains they caught a great number of rats, and near here they caught five opossums. Distance today, eighteen and a half miles.

March 5. — Camp 19, situated on the right bank of Flinders River. — The horses having rambled a considerable distance out on the plain, Jemmy and Jackey were a long time bringing them to camp, and we did not manage to start this morning until 9.3. At 10, came over two kinds of well-grassed country, in an E. and N. direction, for three miles, the first part wooded with box and bauhinia, the second a plain between belts of timber. At 11 came E.S.E., across a plain, to some extent overrun with roley-poley to a deep stream flowing to the north. Here I swam across to the

opposite bank to a plain, which appeared beautifully level and made
on it the meridian altitude of the sun 75 deg. 36 min., lat. 20 deg. 23
min. Started again at 12.50, and came up along the stream, in a S.E.
direction one and half miles over well-grassed land, wooded with
box, to the outlet of a stream from the river, and encamped.
Distance today, seven and a quarter miles.

March 6. — Camp 20, situated on the left bank of a northern
channel of the Flinders River. — The water having fallen greatly
since yesterday we carried the saddles and packs over, and then led
the horses. As the northern bank was boggy, we had to apply the
whip severely to some of the horses to get them started to ascend it.
At 9.57 a.m., having packed the horses, we started. At 10.58 came
E. and by S. up the left bank of a watercourse, with a thin margin
of box trees, for three miles. At 11.12, Jemmy and I left the party,
and came S. for three quarters of a mile, across a plain, to the right
bank of the river, where halting, I made the meridian altitude of the
sun 75 deg. 6 min., lat. 20 deg. 31 min. 12.40 came half a mile N.E.
At 1.12 came along a plain in a S.E. and by E. direction one and a-half
miles to a deeper and broader outlet from the river than the one we
crossed in the morning. Overtook our party here, and assisted to
unsaddle and unpack. The horses were then driven into the stream,
and swam across. Afterwards we pulled the saddles and packs across
with a rope, and encamped... The country we passed over has the
same rich character as the land I described yesterday. Distance to-
day, four and a quarter miles.

March 7. — Camp 21, situated on the right bank of Flinders
River. — Knowing that plains, with just a sufficiency of trees for
firewood and shade, has proved better than any other for pastoral
purposes, this country delighted me; but I must say it would please
me more if there were a few high hills in the distance. I was,
however, charmed with the landscape around the camp this morning.
In the foreground I saw fine box, excoccaria, and other trees,
festooned with beautiful cumbering creepers, and beyond them the
horses feeding on a fine grassy plain, extending to the north and
eastward, to apparently distant blue mountains.

JOHN McKINLAY, DIAMANTINA RIVER, QUEENSLAND, 1862

Born at Holyloch on the Clyde, Scotland, in 1819, John McKinlay came to Australia in 1836 and immediately set out to get pastoral experience on distant stations. He took up a run on the Murray River where he bred cattle for sale in Adelaide, always doing his own droving. The repeated trips earned him a widespread reputation as a man who could find his way about. By the 1860s, he had bought a station on the Darling and several more on the Murray.

In 1861, the South Australian Government sent McKinley out in charge of a party to search for Burke and Wills. He followed up Eyre's Creek, which receives the overlanding Georgina River among those indefinite watercourses, where Aborigines showed him the grave of Gray, one member of the party. He returned to report that find and learnt that the bodies of Burke and Wills had been found. Anxious to see what country they might have found, McKinley set out for the Gulf of Carpentaria.

They reached the Gulf with difficulty then, desperately short of food, they walked 1100 kilometres southeast to the settled Queensland coast where they caught a ship to Sydney.

McKinlay later featured in a wild venture at Escape Cliffs in Adam Bay, the outlet of the Adelaide River. Absurdly, it had been chosen as the site for the capital of the Northern Territory by Lieutenant-Colonel Finiss, appointed the first government resident.

Those who left the settlement made such trenchant criticism of Finniss and the site that the government recalled Finniss and sent McKinlay to find a better site. Incredibly, he delayed too long there, and then set out east for the Liverpool River, an even more hopeless site. The Wet had set in properly, one of the wettest known. In six months, they travelled 170 kilometres. Floodwaters shut off advance and retreat on the East Alligator River.

'We'll build a boat', said McKinlay. 'What with?' They built a hull of round poles and stretched over them the hides taken from 27 skeletal horses – they had eaten the rest. They stretched a second skin of a fairly sound tent and set sail. Sharks circled them, attracted by the hides that began to stink. They reached Escape Cliffs as the vessel fell apart.

McKinlay's diary of his journey across the continent was published in Melbourne in 1863. In this quote, he is on the lower Diamantina as it floods through a system of wandering watercourses and flood plains.

Tuesday, March 4 [1862]. — Wind a little more east; shod some of the horses yesterday, and some this morning. Four of the party after dinner started to kill the bullock; camp there, and return in the morning with meat, when cold. I, with Poole, rode out to some high stone hills eastward, to endeavor to get a view of the creek, and ascertain, if possible, from which quarter it principally flows. After getting to the top of the highest, from which one gets very extensive view to the north-east, there was a slight haze which prevented me positively ascertaining its actual course; there is very heavy timber on a bearing of 35°, and appears surrounded by hills. The haze so bad that I could not be certain; however, I must travel in that direction first, and trust that it suddenly turns round to the north; from this last point, to a point 20° west of north, is a perfect sea, nothing but isolated trees showing above the water; I found the ground exceedingly soft, almost impassable in many places. On the table-land, at the foot of the high stone hills I ascended, are lines of

LAKE MOIRA, Barmah Lake complex south of Deniliquin, New South Wales
H.G.H. Sandeman, 1882, from *Gone out to Australia*, MS3628a, National Library of Australia
Lake Moira dried up periodically, so trees alternately grew and drowned.

creeks forming the drainage of the country, thickly timbered with myall, and (for the place), a considerable quantity of good grass; abundance of water lying on the top of the table-land with sea gulls, ducks, cranes, &c., about and on the basins; seven black swans passed over the camp in their flight, on bearing of 335°; no doubt to some lake in that direction. Some few days ago not a bird was to be seen scarcely, but a few kites, crows, and gulahs; now the whole country seems to be alive with ducks of various kinds, macaws, currellas, cockaatoo parrots, and innumerable small birds...

Monday, March 10... The journey today was over stony hills and flats crossing several small creeks from the more remote hills, some running tributaries of Burke Creek for twelve and a-half miles, and for three and three-quarter miles further over similar country, but more flat as we are now approaching the creek, and camped on the outside of a flat with some water and a fair supply of feed. I was here before the pack animals arrived, but after waiting for them a short time found that in some of the small water courses the water seemed to be driving as I thought with the strength of the wind, as is not unusual, and took for the time no further notice; the horses came up first and were unpacked, the camels were some time after, and did not arrive until after I had returned from a ride to the top of a hill further up the creek, and at which place I went down to the water, and to my astonishment found that the whole valley was a perfect sea rising fast; on my return to where I had fixed the camp I found that the water had approached rather too close to be comfortable, and on the arrival of the camels had them unpacked some distance out on the top of a mound of stones, and had all the horse gear removed there also...

Wednesday, March 19. [by then they are out of the flooded country] — Started about 10.30, and went about fourteen miles; passed through some magnificent country, one fine plain alone extended for several miles, and well grassed; in the distance could be seen high ranges. The weather magnificent and quite tropical, the perfume from the flowers is quite refreshing. Cut a tree with "13 MK (conjoined), 15 to 19-3-62." Distance travelled to-day, 15 miles. Camped on a creek — fine water.

Thursday, March 20. — Left the camp about 10 a.m., and travelled till we struck a large creek, and went over fine flats and sandhills, covered with a most luxuriant grass and several descriptions of creepers. The blue convolvulus was also seen to-day for the first-time, also a most beautiful small blue flower with a dark purple eye. Plenty of pigeons to-day, some few nests were found on the march. The mosquitoes very bad at this camp. A native was brought into camp by Mr Hodgkinson this evening, and we decorated him with necklaces and gave him a feed. Distance travelled to-day, fifteen miles.

Friday, March 21. — Marked a small bastard sandalwood tree this morning "11 MK (conjoined), 20.3.62". Our journey to-day was over nothing but red sandhills, course north-north-east; had to cross a large sheet of water. Eighty duck eggs were found to-day by the men. The country round about now is very fine indeed, grass as high as the horses' knees. We now every day find fresh shrubs and flowers, everything reminding one of the tropics.

A.C. GRANT, CHINCHILLA AREA IN QUEENSLAND, 1863–65

Nothing seems to be known about this man. He wrote a book called Early Station Life in Queensland or Memoirs of an old Queenslander. *Angus & Robertson turned it down for publication in 1921, but referred it to the Mitchell librarian who bought the typescript for £40. At that time, Grant was living in Los Angeles. Each page of the typescript bears his name and address at the top.*

Chinchilla is about 250 kilometres northwest of Brisbane. The creeks that Grant mentions are still named on detailed maps. Cardaga Creek flows north into the Auburn River and thence into the Burnett; Charley's Creek flows south into the Condamine River. There is a Grant Creek in the area, which was probably named for him.

Cattle ran wild on an extraordinary scale in Australia and constantly moved ahead of settlement.

> The bush around "Cadarga"... in those days was literally swarming with wild cattle, many of which had never seen a white man. This was not only the case on "Cadarga". On many stations, owing to the want of a market, both cattle and horses were so lightly regarded as to be neglected in a similar manner, and immense numbers of them, in a wild or semi-wild state, were to be found all over Southern Queensland and Northern New South Wales. On the western side of the run, Cadarga included two large blocks of country on Stockyard Creek, one of the heads of Charley's Creek. These were on the Darling Downs side of the Main Range. The country consisted of fine open apple tree flats, devoid of scrub, and was well watered. Running on this land, exactly as one may see cattle on a well managed station, were thousands of wild cattle, descendents, not of Cadarga herds, but of those which had made their way up Charley's Creek from "Chinchilla". I remember hearing that at that time, by book muster, there ought to have been fully twelve thousand (12,000) head on "Chinchilla", but that no more than two thousand (2000) head could be mustered, the remainder of the estimated number roaming about "Stockyard", "Sideline", and

"Hellhole" Creeks, and some even making into the "Juandah" scrubs
[west of present Taroom]...

Accustomed to work together, knowing the run well, travelling
light, and riding good horses, we were able to perform wonders with
the wild scrub cattle. Many were the mobs cut out at night and early
dawn from their secluded fastnesses. Not infrequently, some of us
would be overtaken by an enraged animal, and as a result have our
horses more or less badly horned. This happened to me on three
occasions, but hairbredth escapes were not uncommon. There being
so many half-wild lively cattle in the herd, we found them handy as
"coachers" into which to drive the wilder ones, when, after mixing
them up well, we would gradually work them along to the yards.
Some of these creatures were quite as wild as American Bisons,
especially the old cows and bulls. The latter were huge, heavy
animals, with great humps of flesh on their necks, and having
innumerable cuts and scars on their thick hides, savage, gloomy, and
treacherous looking, and ever ready to charge at a moment's notice...

It was a singularly fascinating existence. The bush was full of
life, of beast and bird. The wattles were yellow with bloom and rich
with scent. The long sloping iron bark ridges and shady apple tree
flats were ideal places for galloping. There was just danger enough
in heading the flying animals through the thick difficult country,
which could only be ridden through by practised horsemen, to make
it enjoyable, while the open air life day and night, lent a subtle
charm to everything. It might be that we would hunt a Kangaroo if
he came temptingly near, or we would procure wild honey or scrub
turkey eggs during the noon day spell, or fish in a waterhole which
never previously had been disturbed by the hand of an angler
[Aboriginal Australians often fished with lines]. The chief sport,
however, lay in the bursting gallop through the scrubs, often by
moonlight, and the pleasure we found in the qualities of our horses.
The camps at evening were the most ideal that can be imagined.
Today, those days seem like enchanted times. We would usually pick
a nice spot with abundance of grass, close to a good waterhole,
having a large log with plenty of dead timber near it. After supper,
we lay, and smoked, and yarned, until, falling asleep, we would
waken to find the sky beginning to brighten, and the wild birds

commencing to whistle. Then we would make up the fire, put on the quart pots, and, taking our bridles, set out to catch our horses, often returning wet to the waist. After breakfast, we would saddle up, light our pipes, at the burning coals, and start.

A GOLD DIGGER'S NOTES, VICTORIA, 1864

I have a bound volume of six months of All the Year Round *a Weekly Journal
conducted by Charles Dickens with which is incorporated Household Words.
The issues run from 13 February to 6 August 1864.*

Dickens published the first chapter of *David Copperfield* in the first issue of
Household Words on 30 March 1850. In the bound volume of 1864, he adver-
tises 'New Work by Mr. Dickens OUR MUTUAL FRIEND in twenty monthly
parts'.

No contributors are named. The Gold Digger's Notes appeared on 2
April 1864. He was taking time off to look at what was about him.

On this bright Australian summer's day why should I have anything
to do but wander away on some river bank with a gun, a rod and a
line, taking rests in shady places, and watching the habits of such
live things as one may see? Sometimes a snake gliding through the
grass, and lifting his head up from time to time; then a turtle,
slowly rising to the top of the water, and paddling away, or basking
in one place as he looks about him, and then going down with a
splash. Next a kangaroo fly (a fly something like those bright flies
that make their nests in the garden walls at home) will pounce down
among the flies on one's hand or dress, and carry off a victim; then,
some little lizard from under a loose scale of bark on a gum-tree,
and of the same colour, will dash out and follow his example. To
notice a black band reaching up the same tree, over the rough brown
dead-looking bark at the bottom, and up the smooth white bark
above, in a wavy line, and at last lost among the big branches at the
top, is very amusing. In warm weather there is an endless daily and
nightly procession of little black ants, worthy of note both from
their incredible numbers in swampy places, and from their horrible
stench and taste when crushed. Woe to the man who leaves his bread,
meat, sugar, or anything eatable within their reach!

Perhaps after watching these things, one looks up and finds that
one has been watched all the time, either by a big guana, motionless
on the limb of a tree, or by a pair of eagle-hawks high up in the air.

wheeling in their endless circles, as if they were never tired. A mob of ducks next come up the river, following all its bends, and whiz past with straightened necks as they turn off with one consent, on their way to some rushy lagoon close by. Now is the time, down on one's knees, with hat off, gun ready, and dog crawling behind, one creeps up as noiselessly as possible to the belt of rushes which surrounds the lagoon, then rising gradually, has the pleasure either of seeing the ducks swimming comfortably along, out of range, or of getting a raking shot at them, perhaps killing one, and wounding another. When the dog goes for the wounded one, it will swim awhile, then dive. Looking sharply about, one sees the leaf of some water-plant turn on edge and the upper part of a duck's head and bill appear above the surface. I have known my retriever, Bess, swim for an hour at such times, before I could sight and shoot the duck again.

On my occasional shooting excursions last winter (near Beechworth, Victoria), I saw several birds that were new to me. One, a milk-white spoonbill, about thirty inches in height, and with a bill eight or nine inches in length. They are very handsome birds. I also saw, on the muddy side of the swamp, an ibis, brown with longish black legs, and long curved bill. It stood over twenty-four inches high. The magpies here are different from those in England. There are two or three sorts of them; the pied, which are the commonest, always go in pairs, and make a strange wild sort of whistling, especially before and during rain.

RACHEL HENNING, MYALL RIVER,
NEW SOUTH WALES, 1866

Rachel Henning, daughter of an English clergyman, came to Australia with her brother Biddulph in 1853. Biddulph became a pastoralist in a big way and Rachel lived with him for some years. She wrote many letters, all of which were kept by several family members and eventually brought together by a niece in the 1940s. They are a rich account of social life and scenery. In 1866, at the age of 40, she married Deighton Taylor who was in his early thirties without a secure income. 'Of course', she wrote to her sister Etta, 'it is immeasurably foolish for anyone of my age to enter into an engagement like this, but I don't want to be told so on all sides at once.'

Deighton, always called 'Mr Taylor' by Henning, got a job managing a timber hauling business for a friend named Somerville who later became Lord Somerville. They lived on the Myall River on the central coast of New South Wales where the town of Bulahdelah is now. Rachel wrote to her sister Etta on 16 May 1866:

I wish you could see the Myall. It is quite unlike the deep, dry rocky river-beds of the North, but very beautiful in its own way, not very wide but very deep, so that the great timber-punts can go up and down it, and the banks shut in by dense forest so that you cannot see any light through, the beautiful vines hanging from the trees and dipping into the water. Then you turn a corner and come upon a bright little clearing with a settler's wooden house and patch of maize and perhaps an orange orchard or a vineyard. Further on the forest shuts you in again.

The whole country is covered with dense forest, giant trees and thick underwood and vines and creepers. Here and there there is a settler's clearing for some distance round, as, for instance there are open paddocks down to the river; then, backing up our house and the village, is "Bulladilla", a great rocky mountain with steep sides clothed with forest and a range of perpendicular cliffs at the top which always catch the last rays of the sun long after they have left us, and very beautiful old Bulladilla looks then.

Now known as Alum Mountain, it is directly across the river from the town. As a trooper in a Light Horse regiment in 1940, I scaled it one very dark night. Our horses, bred on the flat, needed mountaineering experience. They survived a sudden introduction. A 12-year-old boy on a mountain pony led us single file up a steep, narrow, rocky, winding track. Aware only of the abilities of his own pony, he took us up full gallop. We followed the sparks flying off the shoes of the horse in front.

In 1866, with some help, Rachel climbed it in search of rock lilies, *Dendrobium speciosum*, a singularly beautiful orchid which sometimes grows on trees, but prefers to grow on rocks where it sprawls its dark green, leathery leaves across two or three metres. Massed racemes up to 60 centimetres long bear white, cream or yellow flowers.

> Last evening we scrambled up one of the lower peaks of Bulladillah, the mountain that rises behind our house, to look for rock-lilies and see the view. It was very steep, but, being pulled in front by Mr. Somerville's stick and propelled behind by Mr. Taylor, I continued to get to the top, a sort of labyrinth of splintered peaks and crags.
>
> The view was magnificent — miles of hill and valley covered with forest, the river winding along, then the blue lakes, and beyond all the sea. The white waves breaking on the Port Stephens Heads. I got plenty of rock-lilies and a large hole in my boots from the sharp rocks, and came down safely and dined upon beef-steak pie, which I manufactured before we went.

WILLIAM ROBERT GUILFOYLE, OFF THE TWEED RIVER, NEW SOUTH WALES 1869, MOUNT WARNING 1871

W.R. Guilfoyle was born in Chelsea, England in 1840. His father migrated to Sydney in 1853 and established a plant nursery at Double Bay. William helped him in the nursery, then began making botanical collections that extended to southern Queensland. In 1861, he accompanied scientists on a collecting trip in the South Pacific.

Guilfoyle then bought a farm on the Tweed River and grew tobacco and sugar cane. In July 1873, he succeeded Ferdinand von Mueller as director of Melbourne's Botanic Gardens. He spent 36 years extending them, redesigning them and laying out the adjoining Government House grounds. He visited England and Europe where he was acclaimed as a landscape gardener.

Guilfoyle published three books on botany beginning with *First Book of Australian Botany*, published in 1874.

The quotes are from his miscellaneous writings. In 1869, he noted the wonderful growth on the coast as he approached the entrance to the Tweed River. His prescient remark about clearing is chilling. Fifteen years after he made it, the destruction of the Big Scrub, to the south of what he was admiring, had begun in earnest. It held 65,000 hectares of the finest timber the world has known, worth today some thousands of millions of dollars. It was destroyed for no gain. In 1871, Guilfoyle tells of climbing Mount Warning, the eagle-beaked stone god who created much of the far north coast. His ejaculations of molten granite covered a circle about 100 kilometres in diameter up to 2000 metres deep.

[1869] Among plants which attracted my attention as we sailed along were some lovely specimens of Acmena pendula [probably *Syzygium australe*], the graceful drooping bough of which, like willows, gracefully curved over the green banks to the water's edge. The bright green foliage of the Castanospermum [*C. australe*] or Moreton Bay chestnut, the stems of the branches of which, clothed with their gorgeous yellow and red flowers, were often visible. But far more beautiful than anything I have ever seen were the specimens of the flame tree (brachychiton acerifolium) in full bloom. A mass of the brightest scarlet, enough to dazzle one's eyes, would now and then present itself, perhaps backed up by the dark foliage of a huge Ficus of which I noticed several species. Many fine tree ferns were seen — they have a beautiful effect when their bold grassy green fronds are surrounded by darker foliage. Seaforthia elegans, one of the most graceful of Australian palms [Bangalow Palm, *Archontophoenix cunninghamiana*], is pretty well distributed throughout the forests, but the Corypha [*Licula australis*], or cabbage tree palm is rarely seen. Chamaedon [*Linospadix monostachyus*], or walking stick palm, is very plentiful, and Calamus Australis, or lawyer palm — a sort of rattan — with other plants of straggling habit, form the brush which covers this fertile district for miles. Ipomaea pendula, varying in colour from the deepest shade of purple and lilac to white, literally covers some of the taller trees — the effect is beautiful. [Now *I. cairica*, this is a vigorous exotic already naturalised in 1869.] Higher up the river I was surprised to find Barkleya syringafolia [now *Barklya syringifolia*, Crown of Gold Tree] which is a splended shrub. Its heart shaped lively green foliage contrasted with its spikes of golden yellow flowers, was a sight worth seeing. The botanical treasures of these forests ere long the hand of man will mow down to replace with things more useful to him. The extreme richness of the land, and the way in which nature has sheltered it, astonished me...

[1871, Mount Warning] This is a delightful place as far as the scenery and fertility of the soil are concerned. The scenery is quite beyond description. In all my travels I have never seen anything to equal the beauty of the vegetation. The banks of the river are clothed to the water's edge with an endless variety of the richest of evergreens, and the gay blossoms of climbing plants, entwining themselves around the larger trees, or hanging from the branches in gorgeous festoons alone would be a subject for the painter. But from the tops of the mountains the scenery is upon a much grander scale. You can see the windings of the river for miles; vast belts of magnificent brushlands, richly clothed mountain slopes fading away into distant dark blue or purple ranges. Looking in another direction the great Pacific opens to view — and grand indeed did this appear from the top of the highest mountain here, Mount Warning, or as the blacks call it, "Wollumbin". It was my lot, through the kindness of some friends, to be able to ascend this mountain, which is 3353 feet above sea level [now known to be 3870 feet or 1179 metres].

WILLIAM HANN, CAPE YORK, 1872

*The Hanns came to Victoria in 1851 with five children. Although they lived there for
10 years, there seems to be no record of what they did until Joseph, the father, bought
Bluff Downs on a creek flowing into the Burdekin River in Queensland. He moved
there with his family to breed sheep, a project he never realised was hopeless. In 1864, he
drowned swimming his horse across the river by night. His wife, Elizabeth, died a few
months later. William Hann, their eldest son, and his new wife took over the property.*

In partnership with his brother, Frank, and Richard Daintree, the well-
known Government Geologist for North Queensland, William also bought
Maryvale, the neighbouring run, and stocked it with thousands of sheep.
Frank borrowed money, bought Lawn Hill Station in the Gulf Country
and was ruined by unexpected drought. He moved to Western Australia in
search of land and mapped the last slab of unknown country in the
Kimberley and the Great Victoria Desert. William put the last few thousand
of their sheep on the road to sell them, and drove them into Victoria before
he found a buyer. Then he stocked the runs with cattle.

In 1872, on the recommendation of Daintree, the Queensland Government commissioned Hann to lead the Northern Expedition Party in search
of land and minerals. He set out from Fossilbrook Creek, an outstation of a
cattle run on the headwaters of the Lynd River, with six men: Norman
Taylor as geologist, Dr Thomas Tate as botanist, Frederick Warner as surveyor, Jerry, an Aboriginal, as guide and two other white men.

It was a successful expedition. They found good pastoral land; they found
gold. Frederick Warner earnt half a pound of tobacco (225 grams) as prize
for washing a few shows of light, scaly gold in a gully off the Palmer River.
Hann's assessment was cautious. The country is inordinately difficult.

I wish to be very guarded in all that relates to these discoveries...
My desire is chiefly to impress upon all, that in this direction there
is as good looking a country to prospect for gold as any that I have
seen; but I do not promise its existence, and I would, moreover
caution any but well-trained and experienced bushmen to venture
into this country... The horses would require to be constantly kept
shod... They should have leather under the shoe to protect the frog
from the cutting slates.

Hann enjoyed the trip. He named many of the Cape rivers, but he was generously conscious that Kennedy had been there before him.

> I found them without names ... The discovery ... of the ... large streams on my line of route are entirely the fruits of the great and memorable journey undertaken by that courageous but unfortunate explorer, Kennedy ... I have no desire to pluck a single bay from the chaplet which surrounds his memory as an explorer.

The quotes are from his report to the Honourable W.H. Walsh, Minister for Public Works and Goldfields, 20 December 1872.

[15 July 1872 on the Walsh River then north on to the Mitchell] Having completed and satisfied myself of the nature of the country up the Walsh, I resolved to move on, which I did on the 15th July, by following down the right bank of the river for three miles, through a poor country; here I came upon a limestone formation, which I found to be similar in character to that on the Flinders and the Barcoo. In passing over the ridges I noticed some fossils, which at once induced me to draw up and prosecute a further search. The camp was fixed on the steep bank of the river, which here presented banks sixty feet in depth, composed, near the surface, of a light calcareous soil a few feet in depth, resting on a deep bed of shale, in which limestone boulders of all sizes were imbedded and suspended, and in which the fossils were mostly found.

A more interesting spot for a scientific man can scarcely be conceived; here he is surrounded by the objects of his interest, they are under his feet like pebbles on a seashore, they are hanging over his head ready to crush him if not careful, he cannot move without seeing them around him on all sides; they were of all sizes, and numbers of them beautifully perfect; what, and how many to save was the puzzle, each new find exceeded the last one in beauty, until all the beautiful ones were sufficient to load a dray, could we have saved them, and, as I had not even one packhorse to carry these and the rock specimens, I was put to my wits' end how many to transport. However, Mr. Taylor and myself collected the best of the various species, which we were content to secure and carry along with us. I found two or three bones of the vertebrae of a large animal, which were attached to each other by limestone...

After devoting one day to this search for fossils, I moved on the following one, on a general direction of north... two more miles brought me to another creek, to which I have given the name Louisa Creek, and here commenced as fine a piece of pastoral country as any I have seen in Queensland. The formation was limestone, soil deep and rich, timbered with mimosas and bauhinias, and carrying many grasses common to the Barcoo. Eight miles of this country was terminated by a creek, which changed the character to open forest with rich alluvial soil, when in three miles a fine running river, 300 yards in width, was reached coming from the north. I estimate the good land on this river at about 500 square miles.

[2 September, near Mount Newberry, north of the headwaters of the Coleman] Here we are at last at the termination of our northern course; of the country passed over and behind us nothing could be seen, but the recollections were pleasing. So far the trip has been one of pleasure, as the travelling, on the whole, has been easy; our larder had been well supplied with kangaroos and fish, nondas [the yellow fruit of *Parinari nonda*] and wild honey, and if our search for gold had not been as successful as we could have wished, it had for the time been exciting. I am at a loss to conceive how men call exploring "monotonous"; there is not a creek or a river that does not lead the imagination to think where it may go, what it may lead to, or what it may contain; there is not a goal or a haven looked forward to that has not some interest interwoven with its locality.

ERNEST GILES. FINKE RIVER.
NORTHERN TERRITORY. 1872

*Giles carried out five major explorations in the most unforgiving country Australia
offers. He was born in Bristol in 1835 and, in 1845, was admitted to Christ's Hospital
in London, that long-lived institution of bad food, extreme discipline and erratic
education, which Charles Lamb immortalised. The evening prayer was not defined
to give easy sleep: 'Lord, let the rest that we are going to mind us of the hour of
death, and now that we are going to lie down let us consider that it may be we
shall rise up no more'.*

However, when his parents with his brother and four sisters emigrated to
Adelaide late in 1848, Giles remained at the school and did not join them
until early in 1851. He tried gold-digging with his brother with scant
success and he worked as a clerk for several years enjoying the high wages
of the gold rush days. Then, deciding that he wanted to discover what was
in the unexplored areas of Australia, Giles went out on to the Darling, and
followed it up into southern Queensland to learn bushcraft from William
Conn, a renowned bushman. Later his resolve was reinforced by a meeting
with Harry Tietkens who features in this book.

VIEW IN THE GLEN OF PALMS [Finke River]
Ernest Giles, 1872, from *Australia Twice Traversed* ..., Mitchell Library,
State Library of New South Wales

Giles spent about 16 years learning the country. He took part in droving trips, made short tours in search of pasture on his own or with other adverturers, and then began his life's work.

He told of it in three, well written, fascinating works: *Geographic Travels in Central Australia* (1875), *The Journal of a Forgotten Expedition* (1880) and his greatest book, *Australia Twice Traversed: The Romance of Exploration being a Narrative Compiled from the Journals of Five Exploring Expeditions into and through Central South Australia, and Western Australia From 1872 to 1876* published in two volumes in 1889.

The fourth and fifth expeditions were amazing feats of endurance. Giles set out from Beltana, Thomas Elder's camel station, east of Lake Torrens, travelled west across the Great Victoria Desert, cut his way for days through the tangle of heath that now grows Western Australia's wheat (that land is now becoming seriously salted and eroded) and southwest to Perth. He rested two months, then travelled northeast and crossed from west to east on a line 700 kilometres higher through the Gibson Desert.

Although Giles had made important geographical discoveries, he had found little extent of new pastures. Parsimonious governments rewarded him with few words and less money. He dug for gold in the Kimberley with some success, visited England, and then settled in Coolgardie as a clerk in the office of the warden of the goldfields on half the pay that he had received 50 years before. He died there, at the age of 62, a disheartened man.

This quote is from Giles's first journey up the Finke River and west to within sight of the Ehrenberg Range. It tells of his delight in finding the Red Cabbage Palms in the Finke River, still a wonderful area to visit. The young palms give them their popular name. They are brick red until they grow to about 60 centimetres.

> Soon after leaving the natives [who had threatened them], we had the gratification of discovering a magnificent specimen of Fan palm, a species of *Livistona*, allied to one in the south of Arnhem's land, and now distinguished as the *Maria Palm* (Baron von Meuller), growing in the channel of the watercourse with flood drifts against its stem. Its dark-hued, dome-shaped frondage contrasted strangely with the paler green foliage of the eucalyptus trees that surrounded it. It was a perfectly new botanical feature to me, nor did I expect to meet with it in this latitude. "But there's a wonderful power in latitude, it alters a man's moral relations and attitude." I had noticed some strange vegetation in the dry flood drifts lower down, and was

on the *qui vive* for something new, but I did not know what. This fine tree was sixty feet long, or high, in the barrel. Passing the palms, we continued amongst the defiles of this mountain glen, which appears to have no termination, for no signs of a break or anything but a continuation of the range could be observed from any of the hills I ascended.

It was late in the afternoon when we left the palm-groves, and though we travelled over twenty miles in distance could only make twelve good from last camp. Although this glen was rough and rocky, yet the purling of the water over its stony bed was always a delightful sound to me; and when the winds of evening fanned us to repose, it seemed as though some kindly spirit whispered that it would guard us while we slept, and when the sun declined the swift stream echoed on...

Today, again following the mazy windings of the glen, we passed through the northern tributary noticed yesterday, and continued on over rocks, under precipes, crossing and re-crossing the channel, and turning to all points of the compass, so that nearly three miles had to be travelled to make good one. Clumps of the beautiful palms were occasionally passed, growing mostly in the river bed, and where they appear, they considerably enliven the scenery. During my sojourn in this glen, and indeed from first starting, I collected a number of most beautiful flowers of every changing hue. Why Nature should scatter such floral gems upon such a stony sterile region it is difficult to understand, but such a variety of lovely flowers of every kind and colour I had never met with previously.

ERNEST FAVENC, BUCHANAN CREEK, NORTHERN TERRITORY, 1878

*Favenc was a writer, explorer and a pastoralist. The three pursuits depended
on each other. He was born in London in 1845 and came to Sydney in 1863
because Australia offered adventure. A few months later, he went to
North Queensland for pastoral experience. It was a new, exciting
frontier at that time.*

Favenc worked on numbers of stations in northern and central Queensland
and took part in overland droving trips. In 1871, he began to write for the
Queenslander, short stories, poems, two serialised novels and two imaginary
diaries. All were based on his experiences, all were written under the
pseudonym Dramingo, the name of an Aboriginal companion. Nevertheless, as his stories show, he sanctioned attacks against Aborigines for cattle
stealing and even took part in murders himself.

Favenc gained such a reputation as a bushman that, in 1878, the *Queenslander* sent him to report on the little known country between Blackall in
central Queensland and Darwin, the route of a proposed railway line.
There were occasional stations on the way – the storekeeper at Cork near
the Diamantina River angered them because he 'liquored up all the evening'
and never offered one of them a drink, and they rode up to Rocklands on
the border of Queensland and the Northern Territory for fresh beef. It was
a difficult trip through country where water was hard to find and spinifex
speared their horses' legs. Nevertheless, they found big areas of good, new
grazing country.

Two horses collapsed and died in one dry stage. On a scouting trip,
Favenc and S.C. Briggs, his surveyor, came to a waterhole that was unexpectedly dry. They rode towards camp until their horses knocked up,
and then walked the rest of the way. Day was breaking when they found it
and they waded in up to their knees scooping water into their mouths.
They had been 24 hours without a drink.

Favenc took up stations of his own. He went to Sydney and married
Bessie Matthews who made a wide name for herself through needlework
classes conducted by the *Sydney Stock and Station Journal*. She also did much
co-writing with Favenc and illustrated much of his work. Sometimes they
swapped talents: she wrote and he illustrated. They still wrote for the

Queenslander, but also for the *Bulletin, Sydney Mail, Evening News* and *Sydney Morning Herald.*

In 1888, Favenc published *History of Australian Exploration from 1788,* judged by H.M. Green as the standard history of Australian exploration.

He took time from writing to make other exploratory trips, both on his own account and for the South Australian Government. In 1883, Favenc led a party across little known country from Normanton west to the Overland Telegraph Line. Harry Creaghe and his wife Caroline accompanied him, the only woman to join an official exploration. She was not impressed by the station manager who had 40 pairs of black ears nailed round his homestead walls.

Favenc discovered excellent grasslands between the Gascoyne and Ashburton Rivers in Western Australia in 1889. That was the last of his exploring. He devoted the rest of his life to writing and died in 1908.

This quote is from Favenc's first expedition. He is on Buchanan Creek, found by the legendary Nat Buchanan who knew of waters in waterless country that no one else dares traverse. Buchanan Creek is 120 kilometres southeast of the famous Brunette Downs. Favenc named Brunette Creek, thus naming the station when it was taken up.

Distance is one of the marvels of the Australian inland. One can sense the curvature of the earth.

> As the sun rose, the view I had that morning surpassed anything that I had ever before beheld. Whether it was that the slope was so gradual, or that the morning was exceptionally clear, I know not; but never did I have such a vivid conception of distance as I got that morning. East and west the level country stretched on and on until it faded away into gray nothingness, and the weakness of our human vision alone seemed to stop the sight from travelling on for ever; only to the south a thin black line that through the field glasses looked so near and attainable bounded me. It grew hotter and hotter, and as I rode on over the level downs country the black line of timber — now shadowy and indistinct, now broad and plain (as the haze that the midday heat creates kept rising and falling) — kept me in a state of curiosity that at 11 a.m. was solved. The well-grassed downs country ran down on the gentlest slope imaginable, the forest rose as softly on the opposite slope, but where they met there was no creek — only the prickly spinifex, the stunted bloodwood, the grotesque anthills, and the red sandstone of the desert.

ROBERT LOGAN JACK, CAPE YORK PENINSULA, 1879

*Born in Irvine, Scotland, in 1845, Robert L. Jack attended Edinburgh University,
then joined the Geological Survey of Scotland where he made such a mark that
he was appointed geologist for Queensland. He arrived in April 1877, with his
bride Martha Love, and was sent to Cooktown to examine its coal resources.
He made two expeditions to Far North Queensland and many lesser trips
in search of payable gold. He was always on the move. He led an expedition to
China in 1900, got caught up in the Boxer War and escaped through Burma.
He later worked in Western Australia.*

Jack wrote several books including *The Mineral Wealth of Queensland* (1880),
The Geology and Palaeontology of Queensland and New Guinea (1892), and *The
Back Blocks of China* (1904). He is always a delight to read. He uses mining
terms as though the words excite him. Reefs are vexed by small faults, drive-
shafts have foot-walls and hanging-walls, slickensides slip away, stone is split
up by a 'horse' with a thick vein of quartz, brecciated slaty gangue is mixed
with quartz in nodules and veins.

This quote is from *Report on Explorations in Cape York Peninsula, 1879–80*
'presented to both Houses of Parliament by Command' and printed in
1881. The party consisted of Jack, 2 other white men, 2 Aboriginal youths
and 10 horses. On 18 August 1879, he was in the headwaters of the
Endeavour River northwest of Cooktown:

> ... we left Mr. Starcke's camp [he was a licensed surveyor], after
> improving a cutting through the scrub on the banks of the Morgan
> River for the passage of the pack-horses. This river and the McIvor
> are clothed with a luxuriant tropical scrub. Tall, dark trees throw a
> perennial cool shade over the rapid stream. Their dense foliage is
> pierced by no ray of light; but the slender stems of lofty palms
> shoot up through the leafy mass and wave their graceful heads above
> it. The spaces between the trunks of the larger trees are choked with
> a tangled mass of vegetation, including nutmeg trees, canes,
> plantains, the graceful but formidable laurier vine, and the large
> heart-shaped stinging tree, whose lightest touch is agonising to man
> and often fatal to horses.

A period subsequent to the denudation of the valleys in the horizontal sandstone has been marked by great volcanic activity, whose effects are seen in great masses of basalt. The basalt has emanated for the most part from volcanic centres, which occur generally in the form of dome-shaped unwooded eminences near the heads of the valleys, denuded out of the sandstone table-land. Conspicuous among these are the "Sisters," at the head of the Endeavour, the "Piebald Mountain," Mount Morgan, &c. These hills do not possess a crateriform appearance, but are mere rises marking the site of the lava-eruption which has spread around them when situated on level ground, or escaped in glacier-like *conlées* down the valleys. The points of eruption bear, in fact, such relations to the lava-flows as the similar *foci* in Auvergne bears to the basalt there. *Conlées* of basaltic lava have flowed from the *foci* above referred down the valleys of the north and south forks of the Endeavour River, and have radiated out from Mount Morgan and other centres to the east and north over the flats between the mountains and the sea, where they form, by their decomposition, a chocolate-coloured soil of great depth, peculiarly fitted for tropical agriculture, and at present supporting grasses of very unusually fattening qualities.

Where the basalt has decomposed into soil *on the spot*, it gives rise to open, well-grassed country, almost bare of trees. But where, on the other hand, the soil has been re-deposited in alluvial flats on the sides of the river courses, it is usually darker in colour, and covered by the dense scrubby vegetation already referred to.

The surfaces of the basalt *conlées*, as well as of the dome-shaped centres of eruption, are frequently scoriaceous in a marked degree, forming spongy masses, light and porous as pumice-stone. In a few places the basalt of the *conlées* is columnar, as at the waterfalls in the Endeavour, between Williams' station and Branigan's. The basalt is of the usual character, but contains occasional hornblende crystals, and much olivine. It also contains lievrite (silicate of iron) in geodes.

Gates' Lookout is a volcanic centre of a different character — the deep-seated stump of "neck" of a crater, which once discharged showers of ashes from its mouth. It forms a conspicuous mountain of tuff, and can be seen from Isabella Creek to cut through the

escarpment of a thick bed of white sandstone. The rock is an
agglomerate of volcanic debris, with a certain rude bedding —
courses of larger alternating with courses of smaller bombs —
having a dip to the east at about fifteen degrees. That the bombs are
not detached fragments of an already consolidated rock, but have
been consolidated from a molten mass while whirling through the
air, is proved by the spherical envelope of vesicular basalt which
invariably enfolds them. The interior of the bombs is a mass of
black and green crystals of augite (?) and olivine. They range from
an eighth of an inch to a foot in diameter.

1880—1910

CHRISTIE PALMERSTON,
MOUNT BARTLE FRERE, 1886

Christie Palmerston was the most extraordinary of the extraordinary Queensland
bushmen and prospectors. He spent years living safely with Palmer River and rainforest
Aborigines, when they were trying to exclude the miners, and spoke several of their
languages fluently. A mixture of adventurer and rogue, he was a well-educated man
with a good singing voice.

Christie was born in Melbourne in 1850 or 1851. His mother, Mary Burgess, was the daughter of a London coachman who emigrated to Van Diemen's Land. She became a noted opera singer and toured frequently through Australia, America and India. After her marriage to an Italian nobleman, Casino Jerome the tenth Marquis de Carandini, she took the stage name of Madame Carandini. The Marquis, exiled from Italy after a rebellion against Austrian overlords, came to Australia in 1842 with a troupe of musicians, and later taught music and dancing. Their son was christened Christofero Palmerston Carandini but he adopted his more Australian name when he went to work as a stockman on the Millanjie run in the Broad Sound country north of Rockhampton. He was amongst the first on the Palmer River goldfield.

And there something put him out of favour with the law. There was a rumour that a Chinese was killed in a fight and Christie was wanted for questioning. No warrant was ever issued for his arrest, but Christie disappeared among the Aborigines and into fable. He might have had Aboriginal pack lines working for him, he might have had 200 to 300 Chinese mining for him, or he might have led parties of Europeans and Chinese to the Palmer and the Hodgkinson.

Sometimes, Christie would ride up to miners going back to Cooktown, hand them orders for stores to be delivered by carrier, then ride away singing. When the carrier arrived at a designated point on the track, Christie would be there with Aborigines to unload him. He wore nothing but a loose shirt with a cartridge belt strapped round the waist.

During the 1880s, Palmerston rejoined European society and more is known of his life. He left two excellent accounts of exploring expeditions. In 1882, he was engaged to find a route for a proposed railway from Geraldton to Herberton. Alexander Douglas had been in there and found the country impossible. He spent days zigzagging about in heavy jungle and lowering himself over precipices and waterfalls with vine ropes. Palmerston went in with two Pacific Islanders (known as Kanakas) and three Aborigines in his usual jungle kit: cartridge belt over a shirt if it were fine, cartridge belt over bare belly if it were wet, Snider rifle in left hand, bush knife in the right, no trousers, no boots, gear supported over head and shoulders like a curved horse collar, and he had no trouble at all.

On 6 December 1886, Christie Palmerston married Theresa Rooney, daughter of a solicitor and member of a family with a big timber yard in Townsville. They had music in common; Theresa was a music teacher and a well-known violinist. She was a forbidding woman, so Marce Coomer, her great-grandniece told me. Christie continued to spend time out in the bush with native girls. The Rooney family disapproved of him. He tried to settle down as a hotelkeeper but found it a dull life. The Straits Development Company offered him a job prospecting in Borneo and Malaya. Christie died there of fever early in 1897. He had the originals of his diaries and other records with him and told a friend that he had no money, but his writings were valuable. Termites ate them. Luckily, there were some copies from newspapers and government reports.

Christie and Theresa had a daughter, Rosina, born in 1889 who made a name as a singer. She never knew her father. She was only a year or two old when he left home.

The Bellender Ker Range, with Mount Bartle Frere at 1622 metres the highest mountain in Queensland and Bellenden Ker only 61 metres lower, is still its own world. The determination required to get in there restricts it to few people. The rainfall is thought to exceed 9000 millimetres and the peaks are nearly always clouded. The flattish top of Bellenden Ker has an almost pure stand of tea tree, *Leptospermum wooroonooran*. They might be 2000 years old and the wind fingers in that time have pushed the trunks flat, spread the limbs and sculpted the tops to a constant level.

Here is how Palmerston found Mount Bartle Frere:

> Really, it was as if we were climbing vast masses of rocks, oscillating with the unfinished tremors of a late avalanche, and pregnant with an unexpected direful crash of new birth. The main south-east saddle's crest is particularly serrated with oblong slabbed stones, arranged on end, with a lean towards the south. It seemed as if they had been suddenly shaken loose from nature's tightly-fitted seams, apparently with the ease and similarity of a slight breeze dividing the tail feathers of a fowl, only requiring a delicate touch

to tilt them over amongst the millions of tons of their more
antiquated parts to remould.

These granite rocks are inclining to red in color, and of rather a
soft, sandy-looking texture, with odd large diamond-like crystals
protruding, — just the kind of rock to be easily burst down by rainy
weather. A little later found us perched upon the top-most poising
rocks without words to convey an adequate idea of the view's
immensity. The barometer now registered 6000 feet above sea level.
Although there have been occasional sunny bursts during the day,
the sky is somewhat cloudy and there is a haze that makes
everything shadowy-looking. Yet this is an accessory in freeing the
sight from a brighter light's mirage, thus making distant objects
more satisfying in recognition. For this, I considered myself
peculiarly fortunate, because this spot is mostly under a cloud. The
most vivid impression made on my mind was freighted with the
familiarity of this giant mass of jungles, nooks and corners,
stretching north and south thousands of square miles, and through
which a fair sunbeam never pierces, excepting where its solid
parasitic foliage is cracked by watercourses — crowding these
moments with partially forgotten years of exploration and
unspeakable hardships. Its mountains, rivers, precipices and jungle
afar and near were now dwarfed in complicity to the one dark
seething shadow that lay before me, to be audited merely by a
passing glance, as it were. It was a sight that might but appear to
others a beautiful vista, one which the eyes of others might merely
roll over with the commoner instinct of a dazed gaze at its
complication, instead of enlightenment. Pondering from this view
to the sea beyond, which was of the stoic calmness of a mirror, or
possesses, rather, a sky's immobility, and where the eyes could
marvel to the scope of allotted enlightenment, was simply
contrasting a side-by-side vision of light and darkness.

WILLIAM HENRY TIETKENS,
WEST OF THE DARLING, 1889

William Henry Tietkens arrived in Adelaide in September 1859 as an undersized,
undeveloped 15-year-old. His father had died and his mother sent him out in the care of
an old friend, George Wood, a rascally actor specialising in Shakespearean roles.
Wood ran up debts and cleared out to Melbourne, leaving the boy behind.
Tietkens did odd jobs for the theatrical company to support himself,
and then followed 'Uncle' George to Melbourne, where a message awaited
him to bring up boxes of costumes to Castlemaine.

To get there, young Tietkens rode on the back of a wagon and looked after
the driver's horses to pay the fare. Wood collected the boxes from him, then
told Tietkens to get out. He worked for a bookseller for a while, sold newspapers around the goldfields and tailed a herd of cows for an old German
couple who had started a vineyard. There Wood looked him up again and
borrowed the £12 he had saved and the watch his father had left him.
Tietkens never saw him again.

Tietkens went to Melbourne and was working as a clerk in a railway
ticket office when he met Ernest Giles, down from the backcountry with a
mob of fat cattle. Both of them had attended Christ's Hospital in London,
the Blue Coat School for the poor, with such extreme discipline it engen-
dered a prison-like comradeship among the boys who went there.

Giles had a commission from a firm of stock and station agents to go
beyond the farthest settlement and take up new country. He invited Tietkens
to go with him. They spent three months of 1865 exploring the northwest
corner of New South Wales. On the way back, Tietkens joined a party
overlanding cattle to Adelaide, and then spent years working on western
stations. In the 1870s, he acted as second-in-command to Giles on an expedition west of Alice Springs and on the tremendous expedition with camels
from Port Augusta to Perth along the northern edge of the Nullarbor Plain
and the southern edge of the Great Victoria Desert. It is difficult country.
To misread it and miss water, some of it very hard to find, is to die. Rivers
that flood kilometres wide every 20 years or so drain into lakes that, most
of the time, are beds of glistening salt up to 200 kilometres long.

Tietkens spent a year on the Nullarbor Plain sinking unsuccessful wells
in an attempt to get water for pastoralists who wanted to stock it. In 1889,

the Central Australian Exploring and Prospecting Company sent him in charge of a party to explore the McDonnell Ranges and the country to the west and south of it. He came back with valuable geological specimens and a collection of 250 plants, some previously unknown. Then he studied surveying and settled down to peg out land.

Tietkens loved the dry country and enthusiastically endorsed another's statement that 'the so-called desert country is not to be found! In its place you will find saltbush, cotton bush, native grasses, wild carrots, and a variety of herbage'.

The quotes are from his journal of the 1889 expedition:

Sunday, May 5th [1889; he is in the Northern Territory west of Gardiner Range and north of where the West Meereenie oil and gas wells are now]

I deem myself the most fortunate of travellers to have heard the sounds of running water in such a country as this. At daylight this morning water could be heard running from the hills and gorges, discharging streams of beautiful clear water into the thirsty sands. The only reading I have is Mr. Gosse's diary, and if it rains much longer I will know it off by heart. [In 1873, William Gosse led an expedition from Alice Springs in a hopeless bid to find a route to Perth]. Steady rain fell uninterruptedly the whole day; the camp could not have been pitched in a better place for such an occasion: upon the lee side of a high sandhill, abundance of firewood ten yards in front, and running water in every direction.

Monday, May 13th [Near the Cleland Hills, west of the McDonnell Ranges]

Started at 8.40. This camp is situated at the south-eastern end of a line of hills running towards the N.W., and presenting a line of cliffs to the southward. To examine a remarkable part of this range I turned upon a bearing of N. 37° W., travelled over open spinifex sandhills for ten miles, then turned northerly for half a mile when we came to a gum creek running south-westerly; I was in hopes of obtaining sufficient to fill my kegs, but was very agreeably surprised to find a stream of beautifully clear water coming from a glen in the hills. I have never seen such magnificent bean trees as those growing on the banks of this creek, besides gum trees of majestic proportions luxuriating in the richest brown loam imaginable. There were grasses, shrubs, and undergrowth of the most vigorous growth, low pine clad sandstone hills on either side, completing a landscape only too seldom met with in Central Australia. We had travelled but a short distance it is true, but it was impossible to pass this spot without examining it in detail, besides my ailing camels would benefit by a day on such magificent feed; so at the entrance to the glen we turned them out. Travelled thirteen miles. Collected rock specimens Nos. 38, 39, and 40. Bar. 280.00in., ther. 68° at 5 p.m. Heard some curlews in the evening.

Sunday, July 7th — Mount Olga [west of Uluru]

The little streamlet that here leaves the mountain runs over a stone pavement for 200 to 300 yards, shaded by the smooth and perpendicular cliffs. We imagine what a cool, clean retreat this must be from the blinding rays of the summer's sun — "The shadow of a great rock in a weary land." Being cold weather we seek the sunshine and watch for the sun's rays to reach us. As the great shadow is gradually withdrawn from the plain it reaches its base about 9 a.m. Went up the gorge to take some photographs, and in one or two small hollows was some crystal clear water about three or four inches deep. The bottoms of these little rock basins had all the appearance of the most exquisite mosaic work. The water rushing from the surrounding slopes in time of rain had forced out every particle of sand and foreign matter and left the many-coloured conglomerate perfectly clean, and seen through the clear water was a most beautiful sight...

Monday, August 5th [north of Ayers Range which is on the border of the Northern Territory and South Australia, west of the present Stuart Highway]

From the top of a low sandstone ridge that was here met with I obtained a more extensive view of the eastern horizon than I have had for a long time. North-easterly is a line of hills of considerable height, though apparently of no great extent. Upon a bearing of S. 55° E. I observe some masses of bare red rock, apparently granite, and I decided to visit them with the hope of finding some feature of value and interest; travelled over flat, well-clothed pastoral country, which is now looking its very best. Bright flowers blossom all around; their varied hues and delicate tints present a brilliant and ever-varying panorama of splendour. It was a scene specially attractive to us, so long accustomed to the sombre and irritating spinifex. In six miles we were close to the rocks, and here the growth of grass, crowfoot, and other plants was most luxuriant; eclipsing all by the brilliance of their blossom was the vetch, a pea so plentiful in the Musgrave Ranges, and which here grows in large patches of an acre or two. In color the flower is a bright carmine, and forms quite a feature in the appearance of the landscape. The camels while walking on them snatch up huge mouthfuls as opportunities offer. Arriving at the rocks I found many traces of blacks, but no water. Turned south for half a mile to examine another mass of bare granite. Before I had time to get near it Billy, who was ahead on foot, had found all there was to find, and that was a fair-sized rock hole containing sufficient for our night's requirements, and to replenish the kegs. The camels have been tied up every night since leaving Erldunda, and were entitled to a little consideration, so they were let go upon such feed that it has never been their lot to graze upon since we have had them.

JOSEPH BRADSHAW, PRINCE REGENT RIVER, 1891

*On 9 March 1891, Joseph Bradshaw and his brother Fred landed at Wyndham in
the Cambridge Gulf and rode west in search of pastoral country. There were other
Europeans in the party and several Aboriginal Australians from Palmerston.
The Bradshaws owned a run named Bradshaw on the Fitzmaurice River between the
Daly and the Victoria in the Northern Territory. Altogether they rode more than
600 kilometres. Joseph Bradshaw read a paper based on the trip at the 21st Ordinary
Meeting of the Royal Geographical Society in Victoria on 10 September 1891.
He was a member of the Society.*

An astonishing number of others had been exploring that difficult country.
Bradshaw told the meeting: 'The Forest and Drysdale Rivers are both
fine permanent streams but run through poor, unprofitable country.
Forrest, Stockdale, Woodhouse, Button and others explored this part of the
Kimberley a few years ago and named these rivers'. He did not say whether
he intended to take up any of the country he found, but Fred was speared
to death on their property shortly after the trip so his plans altered.

The most amazing discovery was not of new country, but of a different
type of Aboriginal art, now known as the Bradshaws. Grahame Walsh, who
has spent years studying these works, believes them to be more than 50,000
years old. They tell the story of an unknown people.

We struck the main Prince Regent in about five miles. At this point
it is a fine stream about three chains wide, and seemed to be very
deep at most places. The water was quite fresh, but there were
appearances of its having been periodically backed up above its
ordinary level by the salt water at high tides, and mangroves grew
in small patches along the banks. About a day's journey above the
junction of salt and fresh water we came to a cascade where the
whole volume of the river passes over a perpendicular ledge of rock
about 21 ft. in height from the surface of the water below. On a
calm night the roar of these falls was audible eight miles away.
We followed the course of this river for upwards of five days, and
found that it emerged in an immense volume from a gorge in some
inaccessible ranges, which we penetrated for several miles on foot

without finding any change in the character of the country. We saw
numerous caves and recesses in the rocks, the walls of which were
adorned with native paintings colored in red, black, brown, yellow,
white and a pale blue. Some of the human figures were life-size, the
bodies and limbs were attenuated, and represented as having
numerous tassel-shaped adornments appended to the hair, neck,
waist, arms, and legs; but the most remarkable fact in connection
with these drawings is that wherever a profile face is shown the
features are of a most pronounced aquiline type, quite different
from those of any natives we encountered. Indeed, looking at some
of the groups, one might almost think himself viewing the painted
walls of an ancient Egyptian temple.

Sketch by Joseph Bradshaw of some of the rock paintings that he found on the Prince Regent River,
1891, Mitchell Library, State Library of Australia

ARTHUR MASON. NULLARBOR PLAIN. 1896

In 1896, the Western Australian Under-Secretary for Lands sent Arthur Mason to look for rabbits in unmapped country east of Kalgoorlie. There was a feared invasion of rabbits from South Australia and a crazy consideration, later put into practice, of building rabbit-proof fences to stop them. Overlanders in the hope of easy meals and would-be rabbiters were spreading them much faster than they could manage naturally.

Mason set out from Kurnalpie, 135 kilometres northeast of Coolgardie. It was the most easterly European occupation in that area. Mason's route was unexplored and unmapped, but not all the area was unknown to whites. Delisser had been through some of it, Lindsay had cut across it, Forrest had been through the south and Giles through the north. There were kangaroo-hunters anywhere and Alex Crawford, Chief Inspector of the Rabbit Department with a reputation for getting about, somewhere. Nevertheless, there were 50,000 square miles of country between Forrest's and Giles's tracks about which nothing had been written. Mason found no rabbits until he got to Eucla. Much of the country impressed him.

But it is exceedingly fragile. In the great work *Plant Life of Western Australia*, published in 1990, J.S. Beard, Director of King's Park and Botanic Garden, Perth, published a photograph of the country Mason so admired in a bad season – a more common event than a good season where the irregular rainfall averages 150–200 millimetres a year. A sad-looking Butterbush (*Pittosporum phylliraeoides*), normally a shapely little tree growing four to six metres high, stands in the centre of a red plain strewn with limestone rocks. There might be another couple of Butterbushes on the far horizon. There is nothing else alive.

This is what Mason saw – he is about 40 kilometres east of present Cundeelee Aboriginal community. There is a network of very short creeks in the area.

> Leaving Kalin (Granite Rock) we travelled still Easterly for two days, a distance of about thirty-four miles, arriving at a beautifully green spot which I called "The Oasis". It contains an area of about two hundred acres, and is really one of the prettiest spots that I have ever seen. It is covered with beautiful grass, flowers, and herbage, and is a small Paradise. There are a number of very large salmon

gums growing in a clump about the centre of the patch, one of which we marked A⁴ₘ

There are a great number of small birds and parrots, and their joyous singing makes one feel quite happy and contented. Shortly after leaving Kalin we came to about one thousand acres of granite boulder country, which in the distance appeared to us like an immense graveyard, for the boulders, stuck on end, looked like the monuments and tombs of departed giants, but when we got closer we found that the inscriptions were wanting; it was a sight that one might never come across again in a lifetime.

...We left "The Oasis" on the 30th of June, travelling East for a distance of about seven miles, where I observed for latitude, which I found to be 30° 42' 27" S. We then journeyed on a bearing of about 120° through fairly good grazing country, consisting of blue, needle, and salt bush and grass, timbered with salmon gums, mulga, mallee, etc., for a distance of ten and three-quarter miles to a spot where we marked a salmon gum A⁵ₘ, around which is some of the best agricultural soil we had seen since leaving Yindi, and would produce magnificent cereal crops if only there was a supply of water. Still journeying on the same bearing for eight and a half miles through similar undulating gazing country, we found it advisable to alter our course to 145°, and proceeded on that bearing about ten miles. At a mile's distance we crossed a camel pad, which we supposed to be Crawford's. During the remaining nine miles we passed through good sheep and cattle country, with clay-pans, on which we found innumerable tracks of kangaroos, finding natives' fires still burning, and a number of natives' tracks, some old heaps of mallee roots, but not the slightest indication of water, although there had evidently been a good rainfall. We changed our course next day, and travelled East for a distance of fifty-six miles through gently undulating country, possessing no distinct features of any sort; for although one could see occasionally for twenty miles round, there were no hills, valleys, or landmarks to be seen. For the whole fifty-six miles we passed through the most magnificent pastoral downs I have ever seen, and occasionally through small "oases" of from one to ten acres each in area, with beautiful green feed of trefoil [probably a *Tephrosia*] and other grasses two feet high. The country everywhere had the appearance of an immense farm, covered with all varieties of grasses, flowers, and shrubs. The flowers were beautiful to see, and consisted of Sturt peas, marguerites, daisies, and everlastings. Everywhere the eye can reach it is one vast sea of beautiful changing shades of green.

DAVID W. CARNEGIE, SHIDDI POOL, WESTERN AUSTRALIA, 1896

David Carnegie made the last, long exploration of Australia.
His was a great expedition, but it is little known because:

So far, therefore, as being of benefit to mankind, my work has had
no better result than to demonstrate to others that part of the
interior that may best be avoided. No mountain ranges, no rivers, no
lakes, no pastoral lands, no mineral districts has it brought to light;
where the country was previously unknown it has proved only its
nakedness.

Carnegie was born in Scotland on 23 March 1871, the youngest son of the
Earl of Southesk. He completed his education at the Royal Indian
Engineering College at Windsor and then went to work on a tea plantation
in Ceylon. The Western Australian goldfields offered a more prosperous
and more exciting life. He arrived in Coolgardie in 1892 with his friend,
Lord Percy Douglas. He worked as engine driver and learnt prospecting
and mining so quickly that within a couple of years he was leading expeditions in search of gold.

Carnegie found his own goldfield at Lake Darlot, 300 kilometres north
of Kalgoorlie, and formed a company to work it. They sold out at a good
price, then, at his own expense, he fitted out an expedition to explore
unknown country for minerals and pasture. They were out for almost 13
months, travelling through the Great Victoria and Gibson Deserts, to Halls
Creek in the Kimberley, then back again to Coolgardie, a distance of 4800
kilometres. 'I verily believe that so large an extent of country, good or bad,
has never been travelled through by a more cheerful party,' he wrote in his
story of the trip, *Spinifex and Sand*, published in London in 1898.

Fearful of the amount of water that camels and horses drank, Aboriginal
Australians were unwilling to show his party where their scarce waters were.
Carnegie was ruthless in persuading them to lead him to water. He cap-
tured one man, tethered him and led him for hours, feeding him nothing
but salt beef until he was forced to drink to save his own life. Carnegie made
it a rule (dangerous to health) that no matter how hot it was, none of the
party was to drink or eat between breakfast and the evening meal.

He left Australia in 1897, wrote his book, then joined the Civil Service and became Assistant Resident in Northern Nigeria where he was respected and trusted. On 27 November 1900, Carnegie led an exhibition to capture a brigand and was shot in the thigh by a poisoned arrow. He died minutes later at the age of 29.

The scarce waters in the dry country are a marvel of birdlife. In the quote below, the expedition is at Shiddi Pool, 10 kilometres west of Mount Bannerman off the northeast edge of the Great Sandy Desert. Shiddi was the name of his favourite bull camel that died after eating a poisonous plant growing near the water. That caused a sudden move to another water. Carnegie had intended to stay there until Joe Breaden recovered from severe dysentery.

> This pool was a favourite resort for hundreds of birds — crows, hawks, galahs, parakeets, pigeons and sparrows [finches] — and numerous dingoes. Of the bronzewings, which at sundown and before sunrise lined the rocks literally in hundreds, we shot as many as we wanted. How thick they were can be judged from the result of one barrel, which killed fourteen.
>
> It was a pretty sight to watch the birds drinking, as we sat in Breaden's sick-room, the cave. By keeping quite still we could watch them all. All day long the sparrows, diamond and black, are fluttering about the water, chirping and twittering, until the shadows of a hawk circling above scatters them in all directions. Then morning and evening flocks of little budgerigars, or love-birds, fly round and round, and at last take a dive through the air and hang in a cloud close over the water; then, spreading out their wings, they drink, floating on the surface. The galahs make the most fuss of any, chattering away on the trees, and sneaking down one by one, as if they hoped by their noise to cover the advance of their mate. The prettiest of all the birds is a little plump, quail-like rock- or spinifex-pigeon, a dear little shiny, brown fellow with a tuft on his head. They arrive at the water suddenly and unexpectedly from behind rocks and trees, and stand about considering; then one, more ventursome than the rest, runs quickly down to drink, and is followed by a string of others; then they run up again ever so fast, and strut about cooing and spreading their crests — one seldom sees them fly; when they do they rise straight up, and then dart away

close to the ground and drop suddenly within a few yards. Of all birds the crow has most sound common sense; there is no dawdling in his methods; down he swoops with beautifully polished feathers glistening in the sun, to the water's edge, stands for a second to look calmly side to side; then a long drink and away he goes, thoroughly satisfied to mind his own business and nobody else's.

LIONEL GEE, TANAMI DESERT, 1910

*Lionel Gee was a stipendiary magistrate in the Northern Territory. At the end of 1909,
he was made mining warden and magistrate at the Tanami goldmine. H.Y.L. Brown, the
Government Geologist, had inspected the area in June of that year and reported, 'I am
of the opinion that the gold discovery is an important one and that the rich stone
found near the surface and the lodes will continue in depth and can be followed down
by proper prospecting'. Brown was right. Tanami Gold and other companies are now
mining an area stretching about 200 kilometres northwest from hills known as The
Granites, past Mount Tamani and into the Gardner Range in Western Australia.*

Allan Davidson found the Tamani gold in August 1900. An English mining
company sent him out as leader of a prospecting expedition. Using the
Overland Telegraph Line as a marker, he travelled west into Western
Australia, then south, then turned east towards the hills that can be seen
from a distance. Short of provisions, he could do no more than ascertain that
there was gold at The Granites and, most importantly, in that dry country,
two big rock holes of water near Mount Tanami that local Aborigines told
him 'never died'.

Several men in parties of two or three came in over the next few years
and found encouraging colour but the waterholes, unable to cope with
horses and camels as well as humans, soon gave out. A good season in 1908
brought in more men. The government sent out a well-sinking team to dig
a series of wells to furnish a route in from Wave Hill Station on the Victoria
River in the north and to provide substantial water at Tanami. When Lionel
Gee arrived, there were 60 men and 200 horses on the field. Eleven men
died trying to get in there during 1909 and 1910, their names listed with
disturbing notations, 'Died of thirst and exhaustion', 'Lost, and found
dead', 'Died of fever and thirst', 'Fever and exposure', 'Beri-beri'.

Lionel Gee travelled down from Mucka Yard, the Wave Hill cattle yards
on Gum Creek, one of the headwaters of the Victoria River.

In his report to the Premier and Minister of Mines, he included the
following under the heading PASTORAL POSSIBILITIES:

I have mentioned that in travelling from Mucka to Tanami, through
what is generally termed the desert, I was agreeably surprised to find
that this term is a misnomer, as large areas of good and fair pastoral

country exist throughout, so far as the vast extent of waste lands has
been examined; and I have come to the conclusion that, apart from
the mineral probabilities of Tanami — which I trust will be
systematically and thoroughly tested later on — the pastoral
possibilities are great, and that altogether the effect of the Tanami
discovery is to add a new and valuable province to the Northern
Territory.

During the hot and dry time, when there seemed little for the
animals to eat except spinifex, the horses and camels kept in
splendid hard condition, and, to use a bush expression, "you could
ride all day without wetting the saddle-cloth". Up northward in the
Territory the horses are soft, liable to the "puffs", and, except
perhaps at Willeroo, where the country is rather elevated, do not
breed well. Many practical stockmen have expressed to me their
convictions that Tanami district will prove an ideal place for horse-
breeding.

My impressions, as noted at the end of April, after the rains, are
that the country may be classed as rolling downs of considerable
general elevation, determined by the Government Geologist's
barometrical observation as about 1,400 ft. above sea level, with
sandy rises, red loam flats, stony rises, stony and sandy table
country; these alternations extending for vast distances in every
direction. There are occasional bold rough outcrops of red
sandstone, sometimes — as at Tanami — with a cliff-like frontage or
escarpment of 150 ft. or so high, cleft by steep gorges and showing
red boulders fantastically shaped and piled. When travelling, the
horizon is in some directions far away and in others very near. There
are no very distinctive landmarks. Sometimes you can see the
outlines of small hills, like the teeth of a saw, on the horizon line,
and sometimes the line is slightly curved and recurved, showing the
rolling of the country. Low trees, bushes and spinifex are seen
everywhere. Spinifex is generally regarded as an abomination; but
there are three varieties here, two of which contain very nutritive
qualitities and are good fodder plants for stock as a standby. When
in seed after the rains patches look like waving oatfields. There are,
of course, extensive areas of useless desert spinifex. The long red
loam flats which are frequently crossed are well clothed with many

sorts of bunchy grass, bushes and patches of mulga and supplejack —
the two latter being excellent camel food.

The timber consists of white and desert gum, bloodwood,
Stuart bean tree, scattered dense patches and belts of mulga, and
only occasional belts of heaoak (*Casuarina*). The white trunks
and limbs of the white gum stand out gleamingly here and there;
the tree does not attain much size nor is the timber valuable. The
bloodwood, another eucalypt, has a reddish-brown bark, and in

BROLGAS FLYING

Unnamed, undated sketch by Emily Macarthur, 1806–1880, R11334, National Library of Australia

good spots grows to a fair height; it has dense bright-green foliage and is a handsome tree; the timber is useful. The Stuart bean tree is not a eucalypt; it has a cork-like bark, the leaves are large, curious in shape, and emerald green in color; the wood is yellow, and when dry very light and tough. The aboriginals make their shields of this wood. The tree, however, is not very plentifully distributed. The bushes are in endless variety, but a little scrub-wattle seems to predominate; they are generally straggly and bare-looking and give one an impression of dryness.

The country, after the 11½ in. of rain, is, of course, in an exceptionally good state. Everything is green, bright, and at its best. Broad-leaved climbers twine and twist amongst the trees and bushes, creepers sprawl along the ground, curious herb plants and grasses grow between the clumps of spinifex, and patches of luxuriant bunch-grass are seen here and there.

Bibliography

The following references have been listed alphabetically according to the title of the entry in which they appear.

'A Young Commercial Gentleman', Australia, 1838
Johnston, J.G. 1839, *The Truth: consisting of letters just received from Emigrants to the Australian Colonies*, Adam & Charles Black, North Bridge, pp. ii, vii, ix, 11, 12.

A Friend to Truth, Australia, c.1838
A Friend to Truth. 1839, *A True Picture of Australia its merits and demerits*, John Morrison, Glasgow, pp. 16, 26.

A Gold Digger's Notes, Victoria, 1864
A Gold Digger. 2 April 1864, *All the Year Round*, a weekly journal conducted by Charles Dickens, vol. 9, p. 181.

Arago, Jacques, Sydney and Camden, New South Wales, 1819
Havard, Ward and Olive. 1938, 'A Frenchman sees Sydney in 1819 translated from the letters of Jacques Arago', *Royal Australian Historical Society Journal 24*, pp. 22, 23, 34, 35, 39.

Atkins, Richard, Sydney, New South Wales, 1792
Atkins, R. *mss Journal of a Voyage to Botany Bay, 1791–1810*, held by National Library of Australia, pp. 6, 7, 68.

Atkinson, James, New South Wales, 1826
Atkinson, J. 1826, *An Account of the State of Agriculture & Grazing in New South Wales*, J. Cross, London, pp. 1, 2, 5, 20, 21.

Backhouse, James, Norfolk Island, 1835
Backhouse, J. 1843, *Visit to the Australian Colonies*, Hamilton, Adams and Co., Paternoster Row, pp. 270, 271.

Bartley, Nehemia, Tasmania, 1849
Bartley, N. 1892, *Opals and Agates*, Gordon and Gotch, Brisbane; 1896, *Australian Pioneers and Reminiscences*, Gordon & Gotch, Brisbane, p. 44.

Bellingshausen, Captain Faddei Faddeevich, at sea west of Tasmania, 1820
Debenham, Frank, *The Voyage of Captain Bellingshausen to the Antarctic Seas 1819–1821*, vol. I, ed. translation from the Russian, the Hakluyt Society, 1945, pp. 146–148.

Bennett, George, Off the east coast of Australia, c.1858
Bennett, G. 1860, *Gatherings of a Naturalist in Australasia*, John van Voorst, Paternoster Row, pp. 58, 59.

Bennett, J.F., Adelaide, South Australia, 1843
Bennett, J.F. 1843, *Historical and Descriptive Account of South Australia*, Smith, Elder & Co., Cornhill, pp. 32, 33.

Birkby, Thomas, Sydney, New South Wales, 1834
Hutchinson, W. 3 September 1839, Letter to Birkby's father in possession of National Library of Australia.

Boswell, Annabella, Lake Innes, Port Macquarie, New South Wales, 1843, 1844
Boswell, A. 13 March 1844, Nine handwritten notebooks 1839–1853, in possession of Port Macquarie Historical Society.

Bowler, Richard, Broadmarsh, Tasmania, 1835
Bowler, R. 1 June 1835, First of eight letters written from Australia in possession of National Library of Australia.

Bowman, Anne, Australian bush, c.1858
Bowman, A. 1859, *The Kangaroo Hunters*, G. Routledge & Co., London, pp. 158, 159.

Boyes, G.T.W.B., Nepean River, New South Wales, 1821, Hobart, Tasmania, 1831
Chapman, P. (ed.) 1985, *The Diaries and Letters of G.T.W.B. Boyes*, vol.1, Oxford University Press, Melbourne, pp. 182, 183, 406, 496, 497.

Bradshaw, Joseph, Prince Regent River, Northern Territory, 1891
Bradshaw, J. 1891, 'Notes on a recent trip to Prince Regent's River', Paper read by Joseph Bradshaw M.R.G.S.A. at the 21st Ordinary General Meeting 10 September 1891, *Royal Geographical Society Victorian Branch Transactions 9*, pp. 99, 100.

Brock, Daniel George, In the Barrier Range, South Australia & New South Wales with Sturt, 1844–45
Brock, D.G. 1975, *To the Desert with Sturt*, Royal Geographical Society of Australasia, Adelaide, pp. 62, 63, 215.

Broughton, William Grant, Potts Point, Sydney, New South Wales, 1837
Broughton, W.G. 1837, Transcript of letter written 1 May 1837 to 'My dear Keate', in possession of National Library of Australia.

Brown, Eliza, York to Champion Bay, Western Australia, 1851
Cowan, P. (ed.) 1977, *A Faithful Picture the letters of Eliza and Thomas Brown at York in the Swan River Colony 1841–1852*, Fremantle Arts Centre Press, pp. 148, 149.

Bunbury, Henry William St Pierre, Collie River, southwest Western Australia, 1836
Bunbury, H.W. 'Diary of his travels to Genoa in 1828, and to Sydney in 1834, as well as his explorations in Western Australia 1836–37', pp. 4–6, Handwritten diary in possession of Australian National Library.

Bundock, Mary, Wyangerie Station, Richmond River District, New South Wales, 1850s

Prior, Mrs Murray (née Mary Bundock), 'Memoirs of the early days on the Richmond River', pp. 5, 10, 19, Typescript in possession of National Library of Australia.

Carnegie, David W., Shiddi Pool, Western Australia, 1896

Carnegie, D.W. 1898, *Spinifex and Sand*, Hesperian Press, Western Australia, pp. 302, 303.

Carron, William, Cape York, Queensland, 1848

Carron, W. 1849, *Narrative of an Expedition*, Kemp and Fairfax, Sydney, pp. 5–7, 18, 19.

Caverhill, Jane, Berrybank, Western Districts of Victoria, c.1848

Caverhill, J. c.1848, Handwritten reminiscences in possession of the State Library of Victoria.

Clifton, Louisa, Australind, Western Australia, 1841

Clifton, L. 1841, Diary entries for 17 March and 2 April 1841, in possession of National Library of Australia.

Cook, James, Bustard Bay, Queensland, 1770

Russell, H.S. 1888, Extracts from Cook's journal, *The Genesis of Quensland*, Turner & Henderson, Sydney, p. 516.

Cox George, From Bathurst to the Talbragar River near Craboon, New South Wales, 1821

Cox, G. 1821, *A Journal kept by Mr. George Cox on his late Tour to the Northward and Westward of "Bathurst"*, December 1821, pp. 1, 4, in possession of Mitchell Library, Sydney.

Cox, Jane Maria, Sydney, New South Wales, c.1814

Houison, A. (1912?), *The Cox Family: ms compiled from various sources* (c.1877), in possession of the Mitchell Library, Sydney.

Cox, William, Fish and Campbell Rivers, New South Wales, 1815

Cox, W. 1979, 'Journal kept by Mr. W. Cox in making a road across the Blue Mountains from Emu Plains to a new country discovered by Mr. Evans to the westward', *Memoirs of William Cox, J.P.*, facsimile reprint of 1901 edition by the Library of Australian History, Sydney, pp. 99–101.

Cunningham, Allan, Liverpool Range, New South Wales, 1823

Field, B. 1825, 'Journal of a Route from Bathurst to Liverpool Plains, in New South Wales explored by Mr. Allan Cunningham', *Geographical Memoirs On New South Wales: By Various Hands*, John Murray, London, pp. 172–176.

Dangar, Henry, Hunter River, New South Wales, 1827

Dangar, H. 1828, *Index and Directory to Map of the Country Bordering upon the River Hunter...a Complete Emigrant's Guide*, Joseph Cross, Holborn, p. 42.

de Satgé, Oscar, Peak Range, Queensland, 1861
de Satgé, O. 1901, *Pages from the Journal of a Queensland Squatter*, Hurst and Blackett Ltd, London, pp. 142, 145.

de Vlamingh, Willem, Rottnest Island, off the coast of Western Australia, 1696–97
Schilder, G. (ed.) 1985, *Voyage to the Great South Land*, trans. by C. de Heer, Royal Australian Historical Society, Sydney, pp. 60, 125, 126, 155, 223.

Elliott, Joseph, Adelaide, South Australia, 1860
Elliott, J. 1860, Illustrated letter written to his mother, pp. 1–5, in possession of State Library of South Australia.

Everingham, Matthew, Blue Mountains, New South Wales, 1795
Everingham, M. 1985, *The Everingham Letterbook*, Valerie Ross, Anvil Press, pp. 36, 37, 51–55.

Favenc, Ernest, Buchanan Creek, Northern Territory, 1878
Frost, C. 1983, 'The Last Explorer: The Life and Work of Ernest Favenc', *Foundation for Australian Literary Studies Monograph No 9*, James Cook University of North Queensland, Townsville, p. 18.

Field, Barron, Sydney, New South Wales, c.1824
Field, B. 1825, 'First Fruits of Australian Poetry', *Geographical Memoirs On New South Wales: By Various Hands*, John Murray, London, pp. 489–491.

Flinders, Matthew, Barrier Reef, Queensland, 1802
Russell, H.S. 1888, 'Captain Matthew Flinders' Journal – in Investigator of 334 tons, 1801', *The Genesis of Queensland*, Turner & Henderson, Sydney, p. 572.

Gee, Lionel, Tanami Desert, Western Australia, 1910
Gee, L.C.E. 12 April 1911, 'Tanami Goldfield and District', Report to the Hon. J. Verran, M.P., Premier and Minister of Mines, Adelaide, pp. 14–16, in possession of Northern Territory Archives.

Giles, Ernest, Finke River, Northern Territory, 1872
Giles, E. 1889, *Australia Twice Traversed*, Sampson, Low, Marston, Searle & Rivington, London, vol.1, pp. 24–27.

Godwin, Van Diemen's Land, c.1822
Godwin. 1822, *Godwin's Emigrant's Guide to Van Diemen's Land*, pp. 12–14, 54–56.

Grant, A.C., Chinchilla area in Queensland, 1863–65
Grant, A.C. 'Early Station Life in Queensland' or 'Memories of an old

Queenslander', pp. 48, 49, 51–54, typescript in possession of Mitchell Library, Sydney.

Greenway, Francis, Sydney, New South Wales, 1835
O'Shaughnessey, E.W. (ed.) 1835, 'Colonial Architecture', *Australian Almanack and General Directory for the Year of our Lord 1835*, Sydney, pp. 216, 217.

Gregory, Francis Thomas, on the Gascoyne, Lyons, Fortescue and De Grey Rivers, Western Australia, 1858 and 1861
Beal, J.C. 1884, *Journals of Australian Explorations*, (Augustus Charles & Francis Thomas Gregory), Government Printer, Brisbane, pp. 47, 62, 63, 86, 87.

Grey, George, Near the head of the Glenelg River, Western Australia, 1838
Fitzpatrick, K. 1959, *Australian Explorers*, Oxford University Press, London, pp. 164, 165.

Guilfoyle, William Robert, Off the Tweed River, NSW, 1869, Mount Warning, New South Wales, 1871
Hewitt, N.C. *Centenary Supplement 1823–1923 Tweed River*, (William Robert Guilfoyle), pp. 23, 28, in possession of Mitchell Library, Sydney.

Gunn, Ronald Campbell, Port Phillip and Western Port, Victoria, 1836
Gunn, R.C. 1987, 'Extracts from a journal of a visit to the South Coast of New Holland in February and March 1836', *Venturing Westward*, Tasmanian Government Printer, Hobart, p. 23.

Hahn, Englebert and Frauenfelder, Johann Peter, New South Wales, 1849
Nadel, G. 1953, 'Letters from German Immigrants in New South Wales', *Royal Australian Historical Society Journal 39 part v*, pp. 260, 261, 266.

Hann, William, Cape York, Queensland, 1872
Hann, W. 'Report from Mr. W. Hann, Leader of the Northern Expedition Party', *Queensland Legislative Assembly Votes and Proceedings 1873*, pp. 1033–37.

Hellyer, Henry, Surrey Hills, Tasmania, 1827
Binks, C.J. 1989, *Explorers of Western Tasmania*, Taswegia, Devenport, p. 93; 'Report of Mr. Henry Hellyer', Circular Head, 13 March 1827, *Venturing Westward*, Tasmanian Government Printer, Hobart, 1987, pp. 29, 30.

Henning, Rachel, Myall River, New South Wales, 1866
Henning, Rachel. 1952, *The Letters of Rachel Henning*, The Bulletin Newspaper Co. Pty Ltd, Sydney, pp. 93, 96.

Howe, John, Hunter River, New South Wales, 1819
Campbell, J.F. 1928, 'John Howe's Exploratory Journey from Windsor

to the Hunter River in 1819', *The Royal Australian Historical Journal and Proceedings, Vol. XIV, Part IV,* pp. 239, 240.

Howitt, William, Victoria, 1852
Howitt, W. 1866, *A Boy's Adventures in the Wilds of Australia*, Alfred W. Bennett, London, pp. 102, 138.

Hull, Hugh M., Tasmania, 1859
Hull, H.M. 1859, *The Experience of Forty Years in Tasmania*, Orger & Menyon, pp. 27–29.

Hume and Hovell, Snowy Mountains, New South Wales, 1824
Andrews, A.E.J. (ed.) 1981, 'Bland's Account' & 'Hovell's Journal', *Hume and Hovell 1824*, Blubber Head Press, Hobart, pp. 108, 110, 177, 179.

Jack, Robert Logan, Cape York Peninsula, 1879
Jack, R.L. 1881, *Report on Explorations in Cape York Peninsula, 1879–80*, p. 2, presented to both Houses of Parliament (Queensland) by Command.

Jameson, R.G., Adelaide, 1838, Sydney, New South Wales, 1841
Jameson, R.G. 1842, *New Zealand, South Australia, and New South Wales: a record of recent travels in these colonies*, Smith, Elder, and Co., London, pp. 16, 17, 69, 121–123.

Jamison, John, Warragamba River, New South Wales, 1818
Jamison, J. 1834, 'Journal of the First Excursion up the Warragamba', *The New South Wales Magazine*, no. 6, vol. 2, pp. 54–60.

Jeffreys, Charles, Hobart to Port Dalrymple, Tasmania, c.1819
Jeffreys, C. 1820, *Van Dieman's Land*, J. M. Richardson, Cornhill, pp. 60, 61, 64–66.

King, Phillip Parker, South Goulburn Island, Northern Territory, 1818
King, P.P. 1827, *Narrative of a Survey of the Intertropical and Western Coasts of Australia performed between the years 1818 and 1822*, John Murray, London, vol.1, pp. 62–64.

Kingdom, William Jun., Bathurst Plains, New South Wales and Van Diemen's Land, c.1818
Kingdom, W. Jun. 1820, *America and the British Colonies…*, 2nd edition, G. and W.B. Whittaker, London, pp. 257–259, 296, 297.

Kirby, Captain, Bountiful and Sweer's Islands, Gulf of Carpentaria, Queensland, 1861
Kirby, Captain (of the ship *Firefly*) 1862, *Narrative of a Voyage from Melbourne to the Gulf of Carpentaria*, printed at the Herald Office, Bourke Street East, Melbourne.

Landsborough, William, Flinders River, North Queensland, 1862
Landsborough, W. 1862, *Journal of Landsborough's Expedition from*

Carpentaria in Search of Burke and Wills, Wikson & Mackinnon, Melbourne, pp. 79, 80.

Lang, John Dunmore, Hunter River, New South Wales, c.1832
Lang, J.D. 1834, *An Historical and Statistical Account of New South Wales both as a penal settlement and as a British Colony*, vol.2, Cochrane and M'Crone, London, pp. 94, 95.

Leichhardt, Friedrich Wilhelm Ludwig, Lynd River, North Queensland, 1845
Leichhardt, F.W.L. 1847, *Journal of an Overland Expedition in Australia, from Moreton Bay to Port Essington, a distance of upward of 3000 miles, during the years 1844–1845*, T. & W. Boone, London, pp. 280, 281.

Leslie, Patrick, Darling Downs, Queensland, 1840
Russell, H.S. 1888, 'Patrick Leslie's Diary', *The Genesis of Queensland*, Turner & Henderson, Sydney, pp. 165, 167.

Lockyer, Edmund, Brisbane River, Queensland, 1825
Russell, H.S. 1888, 'Journal of an Excursion up the River Brisbane in the year 1825 by Edmund Lockyer', *The Genesis of Queensland*, Turner & Henderson, Sydney, pp. 591–594.

Macquarie, Lachlan, Illawarra Range, New South Wales, 1822
Macquarie, L. 1979, 'Journal of a Tour to the Cow Pastures and Illawarra in January 1822', *Journals of His Tours in New South Wales and Van Diemen's Land 1810–1822*, Library of Australian History in Association with the Library Council of New South Wales, Sydney, pp. 239–241.

Mann, David Dickinson, New South Wales, 1810
Mann, D.D. 1979, *The Present Picture of New South Wales 1811*, John Ferguson, Sydney, pp. 46, 61.

Mason, Arthur, Nullarbor Plain, Western Australia, 1896
Mason, A. 1897, *Report of an Expedition into the S.E. Portion of W.A. to Enquire into a Reported Incursion of Rabbits*, Government Printer, Perth, pp. 11–15.

McKinlay, John, Diamantina River, Queensland, 1862
McKinlay, J. 1863, *McKinlay's Diary of his Journey across the Continent of Australia*, E. & D. Syme, Melbourne, pp. 17, 18.

Melville, Henry, Van Diemen's Land, 1833
Melville, H. (ed.) *The Van Diemen's Land Almanack for the Year 1833*, Smith, Elder & Co., London, pp. 29–31.

Meredith, Louisa Anne, Spring Vale, Tasmania, 1840s
Meredith, L.A. 1853, *My home Tasmania: nine years in Australia*, Bunce & Brother, New York.

Mitchell, Blanche, Sydney, New South Wales, 1858
Mitchell, B. 1980, *Blanche an Australian Diary 1858–1861*, John Ferguson, Sydney, pp. 94–97, 184, 244.

Moodie, William, Wando Vale, Western Districts of Victoria, 1850
Moodie, W. ?1850, 'Reminiscences of pioneering days in Victoria', manuscript in possession of State Library of Victoria.

Mundy, Godfrey Charles, Sydney, New South Wales, 1846
Mundy, G.C. 1852, *Our Antipodies: or, Residence and Rambles in the Australasian Colonies with a Glimpse of the Gold Fields*, vol. 1, Richard Bentley, London, pp. 41, 43, 74, 75.

Née, Luis, Botany Bay, New South Wales, 1793
Cavanilles, Antonio Joseph, '"Observations on the soil, natives and plain of Port Jackson and Botany Bay"; being mainly a quotation from the general description of the colony made by Luis Née, botanist on the Malaspina Expedition, Mar.-Apr. 1793', *Anales de Historia Natural, no.3*, Mar. 1800, trans. from the Spanish by Robert J. Dorr, c.1955, pp. 2, 3, duplicate typescript in possession of Mitchell Library.

Norcock, John H., Sydney, New South Wales and Melbourne, 1836
Powell, G.T. 1980, 'Journal of Midshipman John. H. Norcock of H.M.S. Rattlesnake on a Voyage to India, Mauritius and Australia 18th October 1835–1st September 1837', pp. 77, 86, 87, transcribed version in the possession of National Library of Australia.

Oldfield, Roger, Sydney, New South Wales, 1828
Oldfield, R. 1828, *South-Asian Register,* October 1828.

Our Correspondent, Thredbo, Snowy Mountains, New South Wales, 1860
Hammersed. 1860, 'Ascent of Mount Inchcliffe', *Alpine Pioneer and Kiandra Advertiser*, 28 December 1860.

Palmer, Thomas Fyshe, Port Jackson, New South Wales, 1795
Palmer, T.F. Portion of a letter dated 'Sydney NS Wales, Sept. 16. 1795' in possession of Harris Manchester College, Oxford.

Palmerston, Christie, Mount Bartle Frere, Queensland, 1886
Palmerston, C. 1887, 'The Diary of a Northern Pioneer, Log of His Doings no.ix', typescript copy of articles in *Queensland Figaro* 18 April 1887, pp. 31, 32, in possession of library of James Cook University, Townsville.

Pamphlet, Thomas, Moreton Bay, Queensland, 1823
Field, B. 1825, 'Narrative of Thomas Pamphlet...taken down by John Uniacke, Esq.', *Geographical Memoirs On New South Wales: By Various Hands,* John Murray, London, pp. 114–116.

Porter, James, Sydney and Parramatta, New South Wales, 1815
Porter, J. 1815, Printed extract from logbook of *Hebe*, 5 November 1815, pp. 1, 3, 6, in possession of Mitchell Library, Sydney.

Smyth, Arthur Bowes, Lord Howe Island, 1788
Paul G. Fidlon & R.J. Ryan (eds.) 1979, *The Journal of Arthur Bowes*

Smyth: Surgeon, Lady Penrhyn, 1787–1789, Australian Documents
Library, Sydney, pp. 82,84.

Stokes, John Lort, Plains of Promise, Queensland, 1841

Stokes, J.L. 1846, *Discoveries in Australia: with an account of the Coasts and
Rivers explored and surveyed during the voyage of H.M.S. Beagle in the Years
1837–38–39–40–41–42–43*, vol.2, T. & W. Boone, London, pp. 316, 317.

Stuart, John McDouall, West of Lake Torrens, South Australia, 1858

Stuart, J. M. 1858, 'Journal of an Expedition into the Unexplored
Country to the North-west and South-west of Port Augusta, by
Mr. J. M. Stuart', Ordered by the House of Assembly (South Australia)
to be printed, November 5th 1858, pp. 2, 4.

Tasman, Abel Janszoon, Tasmania, 1642

Calder, J.E. 1882, *History of the Discovery of Tasmania by Commodore Bel
Jansz Tasman, 24th November, 1642, copied from Woide's Translation of his
Original Journal*, unnumbered, pp. 4, 5.

Tench, Watkin, Sydney, New South Wales, 1791

Tench, W. 1979, *Sydney's First Four Years*, Library of Australian History,
Sydney, pp. 285–287.

Thomas, Mary, Adelaide, South Australia, 1836–39

Thomas, E.K. (ed.) 1925, *The Diary and Letters of Mary Thomas
(1836–1866)*, W. K. Thomas & Co., Adelaide, pp. 50, 51, 131, 132.

Thomas, William H., Bowen Harbour, North Queensland, 1859

Thomas, W. H. 1859, *Journal of the Schooner "Santa Barbara" 9 tons reg
from Rockhampton to the Nor-west Coast of Australia in search of a Safe
Northern Port & Harbour*, pp. 24–28, in possession National Library
of Australia.

Tietkens, William Henry, West of the Darling, 1889

Tietkens, W.H. 1890, 'Journal of Mr. W. H. Tietkens' Central
Australian Exploring Expedition', Ordered by the House of Assembly
(South Australia) to be printed, October 30th 1890, pp. 8, 9, 21, 22, 25.

**Tourle, Thomas, Sydney, Hunter River, New England and Scone, New
South Wales, 1839, 1840**

Tourle, T. 1839–40, Letters dated14 September 1839, 14 September &
22 September 1840. (Large collection of photocopied letters from
Thomas Tourle to his family in England dated 1839 & 1840), in
possession of Mitchell Library, Sydney, originals in National Library of
Australia.

Turnbull, Henry, North of the Mackenzie River, Queensland, 1847

Turnbull, H. 1983, *Leichhardt's Second Journey*, Halstead Press, Sydney,
pp. 45, 46.

Unknown writer, Portland, Victoria, 1841

Mitchell, Major T.L. 1838, 'Method for fully examining the country about Pd. Bay – If arriving by Water', *Three Expeditions into the interior of Eastern Australia*, T. & W. Boone, London, vol. 2, notes handwritten to himself by an unknown person on the flyleaves at the back of Mitchell's book.

Waterhouse, Henry, Port Jackson, New South Wales, 1802

Knight & Frost (eds.) 1983, *The Journal of Daniel Paine 1794–1797*, Library of Australian History and National Maritime Museum, Greenwich, UK & Sydney, pp. 70, 71, 78, 79.

Watson, Henry, Mount Barker, South Australia, 1838

Watson, H. 1838, 'Diary of his Voyage to Australia with his family in the years 1838/9', entry for 26 March 1838, in possession of Mitchell Library.

Williams, Henry Edwin, Chandler Falls, New South Wales, 1851

Williams, H.E. 1851, 'Journal of Henry Edwin Williams covering his voyage from England to Australia and his early days in the colony of New South Wales written during the period 14th September 1849 to 2nd May 1853', pp. 57, 60, 61, typescript in possession of National Library of Australia.

Young, Sir George, England, 1785

Frost, A. 1980, *Dreams of a Pacific Empire Sir George Young's proposal for a colonization of New South Wales (1784–5)*, Resolution Press, Sydney, pp. 33, 35, 37, 38.

Index